LORDS OF
THE LOCKER
ROOM

Other books by the author:

DESTINY'S DARLINGS

SUPERBOWL: THE ILLUSTRATED HISTORY

LORDS OF THE LOCKER ROOM

The American Way of Coaching
and its Effect on Youth

by

Martin Ralbovsky

Peter H. Wyden/Publisher

NEW YORK

LIBRARY OF CONGRESS CATALOG CARD NUMBER: 74-15805
ISBN: 0-88326-071-9
MANUFACTURED IN THE UNITED STATES OF AMERICA

For Susan

Contents

1 · Games Are Too Important to Be Left to Coaches (Which Is Why We're Here)

In the year 1905, the President of the United States, Theodore Roosevelt, summoned to the White House representatives of the nation's major colleges and universities. Roosevelt told them that the game of football was so savage, so violent, so reprehensible to the more sophisticated minds in the country, that he was going to abolish the sport by a Presidential decree unless the schools did something to civilize the game. They did: They put a coach in charge of making the necessary adjustments that would make the game more palatable to the President, and to his enlightened constituency.

The savior was Amos Alonzo Stagg, and he became the leader of a group that was called the National Football Rules Committee. Stagg returned to Washington, D.C., after months of meetings with other coaches, and he told President Roosevelt that the game of football could be totally salvaged if the committee took the following steps: (1) eliminate the flying wedge, (2) eliminate mass momentum plays from behind the scrimmage, and (3) introduce the forward pass. Roosevelt listened, and then he acquiesced. Thus, through the efforts of a coach, was the game of football spared the indignity of becoming the first sport in America to be abolished by a President.

But, as Winston Churchill once said, "Wars are too important to be left to generals." So it could be with sports: Are games too important to be left entirely to the coaches? Since the turn of the twentieth century, when Amos Alonzo Stagg took on the President of the United States, and won, coaches have come to rule our games in much the same manner as lieutenants rule infantry companies and teachers rule classrooms. They are the most visible authority figures in their spheres. As it is, more people seem to be aware of the late Vince Lombardi than of the late Bert Bell, who was the commissioner of professional football for many years. Americans, for whatever reason, seem genuinely to like coaches who are, or have been, successful. The visible end result (winning) has always been more important than the less-visible means (tyranny). So it is: Coaches have become revered figures in American sports, and their status has not been diminished by the swollen ankles, pulled hamstring muscles, and psychic irregularities that hamper their players. Only losing seasons do them in.

In their pursuit of victory, many coaches in America have been known to do some strange things; these strange things have had less than beneficial effects on the people who have been victimized by them, particularly young people in what must be loosely described as "amateur" sports. Sometimes a coach's effect on a young player can last for a lifetime. Witness the Pulitzer Prize–winning play by Jason Miller, *That Championship Season:* The coach had a psychological hold on his former players that bordered on being satanic. They were forever "his boys," and he was forever "the coach"—even when they were in their forties and he was in his seventies. He told them with pride: "I've made you boys what you are today." But what were they? Loyal former players, or approval mavens tortured by insecurity? They cheated to win the championship and then proceeded to cheat, and win, through life. They built Taj Mahals on quicksand, and they were waiting for the columns to collapse. The coach, meanwhile, smiled his approval on them, making the whole charade all right.

To many coaches' thinking, it has become important, indeed, what the boy does to the ball, but not quite so important what the ball does to the boy. Who, then, speaks for the boy?

There are people in America who profess to speak for the rights of fish and assorted reptilian marinelife which are doomed to premature deaths because the rivers and the streams in which they swim are being polluted by poisonous waste materials from factories owned by large and callous corporations. There are people who profess to speak on behalf of the nation's deer and rabbits and squirrels who, likewise, will be meeting violent and untimely deaths because the forests which they inhabit are being polluted by men who carry rifles and kill animals for the sporting joy of it. There are people who profess to speak out in behalf of the rights of oppressed and exploited human beings: migrant farm workers, domestic workers, decimated Indian tribes, poor Appalachian whites, poor blacks everywhere. Even trainees at U.S. Army basic-training posts have banded together and formed soldiers' unions to safeguard against any infringements of their civil rights by their demanding superiors in Smokey-the-Bear costumes. Most of these people are justifiably concerned about their causes, and many of them are sensitive and compassionate human beings who have been motivated into action after having witnessed, or heard about, horrible injustices.

But so far, no group or individual has come forward to speak out in behalf of the civil rights of one of America's largest and most vulnerable minorities: young athletes. During 1973, approximately nine million young American males (and a few thousand females) between the ages of nine and nineteen were engaged in some form of non-professional sports activity, ranging from Little League baseball, Pop Warner football, and Biddy League basketball to their high-school equivalents. Of that group, many suffered injuries that went unreported beyond their own homes or their own doctors' offices. Many others were hospitalized or immobilized with broken limbs, concussions, separations, tears,

pulls, and abrasions. Completely unreported went the mental damage; no school or hospital has compiled statistics on the numbers
of boys (or girls) who suffered through periods of manic
depression, say, after their teams had lost important games, or after
they had failed miserably in a single game, or in a vital situation,
before a large crowd of people. No statistics have been compiled,
either, on the number of boys who, after having been successful at
meting out punishment and pain during games, and after having
been praised and publicized lavishly for it, actually embraced the
practice as being within normal social boundaries. The mental
damage that is inflicted upon thousands of young athletes every
year goes unreported simply because it is not so visible as, say, a
swollen ankle.

According to the National Federation of High School Athletic
Associations, which has its headquarters in Chicago, there are
approximately 3½ million athletes competing in sports at approximately 113,000 public high schools in America every year. The
sports range from badminton (965 high schools offer it on a competitive basis) to curling (711 schools) to riflery (305 schools) to
rugger (16 schools). The biggest high-school sport by far is football; there are nearly 100,000 players every year on five different
levels—eleven-man, eight-man, six-man, nine-man, and twelve-
man. Add to that a total of 4 million junior-high-school athletes,
who play organized sports on the seventh-grade, eighth-grade, and
ninth-grade levels; 2 million Little League baseball players every
summer; 1 million Pop Warner League and junior-league football
players every fall, and another million from assorted programs
such as the Babe Ruth Leagues, the Biddy Basketball Leagues, the
American Legion Leagues, the Connie Mack Leagues, the Pony
Leagues, the Sandy Koufax Leagues, the Mickey Mantle Leagues,
the Catholic Youth Organization Leagues, the YMCA Leagues,
ad infinitum. Put together, all of these programs accommodate a
total of 9 million boys annually.

Nine million boys. Who does speak for them?

Invariably, their coaches do. The American way of coaching
requires that the patriarchs devour their pups. Sports teams are not

constructed along the lines of representative democracies; they are totalitarian in nature. The coach is the dictator. He decides who plays, and for how long; he decides on how players will dress outside of locker rooms and how long their hair will be; in short, he alone controls the apparatus that will determine whether or not a player will be successful on his team. It is no secret that many fine young athletes in America have been denied opportunities to succeed on sports teams because they did not possess personalities that conformed to the image of what the coach had decided the ideal personality was. It is no secret, either, that on sports teams conformity has a higher priority than individuality; there is a superimposed limit on just how intelligent, just how aware, just how inquisitive, just how progressive—just how smart, damnit—a young athlete can be. If he is too egocentric, if he questions the coach's tactics, if he challenges the presumptions upon which the team is constructed (no Taj Mahals on quicksand for him), he will not get the opportunity to succeed, to excel, as an athlete. So, in America, young males had better please the coach first; then, that accomplished, they can proceed to worry about pleasing themselves as athletes. The American way of coaching requires that the pups *allow themselves* to be devoured by the patriarchs. The coaches, then, gladly speak for them.

Now, not all coaches in America abuse this tremendous power; surely, many hundreds of coaches handle young athletes in sensitive, compassionate manners. But there are many coaches who do, indeed, abuse their power and, subsequently, their young players. But when this happens, the athlete has no courts of appeal available to him; he is stuck with the coach's rulings and decisions. Young athletes have no Bill of Rights in America; they live in a subculture that has accumulated its own set of by-laws. Some people in America have fantasized (perceptively portrayed?) sports teams as being fascistic in concept: All the power is at the top, singularly entrusted to one person, and all the powerless are below him and subjected to his whims. There seem to be no checks and balances to the coach's power. One man's will becomes many men's wills. Terror is the lubricant that allows the wheels to grind smoothly. If this vision of the sports structure is accurate, then it is not so radical, not so revolutionary, not so Marxist-Leninist, to assume that many coaches personify something that is very un-American indeed: dictatorial power. If that is true, then millions of young athletes are left at the mercy of one factor: Just how humanely do the coaches handle, and disseminate, all of the power entrusted to them?

Now, to many people in the United States of America, what goes on inside of locker rooms is not too terribly important; sports, they presume, are merely fun and games, and diversions from reality. But in the United States of America, every year, fifteen-year-old boys die from heatstroke and dehydration during hot summer days on football practice fields; fourteen-year-old boys suffer broken ankles and separated shoulders and skull fractures and dislocated knees during basketball practices in showcase gymnasiums; and eleven-year-old boys injure their arms forever by throwing baseballs with such ferocious whiplash motions that they permanently damage their elbow joints. Others suffer mental anguish from situations that they cannot handle, usually resulting from their failure to live up to their own, or to their coaches', expectations; still others accept reduced visions of their worth because they cannot perform well during tense, heavily pressurized situations.

True, the coaches are not entirely to blame for all of this; they are merely the middlemen, for better or for worse. The institutions they represent, the institutions from which they earn their salaries, actually create the circumstances, and then leave the coaches to fend for themselves. In actuality, most coaches function as executors of the institutions' desires; if the high-school principal, or the university president, demands a winning team, well . . . (Produce!)

Too many coaches in America direct all their efforts to pleasing the institution that employs them; that is to say, they direct all their efforts toward producing winning teams so that the institution's image can benefit from them. Those who say, "To hell with winning, I'm going to give the kids a chance to play games and have some fun," are ultimately dismissed by the institution. (What school wants the albatross of losing sports teams?) The coach who produces continuous streams of average teams seems to be in the most comfortable position. He works at neither end of the spectrum—no parades, but no piranhas.

People are suspicious of writers who pay lip service to rationality. At cocktail parties, or over lunches, they say to writers, "I read the introduction to your book, the part where you said not all politicians are crooks, but, c'mon now, tell me, what do you really think?" The writer will then proceed to say that, yes, indeed, he thinks all politicians are crooks, but you know the way publishing is. Editors tell you not to turn people off in the first paragraph, so you suck them in with a few soft lines, pretend to be objective, and then unload. Everybody does it. If writers didn't think politicians were crooks, or that banks were usurers, or that nursing homes were abhorrent, they wouldn't write the damn books in the first place. Get it?

So . . . what do I really think?

I think coaches in America have become too fanatical about winning games. I think winning games is important, sure; but not for everybody. I think coaches miss this point. I think sports are good for kids: the physical activity of it all, the friendships they make. But I don't think too many coaches are concerned, say, about giving fat and flabby kids the opportunity to get into shape through competitve sports. I think coaches discriminate against fat and flabby kids; they cut them from their teams. I think coaches do psychological as well as physical harm to kids who are not perfect bodily specimens. I think these are the kids who need lower-level sports the most. I think coaches are keeping them out of sports on purpose. These kids don't win games for them.

I think competition is good for kids, but only up to a point. I think competitive coaches are wrong in trying to make their players as competitive as they are. I think the so-called competitive spirit—as many coaches envision it—borders on being fanaticism and hysteria. How many kids *really* want to run through brick walls for the coach?

I think coaches have an inordinate amount of power over young people's peer-group relationships. Kids who are rejected by coaches think first about what the other kids will say about them (*He's a loser, a failure, a reject*). I think peer-group acceptance is terribly important to young boys. I think many coaches purposely use this fact to spur borderline cases ("You don't want to be the laughing stock of the school, do you?")—exploitation. I also think it works both ways: Kids who make teams acquire a sense of self-esteem, of self-confidence; making a sports team can actually help them attain a sense of independence from their families, and help them in the process of separation from their parents. I think the whole subject of the power of coaches over peer-group relationships is very important. I think coaches who call kids sissies in front of other kids are contributing to the alienation of minors.

I think some coaches demand unrealistic things from boys; they set impossible goals for them, expect too much from them. When the kids cannot meet the coachs' standards, I think the boys feel inferior, or else they think of themselves as utter failures. I think that in some cases, where a boy has tremendous natural athletic talent, it is desirable to set high goals for him; but in the majority of cases, involving average athletes, it is dangerous to his psyche to tell him that if he doesn't do the 220 in 18 seconds flat by the time he's a junior, he's not trying hard enough. I think coaches should allow most young athletes to reach their own levels of accomplishment.

I think the team concept in sports, as promoted by many coaches, is overrated in its value. I think it's harmful for a coach to demand that a fourteen-year-old boy sacrifice his individuality for the good of the high-school team; I think fourteen-year-old boys should have the option of being individualistic open to them. Learning to work with others is fine; it is highly desirable. But I think that *working with others* and *fitting into the team concept* are two different things.

I think parents have a crucial and often underrated role to play in determining how much influence a coach should have on a young life. I deal with the parental role in sports in detail at the end of this book, but certainly no coach should become what he now does become in many American families: a third authority figure with parental powers in a boy's life. And I keep talking about boys to the exclusion of girls because I think girls are inviting trouble when they demand to be treated as equals in sports. I think male coaches have had very little influence on young girls, and I think that is good. I think the question is this: Do girls want to be subjected to the same distortions that boys have been subjected to? I don't think so. The reverse twist of the girls-in-sports movement is that girls will ultimately become victims of the same winning mania and competitive fanaticism that have hurt so many boys. Will coaches do to girls what has already been done to many boys? I think parents of girls who are aspiring athletes have to ask themselves that question.

I think that nearly every coach in America has been guilty, at one time or another, of doing or thinking some of the aforementioned things, in one degree or another, just as I think all people who travel for a living cheat on their expense accounts (if only on cab fares, or on tips). Nobody's perfect. Not coaches, not writers. I think it would be a good idea if some coach did a book on sportswriting someday. So there.

I also think that a lot of coaches are going to become very angry when they read this book. I think that's good.

II · About Broken Legs, Homosexuality, Backdoor Deals, and Rejection . . .

Jonathan Sharp is an advertising designer who lives in Hollywood Hills, California, with his blond wife, Lynne; they own their own business there. Jon Sharp grew up in an exclusive Connecticut suburb and he played high school football there. Ten years later, he looked back upon that experience with horror. Jon Sharp:

> We had this coach who was a real maniac; always screaming and yelling at us, calling us pussies, kicking kids in the ass—really, kicking them square in the ass with his spikes. We all hated him. But once you got onto the team, there was no escape. He had this thing about quitters, you know; he would make sure that every kid in the school looked down on you if you quit his football team. So there was no escape. I dreaded going to practice. I was an offensive lineman, a guard most of the time. He was on me all the time: "Sharp, you're lazy, Sharp, you're slow, Sharp, you're nothing but a big hairy pussy." I hated him.
>
> O.K., so I put up with the whole thing for two and a half years, as a sophomore, a junior, and half of my senior season.

I felt as if I were in a concentration camp; the fact that there was no legitimate way of getting out of the mess depressed me. I used to walk home at night after practice and say to myself, "How did I ever get into this mess? All I wanted to do was play football. Is this what football is all about?" I knew kids who used to shove their fingers down their throats before practice and throw up all over the locker room, so they could get out of scrimmaging. One kid—he was a defensive line-man—used to bang this sprained ankle of his against a bench in the locker room so that it would swell up; the coach would say, "Get it X-rayed, get it X-rayed. It's gotta be broken." So the kids would go back and forth to this doctor's office, getting X-rays, waiting for the results, missing as much practice as he could. Always, the X-rays were negative. The coach went crazy. He couldn't figure it out. Finally, he took the kid's job away, gave it to somebody else, and told him to sit until the ankle healed completely. This kid missed the rest of the season. He used to walk down the halls in the school, and he'd smile at us—you know, like he was the happiest guy in the world. We envied him.

The thing that made the whole situation impossible to cope with was the way the coach used the peer-group-pressure thing; we were brainwashed to the point where we felt that the worst thing in the world was to be a quitter. If you were going to leave the team, you had to leave it on your shield. Carried away on a stretcher or something. Anything less made you suspect. That's how he got away with the whole thing: He had us believing that if we didn't take everything he dished out, we were less than men. He controlled the view of masculinity that each kid on the team had; when somebody fell short, which was very seldom, the rest of the guys could open season on him—you know, make him feel like a big pile of shit just because he quit the football team.

O.K., so I'm the first-string guard on offense, and it's the third game of my senior season. I had resigned myself at that point to just getting through the season, and then I was going to forget about the whole nightmare and never play another game of football again. Then I got real lucky. In that game I make a tackle, and there was this big pile-up. Somebody—I think it was a guy on my own team—jumped in, knees first, and landed right on my leg. My leg was twisted in a funny position when he landed on it, and I thought I heard this loud snap, like somebody breaking a twig. Then this horrible pain shot up through my leg, right up to my crotch. I knew the leg was broken. They carried me off the field, put me in an ambulance, and took me to the hospital. The nurses cut off my pads; the doctor took one look and said, "It's broken." They put me in a cast right away, and strung the leg up in traction.

So, the next day, I'm lying in this hospital bed, my broken leg strung up in the air, and I'm saying to myself, "You lucky son of a bitch; no more football. It's all over." I was happy as hell. The broken leg saved me from five or six more games, and five or six more weeks of practices. Besides, I went out on my shield; there was nothing to be ashamed of. I was a fallen hero—the perfect way to go. People would come to visit me at the hospital, and I would be smiling and telling jokes, and they would say, "My, you're in good spirits." I used to laugh like hell. Sure I was in good spirits—that broken leg was the best thing that had ever happened to me at that point in my life.

Now I look back on it all, and I say to myself, "Now wait a minute, what the hell kind of stuff was that? Since when does a sixteen-year-old kid go crazy with joy because he's got a broken leg?" That's how distorted the whole thing was. The leg still bothers me at times; it gets stiff some mornings, and I get this dull ache in it when I sit in a car for too long. That's my souvenir from high-school football. But I'll tell you, at the time I felt that a broken leg was a small price to pay for getting out of that situation with my dignity and respect intact.

*

The name "Rick Sennett" is a pseudonym for a man who lives in a small city in Texas, where he is a high-school science teacher. Rick Sennett was born and raised in a small town in western Pennsylvania. He played baseball in what was his town's equivalent of the Little League program; he played basketball and ran on the cross-country team in high school. Now at the age of thirty-six, he has opted for a homosexual life style; he said that he has had a long and satisfying sexual relationship with a man who is approximately the same age, and although they do not live together—"it would be too obvious in this town"—they see each other frequently. Rick Sennett said that he is not entirely happy being a homosexual in a society that is dominated by heterosexuality; he said that he is bothered by feelings of guilt:

I go to a shopping center, say, and I see this suburban-type family, happy little kids, you know, and I feel like hell. Deep down, I'd like to have a wife and kids too, but I know it will never happen. Then I say to myself, "What the hell is wrong with me? Where did I go wrong?" I've been to the Gay Lib meetings and all of that, but I still feel guilty about it. My whole problem, as I look back on it, is that I've never been able to have an honest and human relationship with a woman. My view of women was distorted when I was a kid.

When I was ten or eleven, and I was playing in this Little League, I developed this attitude that somehow girls my age were inferior to me. I was a part of something in town; I had a uniform, and a spot on the team, and people came out to see me play. I even looked down on little boys who weren't playing in the league. It was as if when I put on that uniform I was transformed into Superboy or something; I was important. That sort of attitude was encouraged in us. We were told we were the cream of the crop in town, just because we were good enough as baseball players to make the Little League team.

When I got to high school, I was about five-eleven, and I made the freshman team. When I was a sophomore, I was maybe six-one, and I was put on the varsity basketball team. The coach ... he was one of these guys who was a woman-hater. I suspected back then that maybe he was a latent homosexual, one of those types who felt more comfortable around undressed teen-aged boys than anybody else. He would say things like "Screw 'em but don't marry 'em." He told one kid who was going steady with a girl, "Broads are a dime a dozen. Turn 'em upside down and they all look alike." He saw a guy on the team walking in the hall with a girl one afternoon, and at practice he said, "You chewin' on that, boy?" He called it "cruisin' " when you walked with a girl down the hall. The kid who was the captain of the team—he was so straight-laced, Episcopalian upbringing and all; he's a city manager today—he told us once at practice that the coach had told him to tell us that "Nobody is to jerk off on a game day. It saps all your energy." He never wanted any of us to develop any kind of relationship with a girl, because he said it would hurt us as basketball players.

One day he said: "Guys with steady girls never get scholarships. They never develop as players. Besides, college coaches stay away from guys who have steady girls back home; they think these guys are going to get homesick and go back home and marry the broad."

So, all through high school I stayed away from girls; they were poison. A lot of girls would come around and flirt with us because we were basketball players, but we never did anything back. We'd be coming out of basketball practice at night, carrying our gym bags, and some guy with a souped-up car and long greasy hair, the kind of guy we felt superior to, he'd have three, four girls stuffed into his car. We walked home alone. Looking back on it, and I'm talking about the early fifties, I'd say the best athletes at that high school knew the least about women and sex. The guys with the cars, the guys we used to laugh at for being stupid, they had all the girls. It was just the opposite from what most people thought.

So I was sixteen years old, maybe, and I was a junior in high school, and, like everybody else, I had a pretty good sex drive. But the only people I came into contact with socially were other basketball players. We went to dances and things, but we always clustered together and watched the other people dance, and we'd make snide remarks about how silly these people were, and we'd be thinking how superior we were to them. One night we held this practice during the Christmas vacation; school was out, and nobody was around. The coach went home right after practice (it was seven o'clock at night, maybe), and we were taking showers, about seven of us. We were in the locker room, toweling off, and one of the guys started fooling around with a towel, snapping it, aiming it at another guy's genitals, laughing, you know, horsing around. Then we all started doing it, laughing and snapping the towels, and then one of the guys blurted out, "Let's have a circle jerk." Everybody stopped, and we looked around at each other. I remember being flushed with excitement, I really wanted to do it. One of the guys said, "No, no," but another guy said, "Why not? It's fun." We all started laughing again, and we began masturbating, and we all came right on the locker-room floor. One of the guys cleaned the stuff up with one of the towels, then he put it in the shower and washed it out. When I went home, I felt great; I had had a very exciting sexual experience. Girls were off-limits to us; this was the next best thing.

So that same group of us, every time we saw the coach go home, would lock the door to the locker room and do it again. Before the season was over, this other guy and I were trying other things when everybody else had gone. We'd mastur-bate each other, then blow jobs, and then anal intercourse. He was my first lover.

Now here we were, two of the best basketball players on the high-school team, and we had girls cheering for us, and the teachers were telling us that we were the leaders of the student body, and here we were, sexual partners. By the time

I got out of high school, I wasn't having anything to do with girls at all. Oh, I went to the senior prom, and those things, but it was all a big show. It was a front so nobody would find out the truth. When I got to college, I met a lot of gay people and I was comfortable. I never tried to reverse the process; we'd get together in dorm rooms and in bars and we'd talk about our situations, and we all felt better about it. We were into Gay Lib, in our own way, before it was the "in" thing.

So now I'm pushing forty, and I've never made love to a woman in my life. I'd like to, I really would, but it would probably never happen; even if it did, she'd suspect that I was just using her, which is exactly what I'd be doing. Fucking to see if I like it.

I've come to terms with my homosexuality, and I can live with myself. But I wish I had had the option of heterosexuality open to me. I think coaches are the worst male chauvinists alive, except maybe for career military men. I know I acquired a distorted sense of what women are from that damn high-school coach I had, and I wish to hell today that I had never played high-school basketball. For the damage that man did to us, the bastard should be in jail today.

Billy Murphy was a starting running back on the varsity football team of a large university in Boston in the fall of 1964. Ten years after that season, he looked back upon his old coach with mixed feelings:

The coach, and I think most coaches, make these backdoor allegiances with their players. It's like a sinister, mysterious deal: He's going to protect you from the evils of the real world so long as you do things his way. In the end, you find out the real world is not so evil after all; the coach is.

I remember this one incident—I'll never forget it. We were going lousy, winning one, losing one, and we were supposed to have the best college team in New England. So, we go to Amherst to play the University of Massachusetts. Now, U. Mass. had a hell of a team—Milt Morin, Greg Landry, those guys—and they were unbeaten, if I remember right, when we got there. That game was supposed to salvage our season; if we knocked off U. Mass., which was Number One in New England, we'd become Number One automatically. So, all week at practice, the coach is telling us, "You guys know what you have to do—do it!" All week I psyched myself up; I can't remember ever being so aroused about playing a football game. I wanted to win that game no matter what. By Saturday, the day of the game, I was like a man possessed.

So the game starts, and U. Mass. is running all over us. God, they had a good team. They manhandled us all the way; in the fourth quarter, we were so far behind, I didn't even want to go out there any more. But I did—and I was angry. One of the U. Mass. guys gave me a shot, and I dropped the ball and I went after him, trying to rip his helmet off so I could punch him in the face. That started a riot. Both benches came out onto the field, guys were swinging helmets, cops were running around all over the place, people were screaming—the whole scene. I was thrown out of the game, and we needed police protection to get out of town. The coach never said a word to me.

About two weeks later, I hear this voice bellowing, "Mur-phy, get over here!" It was the coach. He said, "The Administration is up in arms over the U. Mass. fight. They want somebody's head. They're after me to throw the ringleaders out of school, you understand?" I was scared, I figured, "There goes the scholarship." Then the coach looked at me, and he said, "Now, why'd you do it?" I said, "I was angry, coach. They were beating our asses. I couldn't control myself." So then he comes around with his right arm and smacks me over the head with his clipboard—I'm wearing a helmet—and he smiles at me. He says, "Don't worry about a thing. Those bastards won't get a thing out of me."

I loved the guy for that. He was protecting me from the evils of the outside world. Now I look back on it, and I think maybe I made a deal with the devil himself.

"Perry Griswold" is a pseudonym. He is an attorney with a prestigious firm in the Midwest. He was graduated from Michigan State University and New York University Law School and he was an assistant district attorney before going into private practice. When he was a high-school sophomore, he was cut from the varsity basketball team; as a high-school junior, he was cut from the same team; as a senior, he didn't bother trying out. The coach had said that he was too slow to fit into a fast-breaking team. At the time, Griswold said, the rejection was shattering to him; today, he says it was the best thing that had ever happened to him.

When the coach cut me the second time, when I was a junior, I was mortified. I felt inferior, like, two years in a row I'm not good enough to play on this team—something must be wrong with me. God, I spent two whole summers shooting baskets, figuring *I'm getting better.* Looking back on it, I remember telling myself that I had two directions in which to go: I could put my head down and feel sorry for myself, or I could go onto other things and show the rest of the kids, and the coach, that there were other things in the world besides the basketball team. I got involved in other school activities, plays and newspapers; I started dating regularly, I expanded myself. In fact, by the time I got to be a senior I could see that the kids on the basketball team were pretty much stagnating intellectually, and that I had grown beyond them. All they were still worried about was the game on Friday night; by then I had stopped going to the games. My grades improved, and I was accepted into Michigan State with no trouble at all.

Now I look back on the whole thing, and I'd say that the coach actually inspired me when he cut me. He inspired me to prove to the world that I was no reject just because I wasn't good enough to make the basketball team. I guess some kids would have caved in, and begun to look at themselves as failures. That didn't happen to me. I had this feeling all along, anyway, that basketball wasn't the only thing in the world, and to hell with the coach anyway. I ran a little cross-country, and I liked that; it was more individual a sport than basketball, and the cross-country coach was pretty tolerant. He never screamed and yelled at kids, like the basketball coach did. So, anyway, I'm an attorney today, and I've got a nice family, a wife and two daughters, and I've got a nice home in the suburbs, and I've got a good future with my firm, and I'm a pretty happy guy. I've been thinking about getting involved in politics someday, and who knows? it might happen.

One day I get a call in the office from one of the guys who had made the high-school basketball team the years I got cut. He says he wants to see me on personal business. He comes in and tell me he wants me to represent him in his divorce proceedings, and we get to talking, and he tells me he's in debt up to his ears, gambling on football games, he never got the college scholarship he thought he would get from basketball, so he went to this junior college, dropped out, got married, and works in this men's clothing store. He said to me, "You know, you were lucky, you didn't waste your time playing basketball." I said, "Look, I would have except I got cut from the team." He said, "Oh, yeah, I remember that." I asked him if he ever saw the old coach around town. He said, "One day I'm in this supermarket and I bump right into him. I say, "Hi, Coach." He looks at me and he doesn't even remember me. How's that? Three years I played for the guy."

If I had played basketball in high school, I still might be in the situation I'm in today. I don't know. But I do know that getting cut in basketball inspired me to succeed in other areas; it gave me a drive I'm not too sure I had before that. I was so damn mad, so hurt, maybe even humiliated, that I said to myself, "Son of a bitch, I'll show him. I'll show them all." I think to this day that feeling is still with me; the coach gave me the taste of failure very early in life, and I've been out to get rid of that taste ever since.

He doesn't know it today, but the coach did me a tremendous favor when he cut me. I love the guy.

III · A Little Foul Play, the Coach's Way

By the turn of the 1950s, thousands of veterans from World War II had used their GI loans to transform the forests and the farmlands of rural America into what is now known, somewhat derisively, as Middle America. They left their rented cold-water flats in the decaying cities, and they moved their families out to suburbia. They bought their own homes. In 1952, my family moved from the ethnic ghetto that was called Flockie Boulevard in Schenectady, New York, to a suburb of that city called Rotterdam. (People in upstate New York were very big on naming their cities after current or ancient European capitals; besides Rotterdam, there are now, in upstate New York, an Amsterdam, a Berlin, a Rome, a Naples, a Troy, a Carthage, an Athens, a Warsaw, a Hamburg, a Dunkirk, and, of course, an Attica.)

It was in Rotterdam, in the middle of the 1950s, as I entered a junior high school named after some fellow named John Bigsbee, that I encountered my first real, live coach. Everybody said he was a nice guy. Everybody said that Sunday followed Saturday. His name, let's say, was Benchley Steele. In gym classes, Benchley Steele made fun of kids who happened to be lacking in coordination; he had derogatory nicknames for kids he didn't particularly like; he swore regularly at kids who happened to be rowdy, and every once in a while he would punch one. Benchley Steele was a fanatic about the game of soccer; most of the time, at the beginning of gym classes Benchley Steele would throw out a brown soccer ball, blow his silver whistle, and instruct us to go at each other with maniacal fervor. Benchley Steele would stand off to the side, chain-smoking cigarettes, and watch the mayhem that ensued, with, I always suspected, a certain amount of sadistic pleasure. Whenever a kid got kicked in the shins and started to cry, Benchley Steele would berate him for acting like a sissy. Nice guy, my first coach.

But it wasn't until my sophomore year in a spanking, new high school, in the late 1950s, that I experienced rather genuine problems with Benchley Steele. (The spanking, new high school was christened "Mohonosen"; they held a contest, and a kid named Vincent Bowers thought up the name, splicing together the first three letters of three decimated Indian nations that had once occupied the very same land, the Mohawks, the Onondagas, and the Senecas. He won five dollars.) The coach, Benchley Steele, followed us from the old junior high school to the spanking, new high school, and he became the head coach of basketball there. Now, since I was a kid who had roots that traced back to the obliterated inner city, I already was something of a fanatic about the game of basketball. I was totally obsessed with it. By the time I got to the tenth grade, I already had five or six years of shooting jump shots under my belt; the jump shots were not merely shot in the stifling heat of summer, or in the gentle warmth of spring, or in the rustic coziness of autumn. They were also shot in the dead of winter, in temperatures that were twenty-three degrees below zero, with my hands wrapped in gloves, a skiing cap pulled over my head and ears, two sweaters and two jackets covering my chest, black, buckled galoshes over dirty black sneakers on my feet. I shot jump shots on large patches of ice, dribbling the ball deftly, bouncing the ball off cracks in the ice and using the ricochets as lead passes; if you knew how to use the ice to your advantage, and you bounced the ball at the right speed and the right angle off the cracks and the crevices, the ricochets would come back to you in the form of perfectly thrown lead passes from imaginary teammates. My nose would run, the mucous would freeze in a straight line between my nostrils and my lips. My face looked like Niagara Falls, frozen over. People did not know whether my nose had suddenly begun to grow stalactites or my upper lip had suddenly begun to grow stalagmites. But I loved it. The neighbors, of course, recommended to my parents that I be whisked off to undergo psychiatric examination; surely, normal kids were not to be found outside during roaring blizzards, shooting a basketball, while dressed to resemble a refugee from Outer Mongolia. I got even with my neighbors during the summers. They mowed their own lawns.

After a while, I could shoot jump shots quite well in such things as freezing rain, sleet, high winds, and snowstorms. Wearing sneakers and shorts, and being inside a warm gymnasium, and shooting at a basket that happened to have a net dangling off the end of it were luxuries. I used to shoot two hundred jump shots a day, every day; I used to run off streaks of thirty-five or forty-five in a row. I kept score on myself. I never went into the house to eat supper (or because of darkness) without first popping a parting jumper. *Swish.* Even though there was never a net on the basket in my backyard, the imagined sound of rippling cords brought about by a soft-touch jump shot set the tuning forks in my brain to gyrating, and *that sound* made all the more palatable the waiting bowls of hot chicken soup. To this day, I can go over to the schoolyard in my neighborhood, bounce a basketball a few times, and start popping jump shots, stringing together seven, eight, and nine in a row. A boyhood spent in a blighted industrial city shooting jump shots is a boyhood not altogether wasted; little kids in my neighborhood are impressed today. My coach back then wasn't.

He cut me from the basketball team.

I remember the tryouts as if they occurred yesterday. It was a three-on-one drill that did me in. There I was, in my brand-new white, high-topped P.F. Keds, wearing red satin shorts with white stripes down the sides and a sparkling white sweatshirt, dribbling up the court in the image of Mr. Jump Shot himself, Paul Arizin. There was a kid on my right, streaking down the right side of the court; there was a kid to my left, running down the left side of the court. In front of me was the defensive player, tall and strong and experienced, with airplane wings for arms, stretched out wide like a middle linebacker waiting to devour his prey. I dribbled to the top of the key; the defensive player approached me, stalking, and trying to look intimidating. The other two kids were free, waving their arms in each corner of the court. I ignored them both. I opted for the jump shot; the ball left my fingertips softly, and it was perfectly arched and perfectly aimed. Impeccable trajectory. *Swish.* The cords rippled sensuously. The kids on the sidelines began cheering wildly. They appreciated artistry, no doubt.

Benchley Steele blew his whistle. He ordered me off the floor.

"Drive, goddammit, drive," he yelled at me.

The next day, I got a second chance. Three-on-one drills again. I was placed in the middle again, and I started dribbling up court as soon as the coach yelled, "Go!" I didn't want to drive smack into the defensive player. I didn't want to challenge him and run the risk of his getting his hand on the ball and cramming it straight back down my throat, which happened to be the insult of all insults. No sir. The jump shot was my equalizer. I had such confidence in the accuracy of my jump shot that I was convinced it was the most accurate thing inside that gymnasium; I was convinced that its chances of going into the basket were just as good as any other kid's layup was. But coaches such as Benchley Steele, I discovered, preferred layups to jump shots; percentages, the cliché goes. So I came up the floor, and somewhere around mid-court I decided to prove my point. Dribbling to my right, to my favorite spot on the floor, three feet beyond the perimeter of the keyhole, I went up. The ball sailed toward the basket with the lightness of a floating feather; the cords of the net danced ever so slightly—that soft *swish* was the result of a shooting touch that every kid in the gymnasium envied, which is why every kid in the gymnasium broke into spontaneous applause as soon as the ball had dropped through.

Benchley Steele blew his whistle again.

"Out!" he said, bristling. "Get out!"

I showered and got dressed, and I cried all the way home. The tears froze to my cheeks. I could not understand what had befallen me. This coach, this Benchley Steele, had just rejected the best damn jump shot in the whole school, and he was settling instead for a bunch of tall, strong, unpolished goons who had spent their summers husking corn instead of shooting baskets. He was picking the plumbers over the artist, damn him. I was convinced that there wasn't a kid in the school who could have beaten me in a game of one-on-one; I knew—and all the other kids knew, too—that I could string together seven, eight jump shots in a row and totally de-moralize them, which is the secret to winning in one-on-one. (I already held the school record for winning the greatest number of unfinished one-on-one matches; with the scores at 9–2 or 8–1, my favor, my opponents would quit, rather than suffer the embar-rassment of consummated defeat.) Size is not necessarily a factor in being successful in one-on-one; talent most definitely is. But size certainly was a factor in making the junior varsity basketball team; talent, I concluded that night, wasn't. I pretended I was sick when I got home. I took the next two days off from school, and I sulked. I could not bear to face the humiliation that I knew was waiting for me at school, at the hands of my own peer group. I knew that dozens of kids were salivating at the very prospect of my showing up at school, so that they could ease up beside me in the hall, between classes, and say, "Best jump shot, my ass."

A couple of weeks later, one of the kids who had made the junior varsity team stopped me in the hall and said, "Coach wants to see you."

I immediately presumed that Benchley Steele had finally reac-quired his senses; surely, nobody, not even Benchley Steele, could pass over such a jump shot—he was just teaching me a lesson, Mr. Steele was, for not following orders. I ran down the hall to the gym. I stopped abruptly at the door. I took a deep breath. Then I walked through the swinging doors, with all of the correctness and the composure of a British butler. The coach was sitting on the bottom row of the bleachers; the rest of the bleachers were folded up into the wall. I calmly walked over to him.

"You want to see me, Coach?" I asked, faking nonchalance.

"Sit down," he said.

I suspected that Benchley Steele was going to give me that old have-you-learned-your-lesson? routine. (I had been through that once already, in Little League, swinging at a 3-and-0 pitch instead of taking.) I wanted to spare him the embarrassment of elaborating on the merits of humility and conformity; I was quite willing to say, "Yes, Coach, I have learned my lesson. Layups from now on." But he surprised me; Benchley Steele did not say what I was expecting him to say.

He said, "I need a manager."

A manager? *Manager!* I was simultaneously mortified and outraged. Who in hell wanted to be a manager? Gathering up all of the dirty, sweaty, stinking towels after practice; sweeping off the court; pumping air into lifeless basketballs; keeping score at games. How could he do this to me? I felt that he was insulting me with his offer. *Manager.* Managers were gawky kids who had trouble with their eyesight, or else they were elfish kids who had no talent whatsoever but wanted to be a part of the team anyway. Jock-sniffers. Kids who had the best jump shot in their schools definitely were not managers. No sir. It was clearly a matter of pride with me.

I did not answer him.

Then he said, "Look, I already got kids who are going to collect towels and sweep and all of that. I need somebody to be a score-keeper at games. You're the only kid in school who seems to know what a box score is." He was pretty close to being right; most of the kids in that school didn't read newspapers. "I'll let you practice with the varsity every day. Then, next year, you'll have the inside track at tryouts. What more can you ask for? You go to all the games, home and away, free, and you practice every day with the varsity. All you have to do is keep score at games. What do you expect me to do? Make a scorekeeper out of Nicky Bernardino? He can't add four and six."

The coach had thrown me a curve. He had offered me a spot on the periphery: part of the team, but not really part of the team. I immediately envisioned myself working out with the varsity, tossing in endless strings of jump shots over the distorted and frustrated faces of first-stringers, looking so impressive and so confident and so suave that Benchley Steele would finally take me aside some afternoon after practice and tell me to suit up for the game on Friday night. Then, of course, there was the prospect of all of those one-on-one games before practices began; whoever heard of a manager beating the varsity star in one-on-one, in front of the rest of the team? *I'll show them,* I said to myself, *I'll show him. Head manager. . .*

"Yes, I'll do it," I said to him.

The coach smiled at me, and he tapped me on the knee.

"Good," he said.

The first game that season was against Heatly High School in Green Island, New York. Now, if you happen to know where the city of Cohoes, New York, is located, or where the city of Lansingburgh, New York, is located, or where the cities of Watervliet, Menands and Mechanicville, New York, are located, then you certainly will know where the village of Green Island is located. If not, suffice to say that the village of Green Island is located on the northernmost banks of the Hudson River. Green Island is not green; it is burned-charcoal gray, courtesy of the belching smokestacks of the Ford Motor Company plant there.

Before the game, Benchley Steele gave me my instructions: He said that he wanted to personally inspect the scorebook at half time of every game; he said that he wanted to see exactly who was doing what. Now, keeping score in basketball is not a difficult assignment. When a player makes a basket, you make an entry that looks like this: X. When a player attempts a free throw, you make an entry that looks like this: O. If the player makes the free throw, then you fill in the O with an X. So, if a player named Kelly, say, scores four baskets and converts three out of five free throws, for 11 points, his line in the scorebook would consist of the following:

	G. (Goals)	F. (Free Throws)	P. (Points)
Kelly.	4	3-5	11

Heatly High School had a tremendous player on its team; his name was Dick Kendall. He scored 22 points in the first half. I dutifully brought the scorebook to the coach at half time; smoking a cigarette in the hallway, adjacent to the locker room, he scanned the X's and the O's. He also scanned the column that was reserved for each player's personal fouls; when a player committed a foul, the entry was: p-1. The second foul was p-2. And so on. Five fouls and he was out of the game. I quickly learned that Benchley Steele liked the personal-foul column the best of all. He liked to see a lot of p-5's in the personal-foul column. Of the other team.

As he scanned the personal-foul column, the coach abruptly stopped, and he began screaming at me. Benchley Steele bellowed:

"What is this, two fouls on Kendall? *What is this?* Are you daydreaming or something? The kid's been fouling all night long; he must have four on him by now. Whose side are you on, anyway? Goddammit!"

I gulped.

I was sure that Dick Kendall had committed only two fouls. He had been too busy scoring points to commit fouls. Then I realized what my coach was up to: He was intimidating me. Benchley Steele was intimidating me for a reason. He wanted me to think that I had incurred his displeasure; he wanted me to go out there in the second half and eliminate Dick Kendall from the game with my mathematics. Then he would be happy, and I would be vindicated in his eyes. He wanted me to go out there in the second half and sneak in a quick p-3 and a quick p-4 on Dick Kendall when the other scorekeeper wasn't looking. That way, Dick Kendall would foul out of the game quicker. When Dick Kendall fouled out of the game, he would have to sit on the bench. He couldn't score any points while sitting on the bench. Then, my team could win the game.

Benchley Steele wanted me to cheat.

In the second half, he kept leaving the bench and coming over to the scorer's table. He kept asking me the same question:

"How many fouls on Kendall?"

"Two."

"Two? *Two?* Can you count past two? It's three."

After a while, I was afraid to answer him. Dick Kendall wasn't fouling anybody. He was just scoring points. He had 34 points after three quarters. My team was being obliterated by one player. Nobody could have stopped him but me. I could have penciled him out of the game. I didn't have the guts to do it. We lost. Dick Kendall wound up with 44 points in the game. I wound up with a tongue-lashing from Benchley Steele after the game. He was not very happy with me. He said:

"I got a moron for a scorekeeper. I not only get beat badly, but I got a moron for a scorekeeper. A *moron!*"

I had to make a decision that weekend. It was a pretty big decision for a fourteen-year-old boy to make: Either I was going to give the coach what he wanted, and I was going to cheat and doctor up the scorebook to foul out the other teams' best players, or else I was going to have to turn in my pencil. I wrestled with the decision all weekend. Integrity was not the only thing at stake. My future as a basketball player was on the line as well. If I quit, and if I told the coach to shove his pencil into a dark and creviced spot, my chances of making the team the following year would be nil. I could swish fifteen jump shots in a row, I could bank layups, play defense, and throw perfect lead passes, but I still would be cut. The coach had placed me in one hell of a spot.

There was no one with whom to discuss the situation, either. My father, a reasonably honest man, would have advised me to quit immediately. He always told me that man could not live by basketball alone. If I had gone to the school principal—which I considered doing for a moment or two—he would have called the coach into his office and confronted him with my verbal evidence. Then the scenario would have gone like this: The coach would have said, "The kid's lying. He's just trying to get back at me for cutting him from the team. He thinks he's got a great jump shot, you know. You don't really think I would tell him to cheat, do you?" Then the principal would have agreed with him. I would have been out as the scorekeeper, too.

So, I did the only thing that any other fourteen-year-old kid with a great jump shot would have done under the circumstances. I decided to cheat.

The first time I did it was in a game against the Pebble Hill School in Syracuse. How a private, affluent, elite, Anglo-Saxon preparatory school ever wound up on our basketball schedule mystified me anyway. It was an all-male school; on the day we played them, a Saturday afternoon, the school had imported some cheerleaders from a private, affluent, elite, Anglo-Saxon girls' prep school nearby. The kid who was the scorekeeper for Pebble Hill was paying a lot of attention to the girls; it looked as if he had never seen any before. Every time there was a timeout, he would ogle the cheerleaders. While he was ogling, I was finagling.

I got the two best Pebble Hill players out of the game early in the third period. They never knew what hit them. As they left the floor and headed for the bench, they had bewildered looks on their faces. They said, "I've only got three, Coach; I've only got three." The scorebook said five. Out. The Pebble Hill coach, however, was a gentleman. He never came over to the scorer's table to demand a detailed accounting. It was obvious to me that he was so much of a gentleman that it never dawned upon him that a fourteen-year-old scorekeeper that he had never seen before was actually cheating him out of the game right before his very eyes. My school won that game.

After the game, my coach winked at me; it was one of those "nice job" winks. I got the message.

The second time I did it was in a game at Waterford, New York. Waterford is near Green Island; it is landlocked. Waterford High School had a superb basketball player named John Anderson. He had 12 points in the first period. I knew he had to go. Now, Waterford High School apparently didn't have enough boys in its student body to spare one as its scorekeeper; either that, or the male students were very poor in math. The Waterford scorekeeper was a girl. It was like taking candy from a baby. During a timeout in the second period, I slipped in a p-3 on John Anderson. Early in the third period, while the coaches and the referees were discussing a slippery spot on the court, I slipped in a p-4 on John Anderson. Just before the third period ended, damned if John Anderson didn't go ahead and commit p-5 himself.

I pressed the button that sounded the buzzer. The referee came over to the scorer's table. He asked what was wrong.

"That's five on Anderson," I said.

The girl scorekeeper next to me was mortified.

"Five?" she gasped. "I've, uh, only got him down for three."

She stuttered and became nervous; she just did not have the necessary steadfastness to back up her statistics. She panicked. Besides, she was only a girl. What did she know about keeping score?

"How long you been keepin' score, son?" the referee asked me.

"Two years," I said, lying.

"How long you been keepin' score, miss?" he said.

"I, uh, just started," she said.

The referee called the Waterford coach over to the scorer's table.

"That's five on Anderson," he announced.

The Waterford coach went into a fit of apoplexy. He began screaming at his scorekeeper. She began to cry. Benchley Steele came over to the table, and he told the Waterford coach to stop screaming at that poor little innocent girl.

"What kind of man are you?" my coach asked the Waterford coach.

Sufficiently embarrassed, the Waterford coach apologized to his scorekeeper. He sent in a substitute for John Anderson. We won that game, too.

That summer, while playing basketball at all the local playgrounds, I carried around in the pit of my stomach this horrible feeling. I felt as if I were a criminal. Some days I rationalized my actions by telling myself that what I had done was done in the best interests of my basketball career. Surely, after winning three games for him from the scorer's table, the coach wouldn't cut me again. Surely, I had ingratiated myself with him; there would be a spot for me. I had earned it. I had showed him that I could follow orders correctly; I had showed him that I could be daring and yet discreet; I had showed him what a good scorekeeper could do, and that he could pattern all of his future scorekeepers after me. But meanwhile, it was time I got mine. My reward was going to be a place on the varsity team.

I was wrong, of course.

He cut me from the team again, after a spectacular showing in tryouts. I drove to the basket and feinted, sending defensive stalwarts flying in all directions; I banked layups, dropped in jump shots from the far corners of the floor, and, on defense, stole basketballs from players' grasps or else slapped them loose and scooped them up myself. On the last day, when I was coming off the floor for the last time, all the other players applauded me. The coach then put up three pieces of paper on the bulletin board outside the gym.

The first list was headed by the words: "The following players have been selected to the freshman team. . ."

My name was not on that list.

The second list was headed by the words: "The following players have made the junior varsity team. . ."

My name was not on that list.

The third list was headed by the words: "The following players have made the varsity team. . ."

Nope. Cut again.

I didn't cry this time. I silently thought about cutting the coach's heart out with a pair of scissors and feeding it to the neighborhood stray cat. After having showered and gotten dressed, I walked slowly out of the locker room, hoping to bump into some smallish player so that I could start a fight with him and beat him up. The coach was waiting for me in the hall.

He motioned for me to follow him into the dark gymnasium. He sat on the first row of the bleachers again. He said to me:

"I need you again. Just like last year. You're more valuable to me as a scorekeeper than you are as a player. No way you're gonna win three games for me as a player. As a scorekeeper, you could win six, or eight."

I nodded, not saying a word.

"Now, look," he said, "I know you feel bad. But we'll have the same arrangement we had last year. You work out with the varsity all week. You keep scores at games, I'll get you a letter. I'll get you into the varsity club. I'll get you the sports column in the school paper. Put youself in my shoes. You got a kid like you, what're you gonna do with him? Sit him on the bench as a player? Or let him win games for you as a scorekeeper?"

He put his arm around me, and he said: "I like you. You're one of my favorite kids. I've got a soft spot right here for you."

He pointed to somewhere below his left nipple. I was hooked.

"Okay," I said. "I'll do it."

We were in a new league that year, a league called the Suburban Council. It consisted of schools exactly like mine: new, glass fishbowls of schools that were pancaked over vast acres of rolling grassland. I was in the vanguard of the suburban-high-school explosion in America. The Suburban Council was supposed to be the model organization for upstate New York schools; it was going to be the prestige league. The sophisticated suburban kids were supposed to be more intelligent, more aware, than all of those rowdies left behind in the medieval city high schools. We wouldn't be playing in Green Island or Waterford any more; now we were going to be playing on real farmland, in schools that were called "Niskayuna," and "Shaker," and "Guilderland" and "Schalmont." Even the team nicknames were exotic: One school selected "Sabres," another "The Dutchmen," a third "The Blue Bison."

The gymnasiums were lavish, well-lighted, large, and acoustically correct.

When the basketball season started, I quickly realized that the scorekeepers in the Suburban Council were, indeed, a lot more sophisticated and a lot more aware than the scorekeepers I had bilked the year before.

Everybody cheated in the Suburban Council.

A kid from Schalmont, a tall Italian who said his name was Danny, actually had the audacity to attempt to sneak in a p-3 on me. Niskayuna had two scorekeepers, one to keep score and one to watch the other scorer so that he didn't pull any funny stuff. I realized right away that my work was going to be cut out for me. The other kids apparently had coaches just like mine. Their coaches apparently told them the same things that mine told me.

I ran out the string that season. The next year, my senior year in high school, I took a part-time job as a sports stringer for the evening newspaper in town, the *Union-Star*. Sports stringers are people who cover high-school basketball games on Friday and Saturday nights during the winter. They are paid five dollars a game. The job got me off the hook with Benchley Steele. He got himself a new cheater. I didn't see Benchley Steele much that season. In fact, the last time I saw him and spoke to him at any length was one Monday afternoon in the gym office. I had covered one of my own school's games the Friday night before. I had written the story that appeared in the Saturday paper. My school had lost. When I walked into the gym office, I could tell that Ol' Benchie Steele was mad.

"What the hell kind of headline was that?" he growled at me.

"What headline?" I asked.

"The one in Saturday's paper," he said.

The headline in the Saturday paper, I remembered, read: NIS KAS ROUT MOHONS, 72–58.

"What was wrong with it?" I asked.

He said, "What is this 'rout' business? We were only ten down with two minutes left. Tell me, is that a rout? Now, is it?"

I tried to explain to him that in newspaper offices the people who write the stories do not write the headlines. People who are called "Deskmen" do. Benchley Steele did not believe my explanation. He said:

"You're selling me out, right down the river."

Then he walked away.

But I'm not really mad at my first coach today. In fact, every time I think about him I smile. When he retired, I heard that the people gave him a testimonial banquet. Beautiful. But he taught me one of the first real hard lessons that all young men must learn before they succeed in America: He taught me the art of cheating within the system. There is a big difference between cheating within the system and cheating outside the system. When you cheat within the system, you are praised for being smart, alert, and mature. When you cheat outside the system, you go to jail. Doctoring scorebooks in basketball games is cheating within the system. Doctoring blank checks that belong to somebody else is cheating outside the system. Cheating within the system is very big in America, even today.

Grown men cheat companies with fake expense accounts and by calling in sick when they feel chipper but feel like playing a round of golf instead of working. I knew old ladies who cheated at bingo games; they doctored up their transparent, round tokens with half-numbers. If they needed a 4 for bingo and there was a 1 on the card, they slipped their half-4 button over the 1. Then the 1 would look like a 4. Bingo.

In America today, it is entirely possible that millions of young males acquire their first lessons in cheating in the playgrounds of the neighborhood schools. The coaches do the honors. What do you think players practice every night? How to be nice, and legal, and gentlemanly? No sir. They practice deceptive plays until they get them down pat. Deception in sports, for the ultimate good of the team, is revered. Parents and educators do not question the pick in basketball, or the curve ball in baseball, on moral grounds. But they become outraged when there is a little teamwork in the classroom, in the form of sharing test answers. Sports are separate entities; they have their own moral criteria.

Coaches rule these little empires. The only thing standing between coaches and moral anarchy is the referee. And sometimes even he doesn't help. Benchley Steele used to chew out referees at games very often. He chewed them out so often, and so loudly, that the referees became intimidated. They started worrying if they were going to be invited back to earn their fifteen dollars the following week. Then they started ignoring fouls, or else they started making judgment calls in my coach's favor. When that happened, they were always invited back. Someday Ol' Benchie Steele is going to make a deal with Lucifer—I just know it.

IV · Who Are These Men Called Coaches, and What are They Really Thinking?

Coaches. Who are these men, and what are they really thinking? To define these men, one must go to
where
the
coaches
are.

Every year, late in March, Atlantic City is besieged for four days by approximately five thousand men between the ages of twenty-two and sixty-five. These men walk up and down Pacific Avenue and along the boardwalk, wearing plasticized windbreakers, white sneakers, and chino slacks; many of them have clipboards tucked under their arms. They are coaches. The purpose of their pilgrimage to Atlantic City is to attend the annual National Coaches' Clinic. During the four days and four nights they spend in Atlantic City, they exchange information with each other about job openings; they attend discussions about the intricacies of zone defenses and wishbone offenses; they conduct workshops that specialize in such exotic topics as how to discipline players more effectively; they fill open dates on their schedules; they cluster in groups in the lobbies of the Howard Johnson Motor Inn and the Holiday Inn and exchange gossip about outstanding prospects and fallen comrades; they visit exhibits inside the convention hall and chat with salesmen peddling fifty-five-dollar shoulder pads, and with representatives of the Fellowship of Christian Athletes, peddling jock Christianity. At night, the coaches drink and search the wind-swept streets for available women; since Atlantic City, late in March, has as many available women walking the streets as does Nome, Alaska, the coaches wind up just drinking. Some of them wind up screaming very nasty words and pounding on the walls of their motel rooms at three o'clock in the morning (ninth floor, Four Seasons Inn, Pacific Avenue). The four days in Atlantic City usually wind up as nothing more than a reaffirmation of their allegiance to their own particular male society. They return home and tell their wives that they've accumulated valuable strategic information; they tell their school administrators that they spent the school's money prudently; and they tell their cohorts in town what great times they had in swinging Atlantic City.

So: Who are these men? Where do they come from? What are they really thinking? Coaches, hiding behind windbreakers, clipboards, and unbeaten seasons, have always seemed to escape human definition. They are usually defensive about their personal lives and thoughts; they avoid serious questions with practiced malapropisms, and they volunteer nothing. Circulating among their number in the motel lobbies, on the floor of the convention hall, and in the lunchroom area, I interviewed perhaps two hundred of these coaches, in groups of ten, asking them questions on a variety of subjects, ranging from their financial status to their political views. The ground rule was anonymity; to a man, they did not wish to be identified with their views in print. So, I did not ask them their names. The objective was to find out who these coaches really were and what they were really thinking.

Agreed: this is no representative sample. Quite possibly, diehard coaches are excessively represented at conventions. Yet the following results are not exactly meaningless:

1. *Education.* Ten out of ten said that they were college graduates. Four out of ten said that they had earned master's degrees. Eight out of ten said that they had majored in physical education while in college.

2. *Family Status.* Nine out of ten said that they were married. All nine said that they had at least one child. One said: "That's what getting married is all about, isn't it?"

3. *Income.* Seven out of ten said that they were earning yearly salaries of fifteen thousand dollars. Two said they were earning yearly salaries of ten thousand dollars. One said that his year salary was in the neighborhood of eight thousand dollars.

4. *Religion.* Ten out of ten said that they believed in the teachings of an organized religion. Eight of them said that they were Protestant, which they defined as being either Baptist, Lutheran, Methodist, or Presbyterian—"or anything close." Two said that they were Roman Catholic.

5. *Political Philosophy.* Four out of ten described themselves as having conservative political views. Four said that they had "middle of the road" feelings about most major issues. One described himself as a moderate conservative; he said that he did not think all liberals were bad, particularly the senator from the state of Washington, Henry (Scoop) Jackson. One described himself as a moderate liberal; he said he had been wary of the Kennedys, but that he had had "nothing against" Lyndon Johnson. All ten said that they had voted for Richard Nixon in the 1972 presidential election; four said that they would vote for him again, four said that they had had second thoughts about that campaign, particularly after Watergate first broke, and two said that, if given the choice again, they would vote for George McGovern.

6. *Reading Habits.* Ten out of ten said that they read their local newspapers regularly. Two out of ten said that they regularly read

The New York Times. Four out of ten said that they regularly read either *Newsweek* or *Time* magazine. Three out of ten said that they regularly read *Sport* magazine. Eight out of ten said they regularly read *Sports Illustrated* magazine. All ten said that in their regular newspaper and magazine reading, they turned to the sports section first. None of them was familiar with the *Village Voice* or with *Ramparts* magazine; six of them said that they had never seen *New York* magazine, and two of them said that their favorite magazine was *Life.*

7. *People They Admire.* Ten out of ten said they had a particular admiration for Don Shula, the head coach of the Miami Dolphins. ("A coach's coach," one of them said.) Eight out of ten said they admired Woody Hayes, the head coach at Ohio State University. ("The thing that turned me off on Woody," one of the dissenters said, "was this story I heard at a clinic last summer. Woody was up in the tower and he saw the quarterbacks were screwing up; he yelled down, 'All right, you quarterbacks take a lap. Your coach gets a lap, too.' He made the quarterback coach take a lap along with the players; that's disgusting. How can any assistant coach have any pride working for Woody Hayes?") Six out of ten said they admired Joe Paterno, the head coach of Penn State University. ("Joe's playing both ends," said one of the coaches, who works at a small Pennsylvania high school. "He's paying lip service to the liberals with his cracks about Nixon and Watergate and things. People see right through it. A lot of people I know think Joe Paterno is a big phony.") Nine out of ten said that they admired John McKay, the head football coach at the University of Southern California. (The lone dissenter said: "McKay's cocky, too cocky. He comes around to these conventions and talks down at us like we're a bunch of second-string sophomores.") Two out of ten said that they admired Richard Nixon.

8. *Winning.* Ten out of ten said that winning games was the biggest single concern that they had. Ten out of ten said that everything that they do is designed toward winning games.

9. *Women's Sports.* None of the ten coaches interviewed on this subject wanted to see women's sports programs upgraded to an

equal level with male sports. One coach said: "Girls are the biggest pain in the ass that I've got." Another said: "I'd rather watch a boys' intramural game than a girls' varsity game any day." Ten out of ten said that girls were making demands for better sports programs at their schools. Ten out of ten said that the Women's Liberation Movement was behind it all. (One coach said: "Ten years ago, you never heard any of this talk. Now, that's all you hear, give the girls this, give the girls that. Women's Lib put the ideas in everybody's head.") Ten out of ten said that girls' programs will never reach equality with boys' sports programs at their schools.

10. *Pre-season Camps.* Out of ten Pennsylvania coaches, ten said that they take their football teams to some kind of pre-season camp. One said that his camp was nothing more than a conditioning camp; another said that his camp was a crash course in getting the kids into game shape. Eight of ten coaches said that the players pay for camp expenses themselves. One coach said: "It costs each of my players seventy dollars a week. I tell them to spend the summer mowing lawns, running errands, anything, but report to me on August fifteenth with seventy dollars in their hands. If the kid doesn't come up with it, he stays home. Does it hurt his chances of making the team? You damn well better be sure that it hurts his chances."

11. *Job Security.* Seven out of ten said that they already had tenure in their teaching jobs; three said they were working toward tenure. Ten out of ten said that they felt secure in their coaching jobs only when their teams had winning seasons. "Don't let anybody kid you about this," one coach said. "When schools hire you, they say, 'We're going to give you three years, maybe four, to produce.' You get the message right away. You win, or you're out of a job."

12. *Personal Ambition.* Eight out of ten said that they aspired to coach on a higher level, meaning at a major college or for a professional team. Six out of the eight said that they felt their aspirations would never be fulfilled. ("There's too much politics involved," one of them said. "A guy gets a head-coaching job

somewhere and the first thing he does is hire his old friends to be his assistants. A new guy doesn't have a chance. The only way you make it up the ladder is to ride somebody's coattails. Pro jobs are even worse. You gotta be a former player. Hell, I know fifty high-school coaches who could have done a better job with the [New York] Giants than Alex Webster did.") Two out of ten said that they had no aspirations beyond the high-school level.

13. *"Liberal" Educators.* Eight out of ten said that they felt that "liberal" educators were becoming prominent in high administrative jobs in their states. Ten out of ten said they considered these "liberal" educators as threats to their sports programs. Ten out of ten said that they felt these "liberal" educators were trying to pull back on interscholastic sports programs and build up the intramural programs. (One coach said: "In Pennsylvania, we've got this guy who keeps saying that interscholastic sports is a waste of money, that it benefits only a small number of kids. He wants to use the money to benefit the largest number of kids, in intramurals. He also says that it's time to let everybody get a chance at coaching; you know, guys who once played at Alabama, or someplace, who are insurance men in town. He wants to invite them over and hand them our teams. What he's telling me, then, is that I wasted all those years in college, and that I wasted all those years coaching teams, because some guy can come in off the street and do just as good a job as I've been doing. He's telling me I've wasted my life.")

14. *Won-Lost Records.* Eight out of ten felt that an undefeated season, or a league, playoff, or state championship, was the pinnacle for which to strive. Ten out of ten said that the hardest thing to do was to repeat as a league champion, or to have consecutive unbeaten seasons. One said that he preferred having seasons during which his teams won seven or eight games, but never won a championship or went undefeated. He said: "You win seven, eight games, everybody's happy and you don't have any pressure to repeat. Charlie McClendon at L.S.U. has been working this for years; he's always near the top, wins his seven or eight every year,

goes to some Concrete Bowl or something, and everybody's always happy. He's never unbeaten, never in the big game. But he's never fired, either." One coach said that he prefers having teams which finish around the .500 mark. He said: "Never work either end of the spectrum; never win all the time, never lose all the time. You go six–four one year, four–six the next, five–five the next, everybody's off your back. Nobody's talking championship, nobody's talking losing. You're right in the middle, and safe."

15. *Hobbies.* Eight out of ten said that they had no hobbies that were not related to coaching. Two of them said their hobby was attending coaching clinics, seminars, and conventions. One said: "I'm bringing my family down to this clinic next month, in Wildwood [New Jersey]. Hundred and fifteen dollars for the week for all of us. Where else can you get a week at the shore at those prices?" Two out of ten said that if they had a hobby, it would be playing golf.

16. *Water Breaks.* Ten out of ten said that they were concerned about the recent increase in deaths of high-school players from heat prostration and dehydration due to lack of water during hot practice days. Ten out of ten said that they gave their players regularly scheduled breaks for water and Gatorade. (One coach said: "I had a kid nearly die on me two years ago. He had this pimple problem, this horrible complexion. His doctor told him, 'No salt.' So the kid doesn't take any salt tablets, and he stays away from salt at the training table. One day, during practice, he conks out on me. He goes into convulsions. I was scared. After I found out what happened, I said to him, 'Why didn't you tell me what the doctor said?' He said, 'I didn't want any special treatment, Coach.' You can lead the kids to water, but you can't make them drink it unless you personally pour it down their throats.")

17. *Criminal Immunity.* Ten out of ten said that they have never given any thought to the question of immunity from criminal prosecution that coaches enjoy when they help to incite riots at games or when they hold practices in extreme heat—conditions that can lead to the death of a player. Ten out of ten said that they

could not explain why things that happen at games, or inside the realm of sports, are rarely subjected to the laws that govern the rest of society.

18. *Ethnic Differences Among Players.* Ten out of ten said that kids from poor, blue-collar communities were the best athletes. Ten out of ten said that they were the hungriest and the toughest breed of athlete; all ten said that they were the easiest kids to coach. Seven out of ten said that poor kids of Polish, German, Irish, or Slavic extractions were the best high-school football players; two said that Italian kids were the best, but only if they played visible positions, i.e., running back, quarterback, or receiver: ("Italian kids want the glory; they make lousy interior linemen. Polish kids and German kids don't care about glory so much; they make the best linemen.") One coach said that Jewish kids were the poorest players: ("They don't like to hit; there's something about contact that scares them.") As for black players, three coaches said that they were the most difficult to coach: ("The trouble with blacks is that they're either very, very good, or very, very bad. There's no average blacks. If the black kids like you, they'll work like hell. If they don't like you, they'll dog it.")

19. *Rejecting Players.* Nine out of ten coaches, all of them football coaches, said they never cut players from their team. One of them said: "Look, a kid can be hopeless and he still can help you. You sit him on the bench and keep him there, and then one day you put him into a game and all of the pent-up emotion and anger comes out of him, and he turns into a hell of a tackler or blocker. Besides, in football you can always use warm bodies." Another coach said: "The only problem with cutting kids is in basketball. You got what—fourteen kids? In football, we carry as many as come out."

20. *Motivation.* Ten out of ten said that motivating players to excel is one of the coach's main jobs. Nine out of ten said that screaming, yelling, and verbal harassment were acceptable ways of motivating players. Nine out of ten also said that subtle forms of intimidation were also within the acceptable boundaries. ("You let the kid know right away that you're tougher than he is, that you'll

knock him on his ass if he wants to challenge you, and you've got him. He'll never call your bluff.") Six out of ten said that physical violence also is an acceptable method of motivating players. ("You rap a kid on the helmet, shove him into a contact drill, even kick him in the ass, and it arouses him. He gets mad at you, and takes it out on everybody around him.") Four coaches said that they stop short of hitting their players.

21. *Ethics.* Ten out of ten said that they considered themselves ethical people. Ten out of ten said that they never have asked themselves if what they are doing is beneficial to society or not. Two out of ten said that they have heard of Jack Scott (director of the Institute for the Study of Sport and Society), but they said they were not familiar with his work.

22. *State-by-State Differences.* Ten out of ten said that they were aware of wide disparities from state to state in rules and regulations governing high-school sports. Ten out of ten said that they did not know exactly what was going on in high-school sports outside of their own state. Ten out of ten said that they did not particularly care what was going on in other states, so long as they knew what was going on in their own.

23. *Books.* Four out of ten said they did not have the time to read books for pleasure. Three out of ten said that the only book reading they do is confined to books in the football-strategy genre. Two out of ten said that their favorite book was *Instant Replay* (by Jerry Kramer, about a season with the Green Bay Packers under Vince Lombardi), and one said that he particularly liked *Paper Lion* (by George Plimpton, about filling in as a novice player on the Detroit Lions professional team).

24. *Movies.* Three out of ten said that they do not have the time to watch movies for pleasure. Three out of ten said that the recent movie that they enjoyed most was *The Godfather.* Two said they liked *Billy Jack,* and one mentioned *The Way We Were.* One coach said that he went to movies occasionally, but hadn't seen any in recent years that had impressed or touched him. Ten out of ten said that they would not take their wives to see an X-rated movie.

25. *Budget Problems.* Two out of ten said that their schools were

experiencing serious budget problems and shortages of money. Eight out of ten said that their sports programs would not suffer in the event of cutbacks. ("We make money for the school; we're safe.") Two out of ten said that their programs were vulnerable in the event of budget cutbacks. "(The principal, a liberal, said that sports would be the first to go. He said it was the least-important part of the school curriculum. Of course, he's full of shit.")

26. *Views of Themselves.* Ten out of ten said that they considered themselves moral human beings. Ten out of ten said that they considered themselves to be doing their communities important services. Eight out of ten said that they considered themselves popular among their players. Ten out of ten said that they considered themselves "Middle Americans"; all ten said that they were proud of that categorization. Ten out of ten said that they considered themselves to be the greatest male influence their players have—outside of their fathers. Nine out of ten said that they felt that a woman's place is still in the home, with children. Nine out of ten said that their wives did not work at regular jobs. Ten out of ten said that they considered themselves among the most-respected people in their communities.

V • Little League Baseball: Where Boy Meets Coach for the First Time (So You Really Think You Know What Little League Baseball Is, Do You?)

I trust in God
I love my country and will respect its laws
I will play fair and strive to win
But win or lose, I will always do my best.
—THE LITTLE LEAGUE PLEDGE

Ah, Little League baseball. It is as much a part of the American tapestry as apple pie à la mode, Norman Rockwell paintings of little girls in pigtails eating drippy ice cream cones, and fireworks on July 4th. For thirty-five years it has been packaged as the ultimate haven for American boys between pablum and puberty; the late J. Edgar Hoover, who was a member of the Little League Board of Directors, once said that Little League baseball was the greatest deterrent to crime that America had ever seen. "Keep Kids in Sports and out of Courts," the motto went.

Now, after having digested all of the palatable myths for all these years, it usually comes as a shock to people when they discover what the organization known as Little League Baseball, Incorporated, really is: It is, among other things, a federally chartered corporation that operates in concert with the United States government to promote Americanism in thirty-one countries; it is a franchise business that trafficks in millions of tax-exempt dollars every year; it is a conglomerate that sells the rights to the official Little League trademark to hundreds of companies. In a nutshell, Little League is a hydra-headed enterprise devoted to (1) earning money, and (2) promoting America. Boys and baseball are merely the whipped-cream topping.

On July 16, 1964, Lyndon Baines Johnson signed Public Law 88-378. The law gave the organization known as Little League Baseball, Incorporated, with headquarters in South Williamsport, Pennsylvania, a federal charter of incorporation. Federal charters are as rare in the halls of Congress as the duckbilled platypus; only five have ever been granted, to organizations such as the American Red Cross. The Little League charter was the work of two prom-inent matchmakers, Emmanuel Celler, then a representative from New York, and William Cahill, then a member from New Jersey. Before reaching the President's desk, the charter had to pass through both houses of Congress—with unanimous approval. It did.

The charter, once granted, made all the money that found its way into the Little League headquarters building on Route 15 in South Williamsport tax-exempt. All Little League Baseball, In-corporated, had to do in return for the federal charter was two things: (1) tailor its mission to the wishes of the U.S. government, and (2) file an annual financial (and philosophical) report with the Judiciary Committee of the House of Representatives. So, for the past decade, the largest sports organization on the planet Earth (8,500 leagues in 31 countries) has been a quasi-governmental agency, but it has been such a well-kept secret that the only people who seem to know it are the people in the General Accounting Office in Washington who audit the Little League reports.

Now, if you happen to think that your neighborhood Little League in Syosset or Smithtown runs by itself, you are wrong. Each of the 8,500 Little Leagues pays approximately $68 a year (depending on the number of teams) for the privilege of calling itself "Little League." That's $578,000 off the top, every year, to the headquarters in South Williamsport. Each of the 8,500 Little Leagues, like each McDonald's hamburger stand, becomes a separate entity—under the headquarters' umbrella—once it has paid the franchise fee. But all of the leagues, like all of the hamburger stands, are ultimately ruled by a small group of invisible men who sit high atop the corporate ladder. (Several court decisions have already decreed that the term "Little League" is a corporate trademark and cannot be used for profit without financial reimbursement to the Little League headquarters.)

Next are the all-star-tournament game fees. Every year, after July 18, when the all-star teams begin playing in tournament competition (which culminates in the annual Little League World Series, during the last week of August in the ten-thousand seat Howard J. Lamade Memorial Stadium in South Williamsport), collections from the spectators are taken at each game. From each collection, $5 is sent to the headquarters. Since 50,000 or so all-star tournament games are played (it's a single-elimination tournament) before a world champion is finally crowned, at the World Series, the headquarters in South Williamsport takes in approximately $250,000 from these games alone. Combined with the half-million dollars that it gets in franchise fees, the all-star tournament game fees raise the annual intake figure to over three-quarters of a million dollars—all of which the headquarters gets directly from the local leagues themselves. All of it, of course, is tax free.

Next is the business of subsidiary monies. For all of the millions of official Little League bats that are sold, the headquarters receives royalty fees in return for the use of the official Little League emblem. (In recent years, the Little League headquarters has encouraged the use of aluminum bats; in the next five years or so, most of the 8,500 leagues will make the conversion from wooden bats to aluminum ones. Result: Big profits for the bat manufacturers, big profits for the Little League Headquarters.) Royalty fees are also derived from such things as official Little League baseballs, official Little League batting cages, official Little League awards certificates, books, buttons, decals, desk sets, first-aid kits, gloves, batting helmets, leg protectors, pitching machines (which sell for as much as $650), public-address systems, cassette tape recorders and tapes, rulebooks, rubber-spiked shoes, snack-stand equipment, tumblers, women's-auxiliary jewelry, and athletic supporters.

The Little League headquarters also is in the summer-camp business (it operates several boys' camps in various parts of the country; $150 for ten days); the insurance business (with the American Casualty Company of Reading, Pennsylvania, as a partner, it offers "excess" policies to all of its players; when a boy is injured, Little League headquarters covers what his family's insurance policy does not); the real-estate business (Little League headquarters' propery holdings are immense; in some cases, large tracts of land have been donated or willed to Little League baseball by civic-minded citizens. In the hamlet of South Williamsport alone, Little League headquarters has purchased forty-five acres of land, upon which sit its administrative building, its World Series stadium, and one of its summer camps.). It is also in the publishing business: Over one million Little League manuals are produced and sold throughout the world in various languages every year.

There is also the Little League Foundation. It has over $1 million at its disposal, for the "perpetuation of Little League base-ball." The money was collected over several years during National Little League Week, which, significantly, always coincided with Flag Day (June 14). The money has been translated into market-able securities, common stocks, industrial bonds, and preferred stocks, almost all of which are in a custodial account in the Girard Trust Bank in Philadelphia. Exactly what the Little League Foundation is supposed to do with the money has never been spelled out (recurrent rumors that it is being invested in foreign real-estate have always been denied). But, according to the 1972 Little League Foundation financial report to Congress, as prepared by Price Waterhouse & Company, the Foundation had financial assets of $1,104,852.

In recent years, the headquarters of Little League baseball has moved to monopolize the entire field of boys' baseball. It has launched a Senior Little League, for boys thirteen to fifteen, and already has two thousand leagues in the fold; the Senior Little League World Series is played annually in Gary, Indiana. It also has a Big Little League for boys sixteen to eighteen; its World Series is played annually in Fort Lauderdale, Florida. All of which means that once the Little League headquarters wraps its tentacles around a boy at age nine, it will be able to hold on to him until age eighteen. Perhaps even more important, it will be able to hold on to his family for all of those years; the fathers and mothers of the players do all of the work in Little League baseball—they rake the fields, paint the fences, sell the soda and popcorn at concession stands, solicit the sponsors, etc. None of them is paid for his or her services; the only people who are paid in Little League baseball are the headquarters staff in South Williamsport. Everybody else is a "volunteer."

The man who has run the entire organization since 1955 is Peter McGovern. For twenty-one years he was the president of Little League Baseball, Incorporated, and the chairman of its board of directors. According to the 1971 financial report filed with Congress, McGovern's salary was $25,000 a year, plus expenses. Creighton Hale, the president since October 1973, had been executive director since 1956; in the latter job, he earned $18,750 plus expenses. Robert Stirrat, the public-relations director, earned $16,062 plus expenses. There are approximately sixty other people employed full-time in the red-brick headquarters building, which is the nerve center into which five other regional headquarters complexes are plugged. The others are in St. Petersburg, Florida; San Bernardino, California; Chicago; Waco, Texas; and Ottawa, Ontario. McGovern ran Little League baseball single-handedly from 1955 to 1973; it was in 1955 that he succeeded in ousting the founder, Carl Stotz, after a long and bitter federal-court battle.

Stotz, who was then commissioner of Little League baseball, had filed suit against McGovern to prevent him from turning the program into a big business. Stotz wanted to keep it the way he had envisioned it originally: a grassroots organization for boys and baseball. At one point in the dispute, the Williamsport sheriff actually padlocked the doors of the Little League headquarters to prevent McGovern from leaving town with the cash assets and setting up a new headquarters somewhere else. But when Stotz was finally removed from the scene, McGovern left the United States Rubber Company, where he had been an executive, and took control of Little League himself. (United States Rubber, now Uniroyal, had sent McGovern to Williamsport originally to look after its investment in the rubber-spiked shoes that Little League players wear.) Carl Stotz, who is now a tax collector in Williamsport, said that he hasn't seen a Little League all-star baseball game in eighteen years.

How did it all begin?

It began quite innocently enough in Williamsport, Pennsylvania, a city of 37,918 people, located in a northeastern corner of the state. It began because Williamsport had a citizen named Carl Stotz. He started the balls rolling. Carl Stotz had a common-enough dream in his own childhood, like millions of other little boys before and since. Whenever he played baseball, in his imagination he was a big-league player performing in a big-league park. This took considerable imagining, since his baseball consisted chiefly of impromptu games of "movings-up" in schoolyards and vacant lots. Occasionally, Carl Stotz would promote a regulation game with nine players on each side. But, more often than not, the games fell through because the pitcher had to go home and do his chores, or the boy with the catcher's mask failed to show up.

In the summer of 1938, when Carl Stotz was twenty-eight, his nephews, Jimmy and Harold Gehron, aged six and eight, got the baseball fervor. Carl Stotz decided to see if he couldn't make those old dreams of his own come true for his nephews, and for the other boys in their neighborhood. He began to make the rounds of local businesses, trying to interest them in sponsoring small-boy baseball teams. But the Depression was still on (at least in Williamsport). Nobody gave. Finally, after fifty-six consecutive turndowns, he called at the Lycoming Dairy, where the manager, Floyd Mutchler, contributed thirty-five dollars.

With that money, Stotz bought three dozen baseball-style play suits at the five-and-ten store and used them as uniforms for three teams. Then the Lundy Lumber Company and the Jumbo Pretzel Company came through, with smaller amounts of money, making it possible for Stotz to buy shirt emblems and some basic playing equipment. The first season, in 1939, was just supervised sandlot play. No outfield fences, scoreboards, dugouts, bleachers, or loud-speaker systems. Games were scheduled at twilight—as they still are—when the team managers would be home from work. The men would bolt their suppers and hustle out to the vacant lot with the home plate, the pitching slab, and the bases, bats, and balls under their arms.

By 1947, there were so many leagues that Carl Stotz organized a championship tournament, in which all-star teams from leagues in Pennsylvania, New York, and New Jersey participated. (It evolved into the Little League World Series.) By 1948, the thing had become too large for Stotz and his friends to handle on a spare-time basis. Stotz decided that the resources of some big outside organization were needed. He went to the United States Rubber Company, which was already interested to the extent of developing a special line of baseball sneakers with rubber spikes for Little League players. Carl Stotz asked the company for money.

In 1955, Little League baseball underwent a dramatic change in direction. Carl Stotz, the founder, was removed from the scene. Peter McGovern, of the United States Rubber Company, who had been sent to Williamsport to look after his company's invest-ment in the rubber-spiked shoes that Little League players were wearing, took control of the headquarters and, ultimately, the entire organization. The dispute between Stotz and McGovern created sensational and uncomplimentary headlines in newspapers throughout the country. In all of the law suits, the name-calling, the allegations and counter allegations, Little League baseball lost its innocence. People who had previously looked upon Little League baseball as being nothing more than a charming caricature of the major leagues began looking upon it as the big business it was rapidly becoming. But Carl Stotz did not relinquish his original ideals without a fight; if Little League baseball was going to become a big business, it was not going to accomplish the transition without some resistance. Carl Stotz's official complaint was this: The Little League board of directors was being stacked by McGovern to include people who did not know anything about boys and baseball (but who were, presumably, philosophical allies of McGovern's). That meant that all of the people on the grassroots level, the people who were really the backbone of the organization, were being left without adequate representation on the board of directors. Carl Stotz filed a $300,000 suit against McGovern in a federal court in Lewisburg, Pennsylvania.

Carl Stotz withdrew his legal proceedings, he said, when it became evident to him that the judge would rule against him and he would lose his case. For a while he toyed with the idea of forming his own Little League organization—to be called "The Original Little League"—and encouraged defections from the McGovern-controlled organization. But a federal judge issued a restraining order against Stotz that said, in effect, that Stotz was to have nothing to do with boys and baseball—under the penalty of legal action. So, he abandoned the idea and hasn't been heard from since.

The patron saint of Little League baseball in the House of Representatives in the early 1960s was William Cahill, a Republican from New Jersey. (He subsequently became governor of that state.) In a floor speech which spells out the government's interest in, and use of, Little League baseball, Cahill said:

What better medium [therefore], for improving race relations in the United States and developing better international relationships through the world, than this great sport of baseball played as it is under the ideal conditions prescribed by Little League baseball. Consider, if you will, the rare opportunity of bringing forcefully to the attention of some small South American community, or some village in France, or one of the industrialized cities of Germany, Poland, or even Russia, the rules of conduct, the spirit of fair play and sportsmanship, the competitive spirit and the overall good will of the great American game of baseball as played by their own sons in their own back yard under American rules.

It does seem to me, Mr. Speaker, that the conclusion is self-evident. Here is a built-in, sure-fire, guaranteed-to-succeed implement to develop our relations throughout the world. How much more important is this than some of the ill-conceived projects which have been developed and upon which huge sums have been expended for the purpose of furthering the American image and developing good will among nations? Already Little League on its own, without any Federal contribution of any kind, has developed leagues in twenty-seven countries.

But Cahill's vision of having the U.S. Government employ Little League baseball as an instrument toward bettering international relations did not exactly materialize. In fact, it self-destructed—almost literally—right after the 1972 Little League World Series championship game.

Several Chinese people from New Jersey and New York State were injured in a fight after the championship game, and at least two of them were hospitalized with concussions. Ten minutes after Taipei, Taiwan, defeated Hammond, Indiana, 6–0, the fighting broke out in the southeast corner of the grassy slope behind the Lamade Stadium, site of the World Series. Chinese were involved, according to the Pennsylvania State Police. They were using wooden sticks, beating each other. The sticks, some heavy, others light and easily broken, had been used as staffs to hold Chinese flags and banners.

Sportswriters in the press box above the stadium, who were approximately five hundred feet from the fighting, said they saw a person on the ground being beaten with the sticks. An ambulance, on alert throughout the series, took the injured to the hospital. Finally, a state-police helicopter arrived, and began hovering lower and lower over the troubled area. It finally stayed at a height of approximately a hundred fifty feet. Hundreds of spectators scrambled to get out of the helicopter's prop wash. The fighting stopped.

The state police said it was the third time in the four years that the Nationalist Chinese had played in the series that there had been an outbreak of violence. At least two factions of Chinese were involved, the police said, one the natives of Taiwan, the other the Chinese who came to Taiwan in 1949, when the Communists took over mainland China. The police implied that the two groups had a violent hatred of each other.

A vehicle for international relations, Little League?

Really, now.

VI • How Little Boys Can Be Affected by Baseball—the Stories of Two World-Championship Players

Gene Tenace and Fred Riggi do not know each other. Gene Tenace resides, during the summer months, in Oakland, California, and during the winter months in Lucasville, Ohio. Fred Riggi resides the year around in Schenectady, New York. Gene Tenace is a professional baseball player. He plays first base for the Oakland Athletics. Fred Riggi is a stacker of small and medium-size engines in a General Electric Company factory.

But Gene Tenace and Fred Riggi do have one thing in common: They were both world champions at one time in their lives. Gene Tenace played on the Oakland teams that won the major-league World Series in 1972 and 1973. Fred Riggi played on the Schenectady team that won the Little League World Series in 1954. Both were profoundly affected by their experiences as Little League baseball players. In the case of Gene Tenace, that experience apparently paid off. He is a bona-fide major-league player who earns in the neighborhood of thirty-five thousand dollars annually. In the case of Fred Riggi, it apparently did not pay off. As a factory laborer, his annual salary barely surpasses five figures.

Gene Tenace had a father who wanted him to become a major-league baseball player. One day, when Gene Tenace was thirteen years old, he suffered a stomach spasm and was rushed to a hospital. His physical problem was diagnosed as an unusually large ulcer. After discussions with Gene, the doctor called in the young patient's mother, Mrs. Ethel Tenace.

"The doctor said Gene's problem came from being preached at so much by his father about becoming a ball player," recalled Mrs. Tenace, who lives in a house on Route 2 in Lucasville. "The doctor said that for a child to be so young and have such a bad ulcer was an awful thing. But ever since the day Gene was born, his father wanted him to be a major-league baseball player."

When Gene Tenace was a Little Leaguer, his father, Fiore Tenace, would scold him in front of the crowd if the youngster struck out or made a mindless play in the field. He would especially cuss Gene out if he didn't swing at a third strike. Gene Tenace's mother said: "A boy at that age has fearings. Gene would just stand there and take it, I remember. Tears would run down his cheeks. 'Didn't I always tell you to swing at a third strike? How come you didn't swing?' his father used to scream. Gene didn't say anything except 'I don't know.' If Gene had ever attacked back at his father, he probably would've got a slap across the mouth. His father used to say, 'No kid who lives under my roof is goin' to sass me.'

"I would holler at his father, 'Leave him alone, he's doing the *best* he can.' But his father used to say, 'If he's going to be a ballplayer, he'll do as I say.' "

For one year, at age thirteen, Gene Tenace had to stay out of school, and he was given a private tutor. He could not play baseball. In fact, he could play for only limited periods of time with other children.

"His nerves were so bad," said Mrs. Tenace, "that only once every couple of days could he have maybe two children come in and sit with him. They'd play maybe checkers or some games like that. Then they'd have to leave. You see, he'd be getting excited and his ulcer would flare up."

Gene Tenace was put on a strict diet for one year. "No greasy foods, no salt, no acids, but plenty of ice cream, Jell-o, and cottage cheese. Gene didn't like cottage cheese much," she said.

"I've always cooked lasagna and spaghetti and all the Italian dishes. But Gene couldn't eat any of it, and he loved those foods. So I fixed his meal first, then I sent him into the living room. Then the rest of us ate. I didn't want Gene to be there when we were all eating. He'd smell that food. I know what that would do to him."

Gene Tenace played no baseball that year. When he began playing again, the doctor suggested that his father not go to the games. "He stayed away for a couple or three months," said Mrs. Tenace. "Gene always wanted me to come to his ball game. But he asked me to tell Dad not to come because it made him nervous. The doctor said Gene shouldn't play catcher, that going up and down would hurt his stomach. So that's how Gene learned to play all those other positions."

Fiore Tenace had wanted to become a major-league baseball player, too. But he suffered an injury when he was fifteen years old—a bat swung accidentally cracked him in the base of the skull—and he felt that the injury had stunted his athletic progress. He was the son of a Pennsylvania coal miner, who was killed in a mine cave-in when Fiore Tenace was nine years old. At sixteen, Fiore Tenace quit school and went to work in the mines. In 1939, at the age of eighteen, he joined the Merchant Marine, then entered the Navy when World War II broke out. He also served in the Korean War, and was stationed in Philadelphia when Gene was four years old.

Afterward, he became a laborer in southern Ohio, everything from digging ditches to working on high-rise buildings. He is currently a truck driver, or, as Mrs. Tenace said, "a teamster."

For a while Fiore Tenace had been a semi-pro player around the Ohio-Pennsylvania area. Gene was often the batboy on his teams. As time went on, Gene was able to give his father some of his own medicine.

"Gene used to holler, 'Why didn't you strike at the ball, Dad?' Or something like that," said Mrs. Tenace, laughing. "His dad used to strike out a lot, too. But his dad never took it as sassing. He just figured Gene was hollering to hear himself holler at the ballpark. Gene was afraid of his dad."

Mrs. Tenace recalled that Gene's dad began playing catch with his son when Gene was two years old: "He be throwing an official baseball at him. 'Now you catch this,' he'd say. Well, Gene couldn't catch the baseball. He was two years old. But his dad kept playing with him at three and four years old. I remember one night when Gene was four and we lived in this apartment on Snyder Street in Philadelphia. Gene was at one end of the room, his father was at the other. One time Gene missed a baseball catch. The ball hit him in the mouth. Blood started dripping down and tears did, too. His dad said, 'Don't cry or I'll give you a licking.' Gene didn't holler. I said to his dad, 'I'll take this ball and hit you in the head with it.'

"Gene respects his dad. I know he does, and he tells people he does. Gene's a man now, he's twenty-eight, and things are changing between him and his dad. During the play-offs last year [1972] Gene called the house from Detroit. He talked to his dad. I was in the other room, so I didn't know what they were talking about. But his father was silent, say, for a couple of minutes. That's not like him. When he hung up he looked at me real funny. He said, 'Well, my son really hurt me. He said, "There you go criticizing me again, Dad." ' Gene kind of stood up to his dad; I thought that was good.

"But I guess it all turned out for the best. Gene's ulcer is gone. He can eat anything he wants to now. I think Gene is very much happy with his life. He always wanted to be a major-league baseball player. He's happy for himself, and I know he's pleased for his father, too. And his father! He's the proudest person I've ever seen in my life. When we came back from Cincinnati after the [1972] World Series, after Gene was named the best player by that magazine, you should have seen his father."

*

Fred Riggi did not have a "father" problem. But that world championship at age twelve set him up for a big letdown years later. Fred Riggi:

I've got to say that the whole experience, winning the world championship of Little League, and things, was nonsense. What did I get out of it? Nothing, that's what I got out of it. I'll tell you, it put a lot of ideas into my head, and it set me up for the biggest disappointment of my life several years later. Winning that world championship has had no effect whatsoever on what I do and what I am today. In fact, when I think about it, like now, I get upset. Look, when I was twelve years old, I was a world champion. Now I'm thirty-two, and you know what I do? I stack engines all day, eight hours a day, one pile on top of another, at the G.E. They call me a stacker. So I think, hey, maybe my life has gone downhill since I was twelve years old, and maybe I'm some kind of failure now, at thirty-two. But then I sit back and I think, yeah, when I was twelve I was part of something that was bullshit; the whole thing was made out to be something more important than it really was. So we won a world championship, big deal. You know something? I didn't really realize what a world championship was supposed to mean until five years after I helped win one. World champions, shit. All that experience did for me was fill me up with a lot of false hope, and that false hope led me to the most crushing disappointment of my life.

After we won that championship, you know, it was banquet after banquet, write-ups in the paper every day, all of that stuff. All of it made me think I was a sure bet for the major leagues someday; boy, that's all I ever wanted to be when I grew up, a big-league baseball player. I played baseball in the sandlots around Hamilton School and on Hungry Hill and at Central Park, anywhere there was room, long before I got involved with Little League. I loved baseball when I was nine, ten years old; I didn't get into Little League until I was eleven. I always made the team anywhere I went; I was in that percentage of kids who were good enough to make it anywhere. But today I look around and see where the kids who never made the teams are, making thirty grand a year, holding down big jobs with banks and insurance companies and in business for themselves, and I say, "Shit, I wish I never made all those teams, so I could have developed some other interests in life besides baseball." But when I was growing up that's all I ever did—play baseball. Nobody ever pushed me into it. My father was from the old country—Italy—and what did he know about baseball? Nothing. He never even introduced me to the game; I picked it up on the playgrounds. I remember, when I got to Little League, he used to come and watch me play, and he never really knew what was going on; if I made an error, or struck out, or something, he would tell me after the game, "Nobody is God." That's what he said: "Nobody is God." I never had to worry about going home after a bad game, like a lot of kids on that team did.

I played for two years on the Hershey Beverage team; Mike Maietta was the manager. Now, Mike also managed the all-star team to the championship, and I say today that the only reason we won it was because of him; he was a major-league manager with twelve-year-old kids. I always respected Mike, but I always knew—deep down inside—that he cared more about winning that championship than he cared for us. That's cool. O.K., he wanted to win the world championship and he used us to do it. He called all the pitches, and he drilled us like trained seals. But now I look back on it and I say, "Gee, it would have been nice to win the damn thing on our own, twelve-year-old kids beating other twelve-year-old kids, fair and square." But it wasn't that way. It was Mike beating other twelve-year-old kids with us. Mike put the pressure on us; the kids who choked under pressure weren't around long. To tell the truth, I was never a big part of that team after the very first all-star game; the pressure got to me, and Mike sensed it. I was the regular left-fielder that very first all-star game that year; but then he took me out, and I rarely played after that.

After Little League, I went to Mont Pleasant High School. I played football there—second-string quarterback—but baseball is what I loved most. I was still carrying that Little League dream around, that I would make the big leagues because I was a world champion. I played high-school baseball as a catcher; that's what I wanted to be, a big-league catcher. One day, I got to practice early and nobody was around to pitch; I threw batting practice. Now, why do guys want to pitch when they're kids? For the glory, right? Publicity: "Riggi Fires No-Hitter" in headlines—that's why all the kids wanted to pitch. It was the biggest mistake in my life; I might have made it as a catcher, but, no, I went for the glory. I did so-so in high school as a pitcher; then I played in the Twilight League, this semi-pro league, in the summers, pitching and catching. A guy I met in the Twilight League fixed me up with a working scholarship to Illinois State Normal College, as it was called then. Tuition was something like a hundred and fifty dollars a month, and I got forty dollars a week for managing the other sports teams when I wasn't playing baseball. I went there in the fall of 'fifty-nine. I stayed in a place called Cardinal Court, a old Air Force barracks, five guys in a room—it was the cheapest place I could find. But I never got to play ball there; my marks were low, and, to tell you the truth, my heart just wasn't in it. I never had had study habits anyway, and I failed two subjects, which isn't bad, considering. But who wanted to play baseball for Illinois State Normal College? Me, I wanted to play in the big leagues. So I quit school.

I came back to Schenectady and played in the Twilight League again, this time for a guy named Chuck Esmoke. He managed the best young team in the league; it was sponsored by a radio station. We beat the Yankee Rookies that year, I remember. One day, Esmoke—Smokey, we called him—set me up with a tryout with the Chicago Cubs. A dream come true, I thought. He took me to some place outside New York City, and he introduced me to a guy named Ralph Di Lullo, who was a scout for the Cubs. I threw some for Di Lullo, hit some, ran the bases, did some catching. He didn't say anything to me. He said, "I'll be in touch." I didn't know what to think—did I flunk the tryout, or what? I was depressed. Then, one day, DiLullo showed up at my house; he said he had a Cub contract for me. He said, "I'll give you three hundred dollars to sign, and if you make it to Class A, it's another thousand, and if you make it to Double A, it's two thousand." I signed right away. Hey, this was something I had always wanted. I was twenty years old and the Chicago Cubs were signing me to a pro contract. It was like seeing a dream come true.

The Cubs told me to report to Morristown, Tennessee, in some rookie league; it used to be called the Smokey Mountain League. I flew down there, but I could have walked on the clouds, I was feeling so high. They told me to report to this motel; the guy who owned the motel also owned the ball club. I got down there, and I hung around for three or four days, waiting for other guys to show up; I remember watching them come in, big guys, six-three, two hundred pounds, and here I was, five-eight and one sixty, and I began wondering, hey, what am I doing here? Then, when everybody had arrived, they gave us uniforms—the Morristown Cubs, we were called—and we started two-a-day practices, one in the morning and another in the afternoon. Right away, they asked for pitchers; like an idiot, I said, "I'm a pitcher." I began throwing batting practice; this coach—Martin was his name, he was the pitching coach—he watched me and said, "You got a curve, kid?" I said, "Yeah," but I didn't have any kind of curve ball. I had good control, and I threw with a nice, three-quarter-arm delivery, but the curve just wasn't there. They kept me around for two weeks; then the manager called me in.

He said, "We like you, kid, you work hard and no nonsense, but you haven't got a curve ball. We've got nineteen pitchers in this camp and we need only eight or nine. I hope you understand." I remember saying to myself that I'd be back. I wasn't really crushed until a couple of months later, when I realized, "Hey, Fred, you ain't never going to be back." Then I was really jolted; you spend all those years from the time you're ten until you're twenty dreaming about making the big leagues, and then you get a chance and you blow it. What are you prepared for in life? Nothing. That's where this Little League stuff hurt me; it kept alive this dream about making the big leagues—in fact, it convinced me that, since I was a world champion, I was going to make it a lot easier than the other guys. Then, when it was all over, how does a twenty-year-old kid tell himself that he's just wasted half of his life on a worthless dream?

Now I've got two kids, a boy's who's ten, George—he's my wife's from another marriage, but I've adopted him—and I got a boy who's six, Doug. I bought a house, and I live a quiet life. I don't go out much; we don't socialize with too many people.

Funny thing about the championship team: I haven't seen some of the guys since right after we won. A couple of the guys I haven't seen since I was twelve years old. Wouldn't recognize them, probably, if they walked right into me on the street.

VII • Ten-Year-Old Tom Seavers: Doctors Want Them Relieved

In August 1961, while covering the Eastern Regional Little League Tournament in Haddon Heights, New Jersey, for the newspaper *The Schenectady Union-Star*, I witnessed the following sequence of events, involving a team from Levittown, Pennsylvania:

1. Levittown was the defending world champion of Little League baseball; it had won the Little League World Series the year before. Prior to the opening-round game, a dozen buses brought several hundred adults from that city to cheer, in person, for the Levittown team. Having won that game, Levittown was advanced to the final round, and was scheduled to play the team from Schenectady, which I was covering, on a Saturday afternoon. On Friday night before the game, the players from Levittown were frolicking in the motel at which most of the people connected with the tournament were being lodged. It was a two-tiered motel, with staircases connecting both levels.

2. One of the best players on the Levittown team, a center fielder who was twelve years old, fell down the staircase. He sustained a nasty gash in his head. He was taken to a nearby

hospital in an ambulance, his head swathed in gauze. Adults, presumbly from Levittown, gathered to watch the ambulance drive away. One of them said, "There goes tomorrow's game."

3. The boy's gash required nine stitches to close. He was returned to the motel in the middle of the night, and was instructed by a doctor to stay in bed.

4. The following afternoon, the day of the championship game, was hot and humid. The temperature was in the mid-nineties. Arriving at the makeshift press area, a row of folding tables behind home plate, I asked one of the people from Levittown how the injured boy was. "Fine," he said.

5. The starting lineups were announced to the crowd over the loudspeaker. The injured boy was listed as the No. 2 hitter for Levittown, and playing centerfield.

6. The Levittown team, designated as the visiting team that day, took the field first. The injured boy ran out to center field. He was wearing a blue plastic batting helmet over his head. Under it, bandages were clearly visible. There was outrage in the makeshift press area; one visiting sports writer said that he felt the boy's life was actually in jeopardy: "What if he catches a fast ball in the head?" When the boy came up to bat, in the bottom of the first inning, the Levittown rooting section gave him a standing ovation, presumably for the courage he demonstrated in playing in the game.

7. The boy played in the entire game. Levittown won the game. Levittown went on to play in the Little League World Series.

There is nothing unusual about the aforementioned events. In almost every city in which Little League baseball is played, and taken seriously, there are people quite willing to recite horror stories involving the abuse of little boys by adult coaches and managers. Sometimes the horror stories involve the adults themselves, as was the case during the summer of 1970 in New Orleans. At a Little League game in that city, an adult team manager actually assaulted an umpire with a baseball bat.

The people most vocal in their criticism of Little League coaches and managers traditionally have been educators and medical professionals. But through the years their criticism has been discounted by most of the people involved with Little League baseball, for one obvious reason: The critics, however legitimate or well intentioned their arguments may have been, lacked credibility because they had avoided becoming a part of Little League baseball themselves. That educators and medical professionals do all their criticizing from the periphery of the organization actually brought the people inside the organization closer together; there has since evolved a communal immunity inside of Little League baseball to all forms of intellectual criticism. Little League people have always been quick to point out, "If they're so smart, if they know so much, how come they're not out here, helping us out?" The beleaguered-martyr complex is very popular among adults involved in Little League.

The criticism has almost always revolved around two issues: (1) what the adults, and the game, are doing to the boys psychologically, and (2) what the adults, and the game, are doing to the boys physically. For example:

Dr. Walter F. Char, associate professor at Temple University Medical School said: "Many fathers are using their sons as pawns. The father is playing the game, punishing his son, for instance, when he strikes out. Neurotic parents such as this cannot see the danger of overemphasis on winning. They don't see their child as an individual. A child simply cannot face this kind of pressure and deal with it. I shudder when I think of the pressure put on some of these eight- and nine-year-olds when, having to face a crowd of eight or nine hundred people, they strike out."

Charles A. Bucher, professor of education at New York University: "The drive to win in America is traditional. But a boy will absorb that lesson soon enough in high school. In grammar-school years it is more important that his recreation be guided toward other objectives: the fun of playing rather than winning; the child rather than the game; the many rather than the few; informal activity rather than formal; the development of skills in many activities rather than specialization."

Jack Scott, former director of athletics at Oberlin College and founder of the Institute for the Study of Sport and Society: "Kids who play in these leagues, whether it's football, baseball, basketball, soccer, or swimming, are being put into little slots and having their lives regimented at an age when they should be free to discover the beauty and joy of athletic activity. It should be fun to a nine-year-old or a ten-year-old. There shouldn't be pressure and big games. There shouldn't be screaming parents and dictatorial little men who imagine they're the local Vince Lombardi. The kids are exposed to this type of regimentation through games and athletics and then, when they start developing a consciousness about their surroundings and life styles, some of them rebel and throw off the regimentation. Others don't, or can't. It's too ingrained. They simply accept it year after year, as if this is the proper thing and proper way. And this is what I consider a bad part of the regimentation of these leagues. It restricts thinking at such a young age."

Dr. Joseph Torg, assistant professor of orthopedics at Temple University and physician for that college's sports teams: "One of the most serious crimes of our day is robbing children of their childhood. If I had my way, Little League sports would be abolished. To push kids to the brink of mental and physical exhaustion is absurd. I once conducted a study of a baseball program at a local boys' club. The study showed the eight- to twelve-year-olds who participated in baseball at the boys' club had few problems with elbow and shoulder injuries. Those injuries are common in Little League, because of the emphasis on competition, and not recreation. A preadolescent is not a competitive being. He's not at the stage where he's trying to exert himself and make a mark among his peers physically. Instead, he is trying to learn how to entertain himself, explore the world, and establish relationships with others his own age. I think organized sports, such as Little Leagues, prevent the child from doing this. With adult interference, he doesn't learn how to entertain himself, and he can't establish peer-group relationships. In the Little Leagues, you can see eight-, nine-, and ten-year-olds acting out an artificial situation imposed on them by adults. They are subjected to the influence of coaches. Not men trained to be coaches but, by and large, the frustrated guy down the street who recaptures lost successes and achieves vicarious pleasures by exploiting these young kids."

Torg even recommended that the following measures be taken:

1. Discourage practicing at home before, during, and after the season.

2. Eliminate curve-ball pitching for Little League players.

3. Shorten the playing season, especially in warm-weather climates, where league play begins earlier.

4. Restrict pitchers to only two innings a game.

5. Divide Little Leagues into two groups—one for nine- and ten-year-olds, the other for eleven- and twelve-year-olds.

Dr. Nicholas J. Giannestras, of the University of Cincinnati: "Many young pitchers in Little League risk permanent elbow damage. The elbows of children are immature for such sports. The elbows joints of young pitchers have shown both bone damage and the beginning signs of arthritis. Children under fourteen should not be allowed to throw or experiment with pitches like the curve ball and the screw ball."

Karl K. Klein, a professor in the rehabilitation laboratory of the University of Texas: "I believe that the increasing concern over injuries will force all boys' leagues to adopt limitations. But they won't be worth anything unless we get the message to parents. What's the point of league restrictions if every evening Pop takes Junior out to have him practice pitching for a couple of hours? If parents don't stop pressuring their kids, we'll continue to have fourteen-year-olds with arms you expect to see only at old-timers' games."

Dr. Joesph D. Godfrey, chief of orthopedic surgery at the Children's Hospital in Buffalo, New York: "The possibility of sustaining permanent elbow restrictions of motion, or an abnormal area of the elbow, may definitely stem from throwing overhand at an early age. The thrust of the arm and forearm puts a repetitious squeeze or compression on bone growth plates at the elbows of youngsters. This causes change in the growth center. I don't believe in wrapping the kids in cotton. But some kind of pitching restriction makes sense. I would recommend that methods such as an 'Iron Mike' pitching machine, a tee, as in golf, or a toss-up mechanism be used to set the ball up to be hit in both practice sessions and games. We don't know enough to say limiting pitchers to two or three innings a game is enough of a safety margin."

Dr. Joel E. Adams, a bone surgeon and team doctor for San Bernardino, California, city schools and junior colleges: "Curveball pitching should be abolished on the Little League level, and no practice throwing should be permitted. Too much pitching at early ages often causes boys' arm muscles to pull on the growth center of the bone, which are not yet closed. Too much pitching invites trouble rather than perfection in this age group. I tested eighty pitchers in a study in Southern California, and I found all of them had separated and fragmented bone centers, plus accelerated arm growth that could be painful for the rest of their lives. Throwing a baseball mimics the action of a buggy whip. The shoulder acts like the handle of a whip and the flail of the arm and forearm puts a repeating strain on the elbow and shoulder. Thus, the muscles put a strain on the growth centers of the bones. Boys with arm pains should stop pitching immediately and play other positions until those centers close, and coaches should not dismiss such pain as due to wrong throwing motions or failure to warm up properly. I also feel that the playing season should be shortened, with less stress on playoffs and tournaments, especially in temperate climates such as Southern California, where the picking of players for teams begins as early as February. This encourages youngsters to start practicing throwing at home several months before the season even starts."

Occasionally, an adult who is actually involved in Little League baseball as a coach or manager becomes disgruntled at what he sees, drops out, and becomes a critic from the sidelines. Will Fowler, who quit as manager of the Encino Tigers of the San Fernando Valley (California) Little League a few years ago, said:

"I liked the kids, but I couldn't take the parents. The fathers go out to win at all costs, not the kids. I've seen kids go home crying and not talking to their parents. That's not natural for a twelve-year-old. I've seen one kid climb up a walnut tree after a game and sit there brooding half the night. He just felt he was a misfit, alone in the world. What happens is that a parent whose kid comes home crying or upset usually goes out to the next game with blood in his eyes. Once a father threw insults, then clods of dirt and paper, at a manager who did not play his son. The manager finally took up a bat and chased the father through the fence gate, and nearly clobbered him. Once a mother actually pummeled me. That's when I decided that I had had enough."

All of the criticism from educators, medical professionals, and concerned former Little League adults is doubtlessly well intentioned and designed to encourage—or even force—changes in the program that would be beneficial to the boys playing in it. But apparently it has fallen upon deaf ears. The Little League headquarters in South Williamsport, Pennsylvania, has commissioned its own scientific and medical studies, under the direction of Creighton Hale, the organization president. All the official Little League studies show that the program, as it is currently structured, is not harmful to its participants. (What else did you expect, the Pentagon Papers?) One study, in fact, even brings the medical professionals to their knees; the study shows that 99 percent of all doctors who have had sons playing in Little League baseball feel that the program has been beneficial to their boys. The impression left: If 99 percent of the doctors in America are perfectly willing to entrust their own sons to the program, who are all those other quacks, and what are they talking about?

But no studies, scientific or otherwise, have ever been conducted by the Little League headquarters about the men who coach boys in baseball. These Little League coaches—as many as twenty-five thousand of them in a given year—have never been placed under serious scrutiny, by the organization itself or by any independent agency. That fact alone is one of the shames of Little League baseball.

Some observations about the situation:

1. *Motivation.* Most of the men who become attracted to, and ultimately involved in, Little League baseball as coaches and managers fall into two distinct categories: those with sons who are playing in the league, and those with no sons playing, but are interested both in baseball and in becoming actively involved in the game. Very little has been said, or written, about what really motivates grown men to become Little League coaches and managers. Most of the men who become involved do so because they want to personally look after the safety and the activities of their own sons, and also because they want to personally supervise their development as baseball players—and personally insure that their sons obtain the opportunities to show off their abilities. That is why so many coaches' sons are the best players on Little League teams; Dad the Manager paves the way for them, keeps them in games when they commit errors (when other kids would be taken out), stays with them even though they cannot hit (they stay in there until they start hitting), allows them to play more innings than any other boy on the team, and then discusses strategy and the nuances of the game at home with the boy. But what is overlooked in this relationship is usually the adult's participation in the program: He is just as much a part of it as his son is. In my own observations of Little League, I have seen a tremendous turnover in coaches and managers—based primarily on the sons. When a boy leaves Little League, say, and goes on to the Babe Ruth League, the father inevitably turns up as coach or manager in the Babe Ruth League as well. What motivates most of these men, then, is not the program itself, or the game itself, or the participation in it; what motivates these men is the opportunity to increase their own sons' chances of success. The men who have no sons in Little League are motivated, for the most part, by two things: the

high esteem in which they hold the game of baseball, and the opportunity to find a niche, and ultimately success and satisfaction, within the program while at the same time helping kids learn the rudiments of the game. Most of these men are well intentioned. Most of these men consider baseball more important than it really is. The coaches with sons of their own on their teams are forced to play peculiar roles; they must pretend to treat their own son as just another player on the team (in order to avoid charges of favoritism and nepotism), but at the same time they are obsessed with their sons' development. But the other kids usually see through this and rebel against it; the kids' most-common complaint is about the coach's son getting preferential treatment. In my own experience, coaches who have their sons on their teams turn out to be the most unpopular and the most criticized; sooner or later, their motives are uncovered, and their respectability is diminished.

2. *Community Respectability.* I have found that in working-class, blue-collar communities particularly, Little League baseball affords adults the opportunity of gaining instant respect and publicity within the community as coaches and managers. The less affluent, the less educated, the less socially aware the community is, the greater the opportunity for men to achieve a sense of recognition through Little League baseball. The reason: Winning baseball teams attract attention to neighborhoods that are usually ignored, or discriminated against, by the more-affluent sectors of the community. Little League baseball is very popular in blue-collar, working-class towns and cities; for a Little League team to win a tournament title is very desirable. The publicity from the local media—the recognition, the respect the team engenders—increases the pride of the community. Little League tournaments give kids from less-affluent sectors of a city the opportunity to defeat kids from the more-affluent sectors; it gives these kids from less-affluent areas the opportunity to win state tournaments, sectional tournaments, and, yes, even world tournaments. The adults in these communities react favorably to such things, the theory being that "our kids are just as good as their kids, even better—we beat them eight to nothing." The blue-collar, working-class towns and cities

are the staunchest supporters of Little League baseball, and its most hysterical defenders. A listing of past Little League world-championship teams includes teams from such communities as Birmingham, Alabama; Hamtramck, Michigan; Levittown, Pennsylvania; Schenectady, New York; Wayne, New Jersey; Windsor Locks, Connecticut; and Staten Island, New York. This feeling of instant respectability and/or increased stature in the eyes of neighboring areas that Little League tournaments engender among adults has even affected people outside of the United States. In the late 1950s, people in Mexico were so intent upon winning Little League world championships that they actually went out and began recruiting the kids from all over the country to play for the all-star team in Monterrey. A company in that city even went so far as to give their fathers jobs in that city. The team from Monterrey won the world title twice—and then was set down for a year when the Little League headquarters found out what was going on. The same situation holds true today with a group of people from Taiwan; in three out of the last four years, Taiwanese teams have won the world championship—and the league was under investigation by the headquarters for alleged infractions of age limitations (some people thought the kids from Taiwan were thirteen or fourteen years old). The more-affluent and more-enlightened areas of the country do not take Little League world championships that seriously; there have been no world championship teams from Scarsdale, New York, say, or from Palm Springs, California, or Cambridge, Massachusetts, or Berkeley, California. Little League headquarters is obviously aware of working-class aspirations toward increased status and respectability.

3. *Surrogate Families.* In most Little Leagues, there are such things as adult league officers, women's auxiliaries, annual banquets and field days. All of this contributes to a surrogate-family life style. Little Leagues give entire families places to go and things to do during empty and boring summer months. This leads to problems: One district administrator in upstate New York told me of how he was called in to break up three different affairs that were going on between adult male managers and coaches and adult

women members of auxiliaries. He also told me of league officers who embezzled money from the league treasuries; about a league treasurer who was cashing personal checks against the league's treasury; and about a group of Little League women who decided to switch husbands for a few nights. It is safe to say that when adults become involved in Little Leagues, they do not leave their own personal foibles and faults behind.

4. *The Money Tricks.* I can still remember two things about my own Little League baseball career that I find repulsive today. First, there was a thing called "tag day." The coaches and the managers assembled all of us players, dressed in our baseball uniforms, on a particular Saturday morning and dispersed us to locations around the city with paper containers in our hands. The object was to collect money for the league. Some of the kids had to go door to door and solicit money, ringing doorbells. Some of the kids were called beggars by people who did not appreciate having their doorbells rung, and that insult usually was followed by the sound of a slamming door. Other kids, usually the best-looking or most-aggressive ones, were positioned in front of banks and department stores to solicit money from bankers and shoppers on their way in and out. At the end of the day, the money was turned over to the coaches and managers.

One kid was bitten by a dog, I remember; another fell into a drainage ditch that had been covered over by plywood; and another kid was accused by his manager of dipping into the container and transfering its contents to his own pockets. Little Leagues have always said that collect-money days ("tag day" is merely a euphemism) are necessary if the leagues are not to go out of business.

The second bit of foolishness I remember so well is the opening-day parade through the city's streets. Most of these parades go like this: First a color guard, carrying American flags; behind the color guard is a police car; behind the police car is a fire truck; then an ambulance; then open convertibles carrying the city's dignitaries, politicians, and the adult league officers; then a high-school marching band; then an open convertible carrying the local clerics;

then the high-school majorettes, followed by officers from the local National Guard unit, wearing full military uniforms. Then came the kids. The parade gave the adults the opportunity to strut; the kids were an afterthought.

5. *The Juvenile-Delinquency-Deterrent Myth.* This is one myth, circulated by Little League managers and coaches, that is particularly offensive. The fact of the matter is that, in some communities, Little Leagues actually help increase juvenile delinquency. The reason: Kids who have criminal postures invariably are poor baseball players (presumably, they have been practicing how to steal hub caps instead of bases). So, when they try out for Little League teams, they inevitably get cut; the good kids, who are already familiar with the fundamentals of the game, make the team. That leaves the kids with larcenous tendencies free to break into Coke machines and rifle empty homes all summer long. Little League people have always presumed—wrongly—that they are keeping kids out of trouble; the presumption is wrong, because the kids who keep busy with baseball wouldn't be in trouble even if there were no Little League baseball to occupy them.

Probably, they would be playing baseball on the neighborhood sandlots. But it's the kids who are well along the way on the road to Dannemora who need to be detoured by baseball. They never seem to be. They aren't good-enough baseball players to survive the Little League tryouts.

6. *Cheating and Deception.* Little League coaches will deny this vehemently, but they actually promote cheating in their obsession to win games. In the realm of sports, cheating is often called "bending the rules"; good cheaters are called "heads-up players." Kids who are violent enough to throw something at another player's head, as a form of intimidation, are described as being "mean and hungry." Kids who slide high into second base, to take out, and knock over, shortstops in double-play situations, are called "aggressive" and "miniature Ducky Medwicks," always a compliment. One Little League manager I knew actually encouraged his players to bunt, bunt, bunt in the first inning of every game so that he could get a player to third base early in the game. Then,

that player from third base would come charging home on another bunt, and slam right into the opposing catcher, hoping to knock the wind out of him, intimidate him, and unnerve him for the rest of the game. Once accomplished, the game was virtually won; the catcher would start allowing passed balls, he'd be too shaky to make accurate throws to second base on steals (most of them winding up in center field), and runs would score easily.

In sports, cheating within the rules is not only accepted but glorified. The kids who are the best cheaters are described as being the best players, and they usually populate these all-star tournaments. The closest people in Little League come to describing such actions as cheating is to call the whole concept "deception." Millions of young American boys are acquiring their first authentic lessons in "deception" on Little League baseball diamonds. Even more insidious is the fact that they are being praised and publicized lavishly whenever they execute this "deception" successfully, and whenever it leads directly to victories in games.

7. *The Matter of Policing.* The area in which the Little League headquarters is most negligent, so far as coaches and managers are concerned, is policing. Little League headquarters has no staff members touring the country, studying coaches and managers and making sure that they conduct themselves in appropriate ways. In fact, the Little League headquarters has virtually no power whatsoever over managers and coaches in its domain—what can it do to a manager or a coach who bumps an umpire? Fine him a hundred dollars? The policing of adults in Little Leagues ultimately lies within the local communities; ideally, it would be done by an independent group of men, selected at random from within the community by league officers and answerable only to the league president. If this independent group of observers found a coach or manager's conduct offensive, it could report him immediately to the league president, who, in turn, would take immediate action. (That action, of course, would be to remove the coach or manager from the league.) That some kind of policing agency has not been devised by the Little League headquarters, or even by the local leagues themselves, is astonishing. The way it is today, Little

League coaches can do just about whatever they please with the kids under their control; they are answerable to no one except the boys' parents, who in most cases support the coach fully. Meanwhile, some coaches continue to play boys who are injured and should not be playing; they hide injuries, if they can, and encourage the boys to play anyway. They superimpose themselves on the boys and the game, and expect no internal dissent whatsoever. ("No twelve-year-old kid," a Little League coach once told me, "is going to give me lip and get away with it.")

8. *Community Collusion.* In most communities, people are reluctant to publicly criticize Little League coaches and managers because of the resistance they are going to meet. In most communities, there is a bond of collusion among the Little League people, the people who sponsor its teams, the newspapers who publish the results (and nothing more), the civic leaders who make political hay out of throwing out the first ball on opening day, or at the all-star tournaments. Merchants who contribute money to help support leagues, or who buy advertising on outfield fences, are reluctant to criticize something to which they have donated money. Besides, you can lose a lot of business by criticizing Little League baseball. Newspapers have been particularly ineffective on the subject of child abuse in Little Leagues. In some cities, the newspapers actually are involved in the promotion of Little League baseball. (In New York City, the *Daily News* actually underwrites the annual Eastern Regional Tournaments.) Sportswriters who see abusive coaches or managers do not dare write about them for fear of publishers who will come storming into their cubicle offices, saying: "How dare you write this? You know what you just cost me? You cost me the two thousand dollars I spent to co-sponsor this tournament, and you cost me four thousand dollars in canceled subscriptions and advertising as a result of what you just wrote." Newspapers could be legitimate watchdogs of Little League baseball, and sportswriters could be very effective in policing Little League and in helping to weed out abusive coaches. But they never will be. Newspapers are too deeply involved in passing themselves off as community servants (which means sponsoring Little League

tournaments, not criticizing them), or else they are too intimidated by the specter of lost revenue that would surely result whenever a sportswriter took to questioning the tactics of a coach or a manager in print. People in Little League, newspaper publishers have discovered, particularly in small and medium-sized cities, can swing a lot of advertising in their directions—so long as they print the scores and little else.

9. *Nice Guys.* There are, to be sure, some beautiful people involved in the coaching and managing of Little League baseball teams. They remain oblivious to the distortions surrounding them, and merely perform their duties in the best interests of the boys. They are usually described as oddballs by people in the Little League mainstream. Once I heard a story about one of these sensitive, compassionate men. He had just finished the tryouts and selected his players, and was on his way home. Near the park, he walked into one of the young boys whom he had just selected for his team. The boy was sitting on a tree stump, crying. The coach asked him what was wrong. The boy said that he couldn't play in the Little League, that he didn't own a pair of sneakers, that he had no father, and that his mother was too poor to buy him a pair. The coach said, "So? That's no reason to be sitting here crying. C'mon, hop in my car. We're going downtown." The coach took the boy into a shoe store and bought him a new pair of sneakers. When I retold the story to a man who was deeply entrenched in the very same league's hierarchy, the man listened and then said: "Yeah, but would he have done the same thing if that kid was on some other team?"

10. *The Female Problem.* Little girls have always been left out of the Little Leagues. Not only have they been prevented from playing in games, but the boys who were playing actually acquired a sense of superiority over females in their same age-groups, because, of course, the boys actually were wanted, desired, and encouraged by Little Leagues; the girls were not. All of that may be changing, however. In recent years, there have been several legal actions against Little League Baseball, Incorporated, to allow

girls to play. Representative Michael J. Harrington, a Democrat of Massachusetts, has filed legislation in the House of Representatives that would amend the Little League's federal charter of incorporation to include girls in its program. Harrington said, "Congress has allowed the Little League to exclude girls from its teams and it is time to allow girls to play baseball, and for the rest of society to open itself to women, as well as men, on an equal basis." Actually, the infusion of girls into Little Leagues would help solve the problem of abusive coaches, as well as the problem of excessive emphasis on winning. The very presence of young girls would drive the die-hard chauvinists out of Little League baseball, and with them would go the people who staunchly advocate all-star teams and Little League World Series. They would leave on the grounds that girls would be diluting the level of talent for the showcase event. Also to go would be the men who would not risk losing a game to an eleven-year-old left-hander who happened to be a girl.

Girls would civilize Little League baseball. Little League headquarters has said that twelve-year-old girls are not physically capable of competing against twelve-year-old boys, but many physicians (Dr. Arthur Hohmuth, a child psychologist at Trenton State College, among them) have said that twelve-year-old girls are actually better-developed, more muscular, and more mature emotionally than twelve-year-old boys are. Little League baseball headquarters has also said that twelve-year-old girls have too many vulnerable areas of the body, and might be seriously injured if those vulnerable areas were hit by a fiercely thrown baseball or an errantly thrown baseball bat. But psychiatrists (Dr. Antonia Giancotti of Hackensack, New Jersey, among them) have turned the proposition around: Don't boys have vulnerable parts of their bodies, too?

Edward C. Devereux, of the Department of Human Development and Family Studies at Cornell University, may have laid on the doorsteps of Little League coaches and managers the most important—and deepest—question of all. He said, in regard to coaches and managers in Little Leagues, that the measuring sticks for their effectiveness should not be in how many games are won or lost.

"Ultimately, it's not a question of what the boy does to the ball," he said. "The question is what the ball does to the boy."

VIII · Little-Boys' Football: What Two Pros Have to Say About It

There is a large structural difference between the organization known as Little League Baseball, Incorporated, and the autumnal subculture that is known as little-boys' football. Whereas Little League Baseball, Incorporated, is tightly structured, from South Williamsport, Pennsylvania, on down, little-boys' football is a fragmented genre that consists of many locally controlled leagues and a few others that are controlled by national headquarters. Apparently, the largest national organization is Pop Warner Football, which was founded in the Philadelphia area and still has a headquarters there; in an average year, approximately 600,000 little boys are playing football under the auspices of Pop Warner Football. (You never really know how many kids are involved in Pop Warner Football, because the organization won't release any figures.) But a vast majority of the kids playing football do so under local-community control; these little-boys' football leagues flourish in the newer, suburban communities, particularly on Long Island and in southern California. For example, the Long Island Midget Football Organization in Farmingdale, Long Island, has 450 boys and 100 girl cheerleaders in its program annually; in Huntington, Long Island, a junior football program accommodates 1,100 boys annually; in southern California, the San Fernando Valley Football-for-Youth Conference accommodates several thousand boys (and several hundred girls as cheerleaders). As in Little League baseball, the adult male coaches are "volunteers." Since football (tackle football, that is) is a physical game, the number of injuries annually is staggering—but, again, never are the figures reported publicly.

What do pro players think about all of this? Not much.

Francis Asbury Tarkenton is a quarterback for the Minnesota Vikings. The Minnesota Vikings are a professional football team. Lawrence Richard Csonka is a running back for the Miami Dolphins. The Miami Dolphins are a professional football team. Fran Tarkenton and Larry Csonka have spent most of their lives playing football; they were outstanding players in high school, outstanding players in college, and now they are outstanding players in the National Football League. They are also parents. As professional football players who are parents, Fran Tarkenton and Larry Csonka are not exactly overjoyed at the prospect of entrusting eager little boys to the men who coach junior-league football teams. In fact, both Fran Tarkenton and Larry Csonka have been critical of junior-league football coaches, and of their tactics.

Fran Tarkenton:

> When I was ten years old I played on Saturdays with a Boys' Club team, and that wasn't nearly as much fun as playing pickup games in the park. You just couldn't be yourself . . . you had to do this, and do that.
>
> It was . . . a structured program, and that experience, plus others I've been touched by along the way, have convinced me that structured sports for kids simply won't do. I do not believe in any kind of organized, structured football or baseball before junior high or high school.
>
> First of all, I don't think boys seven to twelve enjoy playing in a structured situation. They do it today because all

their friends are doing it; it's the thing to do, and no kid likes to be an oddball.

But I think they would prefer to go out on the sandlots . . . out there they can play any position, they can devise their own strategy, they can be innovative, they can be creative—they can be all those things. But when they go into organized football, they're no longer on their own, they've got to answer to a coach.

And there's a problem right there . . . I've found most of these [midget-league] coaches are frustrated athletes who always wanted to be a head coach.

They watch football on television and read about Bear Bryant, that tough disciplinarian who has coached Alabama to so many college championships. All of a sudden they picture themselves as Bear Bryants. And that's the way they try to coach ten-year-olds.

Larry Csonka was interviewed on an Eastern Airlines Whisperjet that was flying from Boston to Miami after the Dolphins had just lost a football game to the New England Patriots. The subject of conversation was violence and young people. There had been some distasteful scenes late in the game on that day; young boys in their early teens stormed onto the field and, later, threw beer cans, not empty, and soggy bags of garbage at the Dolphin players as they walked off the field and headed for their dressing room. Larry Csonka:

Those kids were immature and irresponsible as hell. But what do you do with them? Beat them, put them in handcuffs, throw them in jail? I don't know . . . I don't know what the answer is. It disturbs me, this violence, very much. You know what I think? I think those kids are irresponsible, yes, but I don't think they're totally to blame. I think their behavior is the end product of their conditioning. We're raising kids in this country on violence, so what the hell do we expect?

We let our kids go to horror movies and to movies where they see people gouging each other's eyes out and chopping each other's heads off and the blood is gushing all over the place . . . whooopee. That's all right, now, isn't it? But we don't allow the same kids to go see a movie that might have in it two people making love . . . no, we tell them that love is wrong and sex is wrong, and it's bad for them; but blood movies, yeah, they're all right. Now, you tell me where our brains are.

As for football, well, we've got to go down into the junior leagues and the little leagues and clean up the nonsense that is going on. You know what I think about the junior football that I've seen? I think it's ruining a lot of our kids.

I'll tell you a story: These people in Florida invited me over to watch one of their little-league football practices. I'm curious about the whole thing, so I tell them, "Yeah, I'll be there. In fact, I'm looking forward to it." So I drive up to the place, and the first guy I meet is the coach. He's in his twenties, and he's fat, with a pot belly, and he's wearing the sweatpants and the sweatshirt and the whistle around his neck and the baseball cap and the cleats. He says to me, "C'mon, hurry up over to the practice field, the kids are waiting for us; we're gonna have a hell of a practice today." I'm saying to myself: "Oh, oh. I'm afraid this guy is going to put on a show for me at the kids' expense." But then I'm thinking, "Oh, well, maybe not, maybe he's all right. Give him the benefit of the doubt." So the coach blows his whistle and starts screaming. "All right, men, get into formation for drill Number One!"

So two kids, maybe nine or ten years old, line up on opposite sides of the fifty-yard line, and the rest of the team splits up and falls into line behind them. Then the coach yells, "Red-ddie," and comes down hard on the whistle. The kids start going at it, head to head, one on one, and I'm saying to myself: "Is this possible? What is he doing to these kids? He's copying Lombardi's *Nutcracker Suite*. The man is insane." Just then one of the kids catches another one with an elbow in the nose. The kid's nose starts to bleed, and he falls down. The coach goes over to him and starts screaming, "Get up, get up. Show us you're a man and not a quitter." The kid gets up, and the tears are rolling down his cheeks, mixing with the blood, and he goes to the end of the line and waits for his next turn. I can imagine how the kid felt. His nose was broken, we found out later, and he had to stand there and show how masculine he was, especially with the male members of his family, and me, watching him. Now, the kid is ten years old and I wanted to go over to him and tell him that everything's going to be all right, that these things happen in football. But the coach, he's jumping up and down, screaming at me, "Larry, watch these two go at it . . . watch these two, I tell you, they're real tigers."

Well, now I'm thinking of writing a book on the subject, something that would educate parents who entrust their kids to this kind of man. These coaches, so-called, are causing a lot of psychological and physical damage to kids who haven't even reached puberty yet. Hell, I don't want to go through the whole thing and rip it to shreds; I just want to propose an alternative to what we have now. What is wrong with flag football or touch football for kids? Do we really need all the violence and the false character-building and the emphasis on winning that is going on now? No, I don't think we do. Football should be fun for kids, they should be able to play an hour or so a day and enjoy it. The way it is now, they practice more, and do more calisthenics, than my team, the Miami Dolphins, does."

One overlooked person, who helps to establish many of these little-boys' football leagues, is the local high-school football coach. In the end, he benefits from them as much—or more—than anyone else. These local leagues actually work for him—they are his farm systems. They prepare the kids for him; the kids learn the basic fundamentals of the game in these leagues—even something as basic as how to put on a uniform properly—and they save the coach a lot of work and time. By the time the kids get to high school, they are already versed in the rudiments of the game and are advanced to the extent that they know the coach's plays already. Many ninth- and tenth-graders, after spending three or four years in junior football leagues, actually step right into varsity starting lineups upon reaching high school.

It is all intertwined—in many cities and towns, the junior football leagues actually serve as designated minor leagues for high-school football teams. For that reason, many high-school coaches are actively involved in the formation, and the perpetuation, of these leagues, and they are among the leagues' most vocal supporters. They even scout players in these leagues, and some of the coaches can even project their varsity lineups seven or eight years in advance—provided, of course, that the kids do not suffer any serious injuries. All of which points out why most high-school coaches—and sports-minded high-school administrators—refrain from criticizing whatever is going on in these leagues. (Does Pete Rozelle criticize Ara Parseghian?)

IX • A Question of Accountability: To Whom Is the Coach Responsible?

During a three-week period late in the summer of 1973, Robert Blatz, Walter Wilkinson, and Tomas Sanchez died. They were high-school football players. Robert Blatz, who was seventeen years old, died of heat stroke and dehydration after collapsing during a sprint drill on a high-school practice field in Brentwood, Long Island. The temperature on that Wednesday morning was ninety degrees. Walter Wilkinson, who was sixteen years old, died of heatstroke and dehydration after completing a two-hour practice session with his Hamilton High School East team of Trenton, New Jersey. The temperature on that Sunday was ninety-two degrees. The workout was held at Camp Cayuga in Honesdale, Pennsylvania, where the Trenton team was beginning three days of pre-season drills. Tomas Sanchez, who was sixteen years old, died of a brain hemorrhage en route to the Providence Hospital in El Paso, Texas. He had been injured during a game his Anthony High School team had been playing against the Reserve New Mexico High School team. Sanchez had taken himself out of the game in the fourth quarter, and then collapsed on his team's bench.

Every year, according to the National Federation of State High

School Athletic Associations, approximately "16 to 20" high-school boys die as a result of their participation in the game of football. But, the federation is quick to point out, the number of deaths is exceptionally low—considering that there are approximately 1,200,000 boys playing football in public high schools in America every fall. The federation is not so quick to point out, however, how many boys do not die, but instead suffer injuries that leave them permanently damaged: paraplegics, or with severe brain damage, or with limps, or with immobile fingers and joints. The policing of high-school sports is a one-way street—statistics are kept, apparently as a defensive measure, as a precaution against critics; the high-school athletic associations have been formed to *protect* coaches, and not to police them. In fact, few groups of adult males in America have managed to escape both internal and external scrutiny as deftly as high-school coaches have; Marine Corps drill sergeants at Parris Island are watched more closely for evidence of extremism than the average high-school coach is. The average high-school coach enjoys both a civil and a moral immunity from criticism—he usually has various high-school administrators (more than one of whom is a former coach) supporting him from the inside, and he has the parents of players and almost all of the adult males in his community (well-intentioned, but incredibly naive about the nuances of coaching sports) supporting him on the outside. In most communities, the only bloc of people that will openly criticize the tactics of high-school coaches is composed primarily of liberal, professional people with strong academic credentials, and they are immediately dismissed with the usual socio-political description: "Left-wing, commie, pinko sympathizers." Inevitably, their warnings go unheeded.

Nothing can arouse emotions to hysterical pitches in most communities throughout America more than the issue of local high-school sports. In the last few years particularly, that fact has been substantiated by the continuous struggles over school budgets. School districts which have had their budgets rejected by local tax-payers have used sports as a political issue; the administrators have threatened to abolish the sports program at their schools unless budgets are approved the second time around. Usually they are; the threat of no high-school sports in the community brings the voting tax-payers out in droves to cast their affirmative votes. The threatened loss of a remedial-reading program, however, does not stir so much as a ripple.

Indeed, in the hotbeds of high-school sports, the school teams actually dictate the emotional climate in the community by their successes, or their lack of it. The team and the community become intertwined—for better or for worse. In Massillon, Ohio, for example, which is a bastion of high-school football, the mothers of newly born male babies are presented with footballs minutes after being presented with their new sons; the footballs are gifts from the Massillon Men's High School Football Booster Club.

As an example of the extremes to which some cities go to support their high-school sports programs, consider the city of Massillon, which has a population of 32,539, and is located approximately 45 miles south of Cleveland. Massillon, Ohio, prides itself on being known as "The High School Football Capital of the World." The Washington High School Tigers of Massillon play their home games in a stadium that seats 21,345 people, covers 35 acres, and requires 300 employees to service every time Steubenville or Canton McKinley comes to town. The city school system has 15 football coaches—one head coach, four varsity assistants, two sophomore coaches, eight junior-high coaches—and a team dentist, a team chiropodist, and even a team historian on its payroll.

Drive through Massillon on a July afternoon and already the landscape, which is dotted with roast-beef sandwich shops and quickie hamburger stands, is dominated with "Go, Tiger, Go!" signs which include the upcoming football schedule on it and, always, the superimposed Tiger wearing a helmet and a scowl. The results of such community backing, the Washington High School football press-brochure points out, include three adult booster clubs, one of which meets for lunch every Monday noon during the football season, hears a report from the head coach, and

watches films of the previous week's game. But the most unique of
the three is called "The Sideliners," and its function, according to
the same press brochure, is:

". . . to be an adult group of buddies for the football players.
During the season each member of the Sideliners adopts a player
for a buddy. He listens to any complaints a player may have, or
suggestions; greets him before and after games, sits down and eats
with him and takes him to a movie the night preceding each game.
The Sideliners have become one of the most important cogs in the
Tiger Organization."

Winning, as one may suspect, is what high-school football is all
about, in Ohio generally and in Massillon particularly. In 1968,
Washington High School lost two early season games, and later
the big rivalry game against Canton McKinley. The head coach
was fired, and the season written off as a disaster. But for beating
Barberton (Ohio) High School by a score of 90-0 in 1959, and for
beating Struthers (Ohio) High School by a score of 74-0 in 1963,
a man named Leo Strang gained a reputation for being a winning
coach at Massillon who rarely called the dogs off. He was recruited
himself by Kent State University and several other colleges,
offered the head football-coaching jobs at each of them, and eventually accepted the offer at Kent State.

Bob Commings, who coached at Washington High School in
Massillon from 1968 to 1973, received his just reward ten days
before Christmas in 1973. Commings's teams at Massillon had
compiled a composite record of 44 victories, 5 defeats, and 1 tie. In
1970, his Washington High School team won the Ohio state
high-school-football championship, and Commings was named the
high-school football coach of the year in the state of Ohio. Commings had been a 173-pound guard on outstanding teams during
the middle 1950s at the University of Iowa; people in Iowa apparently remembered him. When the University of Iowa had its
worst football season ever in 1973, losing all 11 of its games, the
coach, Frank Lauterbur, was fired; the school authorities said the
reason was because Lauterbur refused to make any changes on his
staff of assistant coaches. Enter Commings. Forty years old, he was

offered the job as head football coach at Iowa, and he accepted it. Very few high-school coaches, with the exception of those who serve their apprenticeships at Washington High School in Massillon, make the jump all the way to become a major college's head coach without first serving as backfield assistant or offensive coordinator at a Muhlenburg or a Middlebury. But such is the reputation of Washington High School in Massillon: Its coaches are considered good enough to step right into major college programs—as the head men. Needless to say, the head football-coaching job at Washington High School is the most-coveted among ambitious high-school football coaches. As a springboard to bigger and better things, it has no equal.

In the rare instances when school budgets were voted down a second time and sports programs actually were abolished, the relationship between the community and the coaches' programs truly became evident. The adults in the community actually went out and raised the money to finance sports in their high schools. To wit:

In Portland, Oregon, when the taxpayers voted down for the third time their school board's proposed budget, one of the first expenditures to go was the $450,000 allotted annually to interscholastic sports at the city's 13 high schools. But, in a period of six weeks, a volunteer group headed by Paul McCall, an athletic director at one of the high schools, raised $200,000 and succeeded in underwriting the sports programs at each of the schools during that academic year.

"It was," said McCall, "an unforgettable display of teamwork. High-school students went house-to-house, ringing doorbells, asking for donations. Two of the city's banks contributed twenty-five hundred dollars each, parents held rummage sales, sold candy bars, washed cars. Even the coaches helped out, by taking hundred-dollar pay cuts. By the middle of August we had enough money to restore sports at every school—frills excluded, of course. There were no new uniforms that year."

In Vestal, New York, a city of 26,000 near Binghamton, with only one high school, $50,000 was raised by a similar group to finance not only the sports program but also the cheerleaders, the marching band, and bus transportation to and from games for everybody. That group was headed by a data-processing consultant named Ray Meyers, and it consisted primarily of members of the Dad's Booster Club.

"The first thing we did," said Meyers, "was open a snack stand near the high school. Since the cafeteria program was wiped out too, the kids had no place to eat lunch. So we killed two birds with one stone. We put canisters inside every business in the city, sent the cheerleaders out to canvas homes, and hit the parents of every athlete up for ten dollars each. We also solicited the professional people in town by letter—doctor, lawyer, and such—and they came through very well for us."

So: If 16 boys die every year in high-school football, then 160 die every decade, and 320 die every twenty years, community support notwithstanding. The victims become statistics for the high-school sports federations and are usually forgotten, except by their families, as soon as their classes graduate (or as soon as the season is over, depending on the community's collective sensitivity and compassion). The coaches go on, and the schools go on, and somewhere near the gymnasium there might be a silver plaque on the wall as a memorial to the fallen player.

When a high school-player dies, the coach seems to be immediately protected by his double-barreled immunity; he is not answerable to civil law, nor is he judged by moral standards. If the foreman of a construction gang, say, sent his workers out into ninety-five-degree heat to dig trenches, and prodded them incessantly to work faster and harder, and if one of his seventeen-year-old workers collapsed and died on the spot of heatstroke and dehydration, there would doubtlessly be a public outcry to indict the foreman for murder. But if a high-school football coach did the same identical thing, sending his players out into the broiling sun in full uniform and prodding them incessantly to win sprint races and to block and tackle with fervor, and if one of the players collapsed and died, the thought of charging the coach with murder or manslaughter would not even arise. Almost always, the death is ruled accidental, and the coach is absolved of any responsibility for it; almost always, coroners or attending physicians will tell the bereaved parents that they do, indeed, have the option of filing a civil suit against the coach or the school—but always, the medical authorities advise, the parents, as plaintiffs, must first prove negligence on the part of the coach. Coaches who have been sued for negligence in the death of one of their players are not about to get very many promotions; the same holds true for school administrators, particularly the status-conscious principals, who encourage high-pressure tactics in the name of victory—the victories, of course, increase the school's prestige in the community and that, of course, increases the principal's own prestige. So, bereaved parents, who are intent upon sparing themselves more grief, almost always avoid the legal avenue of recourse and, in doing so, unconsciously allow the status quo to go unchallenged—until the next boy dies, in some other city in some other section of the country.

The question of negligence on the part of coaches has gone unanswered to date. What constitutes negligence? Is a coach legally negligent when he demands that a fatigued player keep running sprints and laps? Probably so, particularly if the boy collapses and, tragically, dies. But is a coach negligent if he demands that his team merely practice on a sunny, humid day with the temperatures in the nineties? Do the circumstances themselves constitute negligence? The very same coach who demands that his players refrain from smoking cigarettes, or from drinking alcoholic beverages, or from listening to Mick Jagger records, on the grounds that these are physically and mentally unhealthy, will demand that they risk their lives in sweltering heat for the purpose of conditioning themselves for the ultimate betterment of the team and the school and the society. The question for parents, then, could be this: Is a kid better off alive, smoking, drinking and gyrating to Mick Jagger, than he is dead on a football field in the names of Spartanism and conditioning and conformity? The question of negligence, based on circumstances rather than specifics, is a lighted fuse just looking for a bomb. Unfortunately for the sixteen or twenty kids who are destined to die this fall, there has been no determination.

The coroner who handled the case of Walter Wilkinson, the Trenton high-school player who died in September 1973, said that he had pondered, in his own mind, the role of the player's coach in that boy's death. Robert Jenkins, the coroner from Wayne County, Pennsylvania, said:

In this case, there is no doubt in my mind that somebody from the school should have questioned the coach's judgment in allowing the players to practice in such extreme heat. The coach himself told me that the boy had "Gone down" the day before. I asked the coach what "going down" meant. He said, "The boy dropped to one knee and said that he was tired." That was on a Saturday; the next day, a Sunday, the boy collapsed and died. Now, what disturbs me in all of this is not only the coach's lack of judgment; it's the lack of supervision on the part of the school toward the coach. Who is watching him? To whom is the coach answerable? Then there is the question of collusion: After the boy died, the school officials rallied to the coach's support. They even got to the boy's parents, you know, talked to them and smoothed things over. The parents wouldn't say a thing against the coach. Then there was the rest of the team. There were a hundred and two kids working out that day, and not a single one of them, who were interviewed by me, would say that anything unusual had happened. I've talked to other people, other coroners, who've been involved in deaths such as this; they said the same things happened. There is an incredible shield of collusion on the part of school officials, parents, and players to protect the coach; nobody speaks for the dead boy. Who is looking after his rights, and who is looking after the rights of other boys who may be victims of the same thing in the future? The coach, it seems, has absolute rule; if the boy refuses to participate in the drills, he is put off the team. If he does participate, and then dies, the coach is absolved from any responsibility in his death. The whole issue is going to come to a head sooner or later; the question is, how many more boys are going to have to die before it does?

Now, in this particular case the cause of death was clear-cut: heat stroke and dehydration. The boy had a very strong heart, and he was in excellent physical condition; if he had had a heart ailment, say, and was still allowed to play, then the doctor who had examined him before the season would be liable for negligence. But that wasn't the case here. If I thought for a moment that there was evidence of negligence on the part of the coach or the school doctor which contributed to that boy's death, I would have immediately called for a coronor's inquest. A jury of six people would have been convened, and it would have taken testimony under oath; then, if there was substantial evidence of criminal negligence, I would have gone to the district attorney and demanded the arrest of the coach, or the doctor, on charges of murder or manslaughter. Besides the coach's poor judgment, there was only one other question about this case that stood out in my mind, the question of medical examination. The school doctor told me that he examined a hundred and twenty kids from that team in one single afternoon; now, you might expect that in the Army, at an induction center, but not when you're dealing with adolescent boys. It must have been a mass-production physical examination; it certainly could not have been comprehensive. That raises the question in my mind of whether or not school doctors are administering sufficient physical examinations to players.

Either the doctor is fluffing off, or else he has no idea whatsoever what those kids are about to go through. I suspect the latter to be the case. The doctors who pass the kids are not around on the practice fields to make sure the very same kids are not being abused. The whole issue of high-school sports and civil law has not been addressed as yet. But when it does, I'm afraid, it's going to open a tremendous can of worms. All it is going to take is for some parent who has just lost a son, or has had one permanently injured, to take the school and the coach to court. In this particular case involving the boy from Trenton, I thought his parents would have had a good case. My own testimony would have been helpful to their cause. I would not ever recommend to them that they file suit, that is not my job; but if they did I would not consider it as clutching at straws. It is a very serious and profound issue. Somebody has to recognize the rights of the kids, and in the area of civil law an affirmative precedent would go a long way toward preventing other sixteen-year-old kids from dropping dead at a practice session that should never have been held in the first place.

In the case of Robert Blatz, the player who collapsed and died in Brentwood, Long Island, the official cause of death was identical: heatstroke and dehydration. The attending physician, Dr. Arthur Quackenbush, of Bay Shore, Long Island, said, "the heatstroke was fatal because he [Blatz] was so severely dehydrated." The boy's mother, Mrs. John Blatz, said, "football was Bobby's whole life. I should have stopped him the second day of practice, but what can you do? I didn't want him to practice in that heat, but he wanted to be a starter at center and he had to take everything they could dish out. Right now I'm numb. He was so athletic, a surfer, Little League baseball, wrestling. We even took him to the [New York] Jets' camp at Hofstra to watch practice most of our vacation. He was the straightest, best kid you'd ever meet. He wouldn't even smoke, because he felt it would hurt his wind. My husband and he were very close; there was no generation gap. We had a happy life, I guess because of sports. I'm not bitter. We should bury him in his football uniform."

The day after Blatz died, the Long Island newspaper *Newsday* was filled with quotations from people who were either there when it happened, or close by. Blatz's coach was praised by another coach: "Greenie [Dick Green] is a great guy, one of the best. He always had the kids' interests at heart." A fifteen-year-old halfback and teammate of Blatz's said that he brought salt tablets from home and took them before practice started. A sixteen-year-old teammate of Blatz's said that the practices at Brentwood were not that hard. A coach at a neighboring school said that he gave his players a water break every fifteen minutes. Another coach said that his practices included regularly scheduled breaks for Gatorade, a drink that is allegedly designed to increase salt in bodies. Nobody, the newspaper included, raised the question of whether or not it was prudent—let alone necessary—to conduct a practice session in the midst of such an extraordinary heat wave. (The first game of the season was still almost a month away.) On the same pages, there appeared interviews with Long Island workers who said that they were being wilted by the heat. A man who operated a hot-dog stand in New Hyde Park admitted to drinking up his inventory: "I've had seven sodas already today; I'll probably have four or five more." An eighteen-year-old lifeguard in the same community said, "The sun just beats down on you. You can't even breathe sometimes." A flagman on the Long Island Expressway said, "I almost passed out today. You feel like you're not all there." All of them were talking about the conditions on the day Robert Blatz died.

A few days later, a dentist from East Meadow, Long Island, Michael L. Schamis, wrote a letter to the newspaper and expressed his anger over the death of the Blatz boy. He wrote:

> It is a sad fact of life that some people never change their old archaic ways, even in the face of new thoughts and ideas.
> Robert Blatz, the 17-year-old football player, will not be the only one to die in this country during the pre-season practice (Aug. 31).
> His coaching staff, which did not allow the players to have water and ice during the sessions whenever a player felt he needed it, should have some deep second thought on the matter.
> In the past decade or so, various physicians who have

studied the problem in detail have said that cold ice water can't hurt but will definitely aid an exhausted, overheated athlete. The old wives' tale which says that cold drinks are bad for anyone who is "sweated up" was disproven years ago.

When I competed in high school athletics (long ago in 1965), we were ridiculed, prodded, kicked, punched and whatever else the coaches felt was necessary to make us work harder to become better athletes. If anyone talked back, that was the end of their athletic career. Unfortunately, this sort of thing still seems to be present, and the attitudes of coaches who feel that water during practice will not make their players "mean and hungry" enough since they can't suffer properly must be changed and the irresponsible individuals eliminated from today's athletics.

Two of the problems in the Blatz case concerned the lack of available drinking water during the practice sessions, and the players' attitude toward taking any. Players on the team said that the nearest available water was in the locker room; thirsty players, they said, would ask for permission to use the bathroom, and, once inside the locker room, they would sneak a drink of water. To ask the coach directly for water, one of them said, "would not be the manly thing to do." John Blumenthal, a guard on the team, said: "We didn't have any water breaks for the first five days. Nobody really asked for water. We wanted to make ourselves a little tougher." Bob Pavelock, a tackle on the team, said: "If you asked for water, you probably could have had it. But hardly anyone would ask. They would have felt funny. They felt they would be put down by the other guys."

In December 1973, Robert Blatz's parents engaged the law firm of Cordes, Purcell, Fritz and Ingrao of Mineola, Long Island, to prepare a lawsuit against the Brentwood Ross High School. The complaint alleged unlawful death and personal injury.

The Blatz suit asked for $1 million in damages.

The case of Tomas Sanchez, the sixteen-year-old player from

El Paso, Texas, did not include the element of excessive heat. He
died on a Friday night. The chief medical officer in his case was a
justice of the peace, Judge Al Mestan of El Paso. He said the
official cause of the boy's death was "acute left subdural hemorrhaging, between the brain and the skull." He added:

A television station was there, taking films of the game, so
we really got a good picture of what happened. The boy was
a real gung-ho player; really enthusiastic. In the second
quarter of the game, he got into a real good scramble—you
know, piling up and all of that; we saw it in the films.
Nothing happened until the fourth quarter; then he came to
the bench and he told the coach he didn't feel well, that his
head was hurting real bad. He began to vomit. There was a
medical attendant at the game, somebody from the Latuna
Prison nearby. He gave the boy mouth-to-mouth resuscita-
tion. He thought the boy had a concussion. They took the
boy by ambulance to the doctor's office in town, then they
decided to take him to the hospital, Providence Hospital, in
El Paso. He died en route. The nurse who was in the ambulance with him said that before the boy lost consciousness he
was pulling his hair out, his head hurt him so bad. The
pathologist at the hospital pronounced the boy DOA—dead
on arrival. After he performed an autopsy, and after he saw
the films of the game, he issued his verdict right away: death
by brain hemorrhaging. The blow [Sanchez] received in the
head in the second quarter of the game was the blow that did
it.

The doctor said that sometimes it takes a half-hour to an
hour for the hemorrhaging to take its toll visibly. That explained the long delay between the time the boy got hit and
the time he became ill. The hemorrhaging is usually slow, in
an injury such as this, but the result of it all is that the
hemorrhaging creates pressure on the brain. That pressure
caused the boy to see double, to be weak in the knees. I don't
think the boy had much of a chance. Once he got weak in the

knees and he started seeing double, the doctor said that the boy had about ten minutes left before death. We had another case like that a couple years before; a kid in high school was fooling around, and he hit another kid on the top of the head with a science book. The same thing happened. The kid who was hit died. It's one of those freak things.

This boy, the football player, was real poor. All he had was his mother. The coach felt real bad about it. His name's Dewey Whittaker, Anthony High School. The Sanchez boy was the second football player to die around here in two years; we lost another boy in 1971, a kid named Phillips, from Andrews High School. He died after a game, too. The coaches around here, they have this coaches' association and they have insurance policies to protect themselves against getting sued if a kid dies on them. This is big football country, you know. Out here, there isn't much else for kids to do except play football."

Two steps have been taken in an effort to protect high-school athletes from serious injury and death. The first involves a bill in the United States Congress, introduced initially by Representative Ronald Dellums, a Democrat from California, which would "require educational institutions engaged in interscholastic athletic competition to employ certified athletic trainers." Dellum's bill, called the "Athletic Care Act," has already received the support of the National Association of Athletic Trainers and of the National Football Association. The bill would require that each high school with an interscholastic athletic program "maintain in employment at each school at least one person from the profession of athletic training certified by the Education Commissioner."

Michael Duberstein, who is Representative Dellums' legislative analyst, said that of the 14,000 high schools in the country with 11-man football teams, fewer than one per cent have certified trainers. The trainers called for in Dellums' bill, Duberstein said, would be required to attend all football-practice sessions as well as games. He said that the bill would not require school boards to go out and hire new personnel. Said Duberstein: "Ideally, the best situation is to take a current teacher and let him get the training so he can qualify as a trainer. This could be a gym teacher, or almost anyone else on the teaching staff of the school."

Another man who worked closely with Representative Dellums on the bill is Otto Davis, who is the executive director of the national trainers' association and the trainer for the Philadelphia Eagles football team. Said Davis: "We're not saying that every school should go out and hire a man who will be nothing but a trainer. We want a teacher-trainer. A person who will teach —English, biology, physical education, whatever. Then, about two or three in the afternoon, he would go down to the high-school practices. It wouldn't cost the schools that much. It could be done the way some school districts pay assistant coaches. They might get two thousand dollars extra for helping as a trainer. Or fifteen hundred. But we're surely not saying that every school has to go out and find ten thousand dollars for a trainer."

The second step does not have the national implications of Representative Dellums' bill—yet. It is purely regional in scope. It is a medical clinic which is devoted strictly to the treatment of athletic injuries. The first of its kind has been established in Newark, New Jersey, by an orthopedic surgeon named Dr. Max Novich. He runs this clinic on the first and third Wednesdays of every month at the Orthopedic Center of the United Hospitals of Newark. His goal: to establish medical-treatment centers solely for athletic injuries. He said: "In America, about seventeen million people are injured in athletic events, professional and non-professional, every year. I think the time has come for the medical profession to handle these injuries in something other than a routine manner. The whole idea of sports medicine is something that is long overdue, particularly when you sit down and realize just how many people are actively involved in sports these days, whether it's jogging or swimming or skiing or professional football. It's a tremendous number of people."

The patients who use Dr. Novich's sports-injury clinic are not charged for diagnoses or evaluations. Laboratory fees and X-ray fees, however, are billed, but insurance covers athletes in most cases.

Dr. Novich said: "I enjoy working with athletes. Their motivation to get well is high, and they are easy to handle. But it depends on the doctors to send injured athletes here. I would especially like to get to those younger people who play in the Pop Warner football leagues and the Little League baseball leagues. They have no real medical supervision in these leagues. I think this kind of clinic can be particularly geared to these leagues. Someday, I like to think, this kind of clinic will be established in every city in the country in which people play games."

At the end of the 1973 scholastic-football season, a young sports writer for the Wilmington *News-Journal* in Wilmington, Delaware, named Matt Zabitka, decided to do a spinoff on the idea of all-star teams. He chose what he called an all-scar team, consisting of players who had been injured during the season, either at games or at practice sessions. On the first team, for example, he listed a high-school player who had suffered a shoulder separation and had missed seven games. On defense, he chose one player who had a leg broken in two places, and another player who missed four games because of a broken collarbone. He gave a special award to a player who had suffered a cracked vertebra. It was all written in good fun, but not necessarily in good taste. It was merely the writer's way of recognizing all the players who had been injured during the season.

But what followed publication of the article surprised Zabitka. He was deluged with phone calls from parents of injured players who wanted to know why their sons were omitted from the team. One parent said: "My son broke his arm in two places early in the season and couldn't play any more. Don't you think this entitles him to some mention?"

By writing about injured players, Zabitka accidentally addressed himself to a much larger, and sadder, truth:

Once all of these high-school players fall by the wayside, once they are encased in casts and strung into traction, set upon crutches or set into wheelchairs, they are quickly forgotten. In their alienation, broken legs and pinched nerves become not merely serious injuries ... but badges of honor, to be worn proudly, and, hopefully, to be recognized as such.

X • When Coaches Bring Down the House: Inciting Riots at Games

In 1968, a young man named H. Rap Brown was placed on the "Most-wanted List" by the Federal Bureau of Investigation, and he immediately became one of the nation's most celebrated fugitives. The charge against him was inciting a riot in Cambridge, Maryland. While the Federal Bureau of Investigation was conducting its extensive manhunt for H. Rap Brown, many high-school coaches all across America were inciting little riots of their own inside their own little school gymnasiums. But, of course, criminal charges were never lodged against any of these coaches, even though several dozen students and several dozen spectators and a handful of athletes were either assaulted or arrested at each of them because the coach's very actions on the bench inflamed their emotions to fever pitches—and then beyond.

The scenario usually goes like this:

The coach is a man with a volatile personality; he can be described as a high-pressure coach. His team is sluggish on the floor and is losing the game. He feels he must do something to fire up his team, to snap it out of its collective lethargy. He begins by berating the referees, the favorite, oblique target; he questions every call against his team, his demeanor becoming more combative with each protest. Finally, he begins throwing a towel around, or maybe a clipboard. By this time, his team indeed is fired up; so are the followers of his team, sitting in the bleachers. But the other team, and its followers, have become fired up as well—negatively. Their fervor is based on outrage over the coach's actions. Before long, a loose ball collision, or a struggle under the backboards, ignites the players' pregnant tempers; a fight ensues. The people in the stands come out onto the floor and join in; two separate, but intertwined battles are going on—one among the players, the other among the adult spectators. The police are called in to stop it. When it's over, two or three players are thrown out of the game; ten or twelve adult spectators are escorted out of the gymnasium; and the injured people are taken for medical help. The coach stays on the bench; rarely does anything happen to him.

High-school administrators have usually blamed the trouble on "unruly outside troublemakers." That, of course, is nonsense. The blame, in many cases, traces directly to the actions of their own high-pressure coaches. Such coaches are not replaced because they throw towels or clipboards on the bench, or because they berate referees; they are replaced when they have two or three losing seasons in a row. The result, then, is that the specter of violence hangs over many high-school gymnasiums like a London fog; the blame rests with the administrators who condone high-pressure coaches who incite riots as much as it rests with the high-pressure coaches themselves.

Consider, as a case in point, the following report from the records of the North Carolina High School Athletic Association:

At a game between the Edneyville and T. C. Roberson high schools, Edneyville's coach approached officials in an unsportsmanlike manner and used profanity; he went into the officials' dressing room and continued to voice his disapproval. Adult Edneyville spectators had to be restrained by a deputy sheriff when they, too, approached the officials. One Edneyville player threatened the T. C. Roberson coach with a chair. Edneyville's coach was fined one hundred dollars and was placed on probation for the remainder of the school year. Remaining Edneyville games were played in the afternoon, before only the student body and faculty members. The Edneyville player was suspended for several weeks.

True, not all violence at high school games is coach-inspired. Players, in many cases, are not angelic either. Some examples:

• In Kings Park, Long Island, forty-eight seconds before the end of a basketball game, a player from Wyandanch High School threw a chair at a player from Kings Park High School, and fans poured onto the court from both sides. In the ensuing melee, nine persons were arrested and nine others—including two Suffolk County policemen—were injured. Twenty-five policemen were eventually called in to quell the disturbance. As a result of the incident, the schools severed their athletic relationship. The principal of Kings Park High School, Robert B. Cody, said that he would ask that his school be assigned to a new league, and if Kings Park and Wyandanch were ever paired again in any future championship games, he said: "We would petition the league to have the game played without any spectators present. Since I am charged with the responsibility of their safety and well-being, I refuse to subject either players, staff, spectators, or school property to the possibility of further disturbances."

• In Delaware, the state championship team from DeWarr High School in Wilmington was not allowed to have spectators at its last three home games following riots in its gym.

• In Rhode Island, a state basketball championship tournament was interrupted by a student assault on an usher at Providence College, the site of the tournament. Students at Providence filed a protest with their administrators that said, in effect, "Keep the high-school kids out of here."

• In Detroit and Chicago, high-school football games have been played on Thursday afternoons and basketball games on Friday afternoons before students-only audiences for many years.

• In Albany, New York, a basketball game between Philip Schuyler High School and Linton High School was canceled in the first period when spectators ran onto the floor and attacked players. It was replayed three days later in the afternoon—without

anyone knowing it, not even the students who were passing
between classes.

· In Cincinnati, two boys were assaulted and another arrested
after a football game between Purcell and Walnut Hills high
schools played at Withrow High School Stadium. Five students
were beaten near Trechter Stadium after a football game between
Aiken and Woodward high schools. After that incident, Hamilton
County Juvenile Court Judge Benjamin Schwartz issued a "get-
tough" policy for dealing with youths arrested on assault-charges
at high-school football games. He warned that anyone convicted of
assault charges would be institutionalized, even for a first offense.

Some observations on the subject of violence:

1. *Immunity.* High-pressure high-school coaches who ignite,
and then preside over, riots inside of high-school gymnasiums
apparently enjoy the same immunity from civil law as the coach
who conducts a practice in ninety-five-degree heat during which
one of his players falls dead. Unlike such people as H. Rap Brown,
high-pressure coaches are never arrested for inciting to riot. The
high-pressure coach can rant, rave, swear, throw, intimidate, gesture, and demean from his bench; while doing all of these things, he
can inflame the emotions of the crowd to a combative lynch-mob
pitch. But once the fight erupts, he is held blameless. If he did the
same things outside the gymnasium, in the street, he would
doubtless be arrested immediately, but the walls of the school and
the structure of the game immunize him. If he incites a riot from
the bench during a game, administrators will say that he had only
become excited; they will add that the reason he had become
excited was because he wanted to win the game so badly. Police
who storm into gymnasiums to break up such melees always arrest,
or club, the participants; the men who start them go back to their
benches and, more often than not, use the excitement to further
fire up their teams. As a sportswriter, I witnessed three such
melees; each time, the high-pressure coach who was responsible

for starting it escaped without so much as a verbal reprimand from the referees, the police, or the school administrators who were present. The reason, I felt, was because the high-pressure coaches were opportunistic enough not to throw any punches once the fighting began; incredibly, when the riots were at their peaks, the high-pressure coaches began acting as peacemakers. Thus, they neutralized the effects of their previous actions; people actually forgot that it was the high-pressure coach who had started the whole thing.

2. *Referees.* Referees at high-school sports events absorb astonishing amounts of verbal abuse from high-pressure coaches. Some of them fight back; they call technical fouls, eject abusive players from games, and sometimes even remove the insulting coach from the bench and banish him to the locker room. But the result of all of this is that the referee makes it worse for himself—if he cleans out the bench, the crowd unloads on him. Since he has no control over the crowd, the abuse is even worse. So he is faced with a dilemma: either clamp down on the high-pressure coach, and risk inflaming the ire of the crowd, or else keep quiet and let the high-pressure coach bellow and bray. Either choice may leave him with a riot on his hands; once a riot ensues at a game in which he is officiating, he acquires a reputation for being a referee who cannot control the game, or the crowd. His assignments diminish immediately. One referee I knew in upstate New York solved the problem nicely; he became, in the lexicon of his profession, a "homer." This meant that he went out of his way to makes calls that would be pleasing to the home team, and to the home team's high-pressure coach. After a while, high-pressure coaches were falling over each other to hire him for their home games; he was worth, to them, anywhere from 10 to 20 points a game. This referee also happened to be a city policeman, and the combination made him a revered figure in town. That he compromised himself on Friday and Saturday nights, inside local high school gymnasiums, was never a topic of discussion, however; it simply was not mentioned—ever. Referees who work high-school games to supplement their incomes cannot win in their relationship with

high-pressure coaches; they are either routed or corrupted, depending on their own levels of integrity.

3. *Winning.* One of the most nonsensical of all motivations attributed to riotous high-pressure coaches is their passion for victory. In many cases, it is pure nonsense. These coaches are not so much obsessed with winning as with *not losing.* Many high-pressure coaches do not coach to win games; they coach to avoid losing them. There is a fine line between coaching to win and coaching not to lose. Most high-school coaches have not come to terms with defeat; they pigeonhole the word somewhere in between "death" and "despair," and then forget about it. High-school coaches are expected to be overcome with remorse after a loss; their players are expected to cry and be overcome with emotions. It is all a big act. But these high-pressure coaches are avoiding one very important part of their jobs: teaching young men how to come to terms with defeat. They spend all of their time allegedly teaching their players tactics that will enable them to win games, but since a very small percentage of teams go undefeated, losses are inevitable. The most obvious example of a coach who is coaching to avoid losing is the coach who employs the stall in basketball, or the conservative running game in football, as soon as his team has taken the lead. Instead of allowing the kids to play out the victory (and run the risk of allowing the victory to slip through his fingers) he goes into a freeze. He is "coaching scared"; he is afraid to lose. So, then, a lot of what passes for an obsession with winning is nothing more than an obsession with avoiding defeat. The passion for winning is not necessarily a problem among riotous, high-pressure coaches; losing—and coming to terms with it—is.

XI • From a Reporter's Notebook: Jekylls and Hydes and Hatchet Men

During the eight years in which I covered high-school sports for a newspaper in upstate New York, I witnessed numerous displays of fanaticism and extremism on the part of high-school coaches. During this time, I considered myself in the unfortunate position of working for a newspaper that happened to be located in an area that seemed to have the market cornered on coaches who were raving maniacs. But I was wrong. In the late 1960s, while traveling extensively throughout America as a syndicated newspaper sportswriter, I discovered that Chicago and Detroit, and Cleveland and Kansas City, and Akron and Albuquerque, had their shares of overzealous coaches as well; upstate New York, I discovered, was merely a microcosm of the United States of America. During that time, I noticed two things about high-school coaches and athletes that particularly stood out in my mind: (1) Hardly anyone—parents, educators, clergymen, policemen—was openly critical of the coaches' actions, and (2) there was very little joy on the faces of the fourteen-year-old forwards and the fifteen-year-old linebackers when they played their games. The coaches had demanded that the kids sacrifice whatever touches of individuality that they possessed for the good of their teams; the kids did. They had become robotized mannequins, and most of them, I suspected, did not know exactly what was happening to them. They started out just wanting to play games; they were turned into different people along the way. But whatever it was that was happening to them, the kids did not necessarily like it. Looking back over those years, if there was one single memorable fact that stands out above the rest, sadly, it was the lack of joy experienced by the young players. They had become grim, self-centered, tunnel-visioned practioners of the coaches' rules—at fourteen years old. None of the joy that was evident on the faces of students in high-school plays, say, was evident on the faces of high-school athletes.

Following are some personal anecdotes from that period concerning the actions of coaches (they could have been culled, I feel, from the notebooks of sportswriters in California, Wisconsin, Ohio, and Delaware, just as easily):

1. A memorable incident occurred right after a high school football game in the fall of 1963. A suburban school, new and expensive and thirsting for status, had just defeated the old, established football powerhouse of a high school from the inner city. It was a big upset victory, the newspapers were to report. Seconds after the game ended, the head coach from the suburban school and one of the assistant coaches from the city school began exchanging words. Soon a crowd began to gather. The two coaches were nose to nose, and apparently quite willing to go at each other with fists, or whatever. As the crowd encouraged them, a dandy of a bare-knuckled fight seemed inevitable. But a sports writer who happened to be 6 foot 1 and weigh 190 pounds, stepped between them. After separating them, he admonished them both for acting like little kids. Reluctantly, the coaches parted and went their separate ways, glaring at each other as they left, mumbling under their breaths. Today, the coach of the surburban football team is the principal of his school. The assistant coach from the city school is now the principal of *his* school.

2. I had always been amazed at just how badly Roman Catholic schools wanted to embellish their images by having winning sports

teams. The priests and the brothers who ran these private schools were the most vocal and fanatical supporters of their sports teams. From the bleachers, they berated referees, taunted players from other schools, and acted, generally, as if in need of exorcism themselves. Now, these Roman Catholic high schools went to great extremes to insure the success of their sports teams. One weapon they used effectively was the process known as junior-high-school recruiting. Whenever they spotted a kid in junior high school who looked as if he would become an outstanding player in high school, they offered him a scholarship to attend their school. This scholarship included free tuition and free books, and, presumably, only God knows what else on the side. If an outstanding junior-high-school player happened to be of the Roman Catholic faith, the Catholic high schools would almost surely get him as a scholarship student. If he happened to be enrolled at a Roman Catholic junior high school, it was virtually a sure thing. If he happened to be a Methodist, or a Lutheran, or an Episcopalian, it didn't really matter; the Catholics wouldn't discriminate against him—and who knows? The kid might find that he likes what he sees and hears, and he might even turn Catholic himself. By cornering the market on the best Roman Catholic players, the Roman Catholic high schools then proceeded to run roughshod over the public high schools in sports. While the public high schools were prevented from recruiting players from other school districts, the private Roman Catholic schools were not. Result: In most cities where there are Roman Catholic high schools, those schools are among the most successful in sports. The underpinning, of course, is the fact that they can recruit junior-high-school players and offer them these scholarships. And what thirteen-year-old kid isn't going to be impressed by an offer of a high-school scholarship? Religion, it appears, is thicker than region.

3. One spring morning, a basketball player from one of the city high schools stopped into the newspaper's sports department. He proceeded to tell me a story about his head coach, and he implied that he wouldn't mind at all if the story found its way into print. The story was this: At the end of a disastrous season, the coach

called together his entire team. He said, "Now that the season is over, I would just like to know, for my own private information, how many of you people broke training rules during the season?" The kids, knowing that the season was over and nothing could be done to them in the form of disciplinary action, were honest about it. Thirteen of the fourteen players raised their hands. The coach thanked them, and then dismissed them. The next day, he announced to the school that no varsity letters would be awarded that year because of training-rules violations. The player felt as if he and his teammates had been tricked by the coach; so did I. I wrote the story for the newspaper, and the predictable happened: The coach was outraged at me. Confronting me at a track meet, he gritted his teeth (presumably to show me to what extreme he was going in order to hold back his temper) and said, slowly and bitterly: "Where . . . are . . . your . . . *morals?*"

4. The football coach at one of the suburban schools had a typical Jekyll-and-Hyde personality. Affable and friendly during the week, at practice sessions and during telephone conversations, he was transformed into a screaming madman on Saturday afternoon. Games did it to him. Now, on one particular Saturday afternoon, while covering one of his games on the sidelines, I watched him reach a new low. One of his players, an offensive lineman, was flagged by a referee for being an ineligible receiver downfield. The penalty was fifteen yards, and it was a very costly one, since it ultimately stifled a nice drive downfield. The coach immediately sent in a substitute player for the offensive lineman. The player, apparently knowing what was waiting for him on the sidelines, refused to come out of the game. In the huddle, he argued with his replacement; meanwhile, the team had twelve players on the field, and a five-yard penalty was imminent. The coach, apparently anticipating another dropped flag, ran out to within five yards of the huddle and screamed out the offending player's name. Then he proceeded to drag the player right off the field by his jersey. Of course, the player received the tongue-lashing of his young life once they both reached the sidelines. But the ultimate message was missed by the coach, and by the school authorities and the parents

who were present: The kid was afraid to leave the game because he was afraid of the coach.

5. One of the most ridiculous practices known to high-school sports is that of filming games, particularly football and basketball games. Coaches always tell the school authorities that they need the money to film these games for two reasons: (1) To watch the team and detect any deficiencies in it, and (2) because colleges, whenever scouting one of their players with a scholarship offer in mind, always wanted films of the kid in action. Surely, the coaches lament, you wouldn't want to cost a kid a college scholarship because we don't have films of him in action? So the school spends a couple thousand dollars every year filming its games. Now, multiplied by thousands of high schools throughout America, the money spent on filming high-school games boggles the mind. One incident involving game films sticks with me particularly: Two suburban schools had just played a close game on a Saturday afternoon; the final score was something like 14–13 or 13–12. The coach whose team lost called me at the newspaper on a Monday morning; he invited me to his school to watch movies of the game. "It will be very interesting," he promised. I went. He showed me the film of the last series of downs during which his team had the ball. Twice he stopped the film and showed me where a defensive player had been offside; he said the referees should have called those two penalties; had they called them, his team would have won. Sitting in this elaborate screening room at his school, looking at movies that were being played on a large screen that descended from a hidden spot in the ceiling, I realized that he was contesting the outcome of the game with his films. A good story, I surmised. Then I called the other coach; I told him what had happened, and I asked him if I could get his side of the story. He said sure, come on over, we'll show you our films. I went into his screening room, which was not quite so elaborate, and I watched the last series of downs. "See," the coach said, "those kids were not offside." They weren't; his movies were taken from a different angle. Nothing ever happened, except that the losing coach managed to taint the

other team's victory by clouding it with two uncalled offsides penalties. The films were his vehicle.

6. Subtle tricks coaches use during games amount to subterfuge—and the kids pay the price. I knew one coach at a suburban high school who instructed his punt returner to call for a fair catch the very first time the other team punted the ball. It was automatic, no matter where the ball was kicked from. The reason for this was very subtle. The coach knew that the team that was punting away the ball would be quite enthusiastic about covering the kick. The team had just been stopped, it was giving the ball up, but it desperately wanted to make an awesome impression on the other team's offense. What better way to intimidate the offense than to obliterate the punt returner? The coach knew that the opposing team's players would be so fired up, so determined, so hysterical, so hellbent on covering the kick, that they might not even see the fair-catch signal, particularly if his punt returner gave it in a half-hearted way, which he was instructed to do. Then they would obliterate the punt returner in a pile of thrashing, kicking bodies. Then the referee would drop a flag and call a roughing-the-catcher penalty. That meant that the coach would be able to start his first offensive series with a fifteen-yard penalty in his favor. Nobody seemed to be concerned about the punishment which the poor punt returner was receiving on these plays. The coach used the other team's hysteria for his own purposes, and the fifteen-year-old punt returner had all the bruises and bumps to show for it.

7. One coach I knew was a machismo fanatic; he wanted his basketball players to be the roughest and toughest in the league. So every day he would scrimmage with them, one on one. He would berate them, push them, use his body to punish them, intimidate them, curse them, and regularly outscore them. The players then went out on Friday nights and did the same things to other teams. They won a lot of games, to be sure. One day, during one of these scrimmages the coach conducted, he was particularly brutal; his opponent was a gimpy-legged player who couldn't run, and he was used only in games in which his team was ahead by 30 or 40 points.

But the coach apparently concluded that the kid was using his bad leg as an excuse; the kid wasn't as tough as the other kids because, the coach implied, he always copped out in confrontations, using his gimpy leg as an excuse. On this day the coach poured it on; he ran rings around the kid, screamed at him, drove to the basket on him, rebounded with a fury; the kid was humiliated. Finally, the kid rebelled; he called the coach a very bad name. Then he began walking off the court. The coach chased him. Then he punched the kid in the jaw.

8. One of the most interesting examples of coaching compromise I encountered involved the coach at one of the suburban schools. His star basketball player, a 6-foot-3-inch center who had sensational moves and good basketball sense, went out during his summer vacation and got himself tattooed. He reported to practice that fall with a large tattoo etched on to his right bicep. If I recall it correctly, the tattoo was a caricature of Satan. Under and around it, in morose script, were inscribed the words: "Born to Raise Hell." The coach was very distraught; this tattoo would surely sabotage the image he was attempting to project through his players, the image of clean-cut, athletic masculinity. Yet he could not remove the player from his team; the kid was too good, and, besides, everybody in the school knew he had the tattoo (sometimes the kid would show up to school wearing short-sleeved tee shirts). So, after considerable mental anguish, the coach jubilantly reached an acceptable compromise. The kid played the entire season with a white surgical armband on his right bicep. First attempts to use a white knee guard on the arm were futile; the knee guard was too cumbersome to the player. He couldn't shoot well with it on. Still, he was one of the best players in the history of that school, tattoo notwithstanding.

9. Almost every successful basketball team I covered had a reserve player who played the role that was called "hatchet man." This player, usually a brawny, dedicated type who lacked finesse and talent, would be inserted into games by coaches for one purpose: to commit fouls. These fouls were not committed arbitrarily; they were committed with great thought and conviction.

They were usually committed against the other teams' best players, or against a player who suddenly developed a hot shooting hand. These fouls were not "excuse-me" types; they usually sent opposing players three rows deep into the bleachers. The point made—intimidation, of course—the hatchet man would return to the bench. If the opposing player persisted in scoring huge numbers of points, or in amassing large numbers of rebounds, the hatchet man would return to the game. To detect the hatchet man on most teams, one merely has to look closely at the team's box scores in the next day's newspapers. The hatchet man is the player whose name appears regularly . . . next to the numbers 0–0–0. The best hatchet man I ever saw on a high-school team actually received a college scholarship. He averaged 1.3 points a game for the season. Apparently, colleges can always use a well-trained hatchet man.

10. Coaches who handled the select group of minor sports were equally fanatical. I saw a gymnastics coach make a kid with a broken arm work the high bars, cast and all; the coach had told him that he still had to stay in shape, broken arm notwithstanding. Cross-country coaches are a particularly uncompassionate breed. Anyone who has ever witnessed the finish of a large high-school cross-country meet will attest that the sight is not a pretty one. Kids who have just run two and a half miles have blue faces, covered with saliva, which are distorted into sculptures of pain; they have pushed their young bodies as hard as they can possibly push them. Yet, near finish lines, there is always the high-school cross-country coaches, stop-watches in hand, screaming and yelling at the kids to go faster. The kids collapse to the ground, writhing and gasping for breath, and the coaches ignore them, waiting to scream and yell at the next kid that comes by. Once, my newspaper ran a four-column picture of a high-school cross-country runner who had just collapsed after finishing a race; it was a picture of gruesome pain. A week later, the kid's coach, outraged, stopped me at another meet. He said: "You are trying to sabotage my program by running that picture. How in hell is any mother going to let her kid come out for cross-country after seeing a

horrible picture like that, you son of a bitch?" Wrestling coaches, always mindful of weight limits, had kids steaming out in sauna rooms to sweat off excess poundage. That their growing and developing bodies no longer could make the 145-pound limit did not seem to matter; they were going to wrestle at 145, no matter what. Many high-school wrestlers are like professional jockeys; they spent more time sweating than competing.

Almost any city in America with more than one high school has its own versions of the aforementioned events. They are interchangeable, city to city, school to school. One high-school coach I knew, now retired, said that extremist coaches, and extremist tactics, will be around for as long as school administrators opt to embrace that vague phrase known as "a successful sports program." He said: "The trouble is, school administrators do not think deeply enough to decide what is meant by being successful. Is the successful sports program one in which the team goes undefeated and the kids are being turned into little robots, hating every minute of it? Or is being successful having a so-so season during which the kids have fun, enjoy themselves, and expand themselves a little bit as individuals? Me, I got out when I looked around and realized that my bread and butter depended on a fourteen-year-old quarterback. No grown man, reasonably intelligent and reasonably well-educated, should be put in a position like that. The closest I ever came to going mad was when I was a high-school coach. Some guys, they belonged in padded cells."

XII • The Alleged Revolution: Has Anything Really Changed Besides Hair Lengths?

In the years between 1964 and 1974 there has, indeed, been a "revolution" of sorts in the sphere of high-school sports. For one thing, the glamour status of athletes has diminished among their peers; it is no longer fashionable to spend four years in high school aspiring to wear a letter sweater. Needless to say, it is no longer fashionable to be seen wearing a letter sweater while walking (strutting) through the halls of the school. Army-surplus field jackets have been in vogue. Coaches have been affected by this change in values—outwardly, at least. They have let their own hair grow longer, they now wear bright-to-flamboyant sports jackets and slacks with flared cuffs, and a few of them have even been seen wearing platform shoes. The new style of dress is their concession to the times. They have acquiesced externally to the wishes of their players; but that does not necessarily mean that they have acquiesced internally. Quite the contrary; what has emerged now is a legion of coaches that might be described as "pseudo-Vince Lombardis in drag." Dressed like Mick Jagger, but thinking like Don Shula, they still get the same results; their authoritarianism has been blunted somewhat, but the superficial concessions make up for it. In the end, the alleged revolution has changed many coaches only outwardly; inside they are the same people.

Richard Rehberg, an associate professor of sociology at the State University of New York at Binghamton, conducted a study to ascertain the political attitudes of high-school athletes. He interviewed 937 high-school males. He was doubtless prodded into action by all of the talk of "revolution." He presented his report to a symposium on Sport and Social Deviancy which was held at the State University of New York at Brockport. His conclusions:

1. High-school athletes are more conservative politically than non-athletes.

2. High-school athletes are more accepting of "the American way of life" than non-athletes.

3. High-school athletes are less inclined to resist military service than non-athletes.

4. High-school athletes do not consider themselves to be social or political activists.

The same conclusions could have been drawn in the middle of the 1950s, or in the middle of the 1940s Revolution.

Consider, as a popular expression of revolution, the smoking of marijuana. It is no secret that thousands upon thousands of high-school kids in America have at least tried smoking marijuana. It is no secret that many hundreds of athletes have been among them. In the 1950s, it was smoking cigarettes or consuming alcoholic beverages. Now, in the sphere of high-school sports there are such things as training rules; among them is the declaration that players should not smoke marijuana. So what is happening? Kids are smoking anyway. The trick, of course, is in not getting caught. Once a player is caught, the coach is forced to make a decision: either enforce the training rules and boot the offenders off the team, or look the other way and have a strung-out team. Training rules in high school are usually ridiculous; they are enforced only when the offenders are caught. That kids are breaking training rules is no secret; the secret is that many coaches know it and do nothing about it. The reason: The star players are involved. Boot them and kiss off the season. There is a very flexible gray area in high-school training rules; discretion is the solution. Don't get high in public, goddammit; get high where nobody can see you.

One such coach who was forced to make the ultimate decision was Joseph Logue, who coached St. James' High School football team to a championship in the Philadelphia area in 1972. In 1973 he booted 20 players from his team for drinking and drug use. It all started when a group of them was stopped in an automobile by the police; the car reeked of marijuana. Before it was over, 20 players had been implicated and charged with training-rules violations and dismissed. At the time Logue's team had a 1–3 won-lost record, which raised a question in some people's minds in Philadelphia: Would Logue have booted 20 kids from his team the year before, while on the way to a championship season? Logue said: "We're trying to mold men. We may have to bring up some of the JV's. We'll go with clean kids, not trash."

The crime, of course, was in getting caught, not in getting high. Discretion, it seems, is not only the better part of valor, it is the better part of varsities.

So, despite all of the research papers and all of the talk of "revolution," the plain fact is that very little has changed in high-school sports despite the sociopolitical turmoil of the last decade in America. Kids still want to play football and basketball on the varsity, interscholastic level; coaches still want to diagram X's and O's and call plays and dictate strategy. John Jeansonne, a young sportswriter, grew up in a small town in Texas during the late 1950s and early 1960s; he said that high-school football dictated the atmosphere of the town then. In the fall of 1973 he returned to see if anything had changed. Nothing had. He filed the following report, which is enlighting in that it shows just how entrenched high-school football still is in many communities in America, and just how interwoven it still is into the social fabric:

Hereford, Tex.—Anyone who never has had chicken-fried steak just wouldn't understand. Neither would anyone whose morning doesn't begin with pure, cloudless skies, scented by oil refineries or cow manure; anyone who doesn't mark the center of town with the Rexall Drug Store; anyone whose social life runs into more money than a dollar for a movie.

Yet these country constants are not what makes rural Texas unique. They are props for something bigger. Something which is discussed in churches, bars (where they aren't against the law), cafés, schools, Kiwanis Club meetings, oil fields and out on the north forty. Football, particularly high school football, is the staff of life.

While Sunday is the Sabbath on the dusty plains of the Bible Belt, Friday is Game Day, and not even believing in the Spirit quite generates the urgency that believing in team spirit does. Last Friday—in this small cattle town—dawned just as any autumn Friday does in any small Texas community.

Women came to work, at the Hereford National Bank and the Rexall Drug Store and the Christian Book Store, wearing white mum corsages with maroon "H's" on them. Nearly every man not compelled to wear Levi's on the farm opted for maroon slacks or maroon sports coats or maroon ties. "Everybody wears the team colors today," explained Hereford *Brand* news editor Don Richards. Indeed, even the manikins in the two apparel shops' windows on Main Street were dressed in maroon.

Of the 13,414 residents of Hereford, more than 6,000 would be at the Hereford High School football game. "I guarantee," Richards said, "there won't be any no-shows." Hundreds of them would leave work early in the afternoon to attend the pep rally in the high school gym, and more would line Main Street or the parade involving the high school and junior high school bands, cheerleaders and drill teams. Hereford, in West Texas, north of Lubbock, has only 10 traffic jams per year—five after high school parades on Friday afternoons and five after the high school's home football games on Friday nights.

Peering out almost every store window was an eight-by-ten glossy of a high school football player. With a fill-up of gas, customers received a water and oil check, a cleansing of the windshield and a free prediction on the game: "Best damn team we've had in many a moon," it went. "I think we'll whup 'em."

Entire communities like Hereford funnel all of their excess energies into the high school football program for three major reasons:

1) Isolated as they are, more than 300 miles from the nearest professional team and at least 70 miles to the nearest major college team, there is no team other than the high school for a fan to follow.

(2) There is fierce community pride ("I'm From Dimmitt, Dammit" or "Lucky Me, I Live in Lubbock" adorn the car bumpers), probably because most residents spend their entire lives in the same community.

(3) Football reflects the basic belief of small, non-industrialized towns: That hard work and the spartan existence build strong men.

George Kirk, for 14 years a high school coach in West Texas and now an assistant coach at Baylor University, said, "The community EXPECTS a boy who's able to play to play. Football becomes important to him because it's important to the community.

"It's like the feudal times," Kirk said, "and each town is a kingdom at war with the other." Gary Shaw, author of the book *Meat on the Hoof* based on his experiences as a Texas University football players, remembers his high school days in Denton, Tex. "There was a real feeling of community responsibility when you played for the high school team," Shaw said. "You were defending your town against the aliens who were about to attack."

Phil Bonsal, 17, a starting guard on the high school team in the oil and farm town of Dumas (pop. 9,771), is reminded every day that he is representing his town against such invaders as Muleshoe, Canyon, and Levelland. "I guess I know about half the people in town," Bonsal said, "but they all know who we [the football players] are. They stop me and ask me if I'm ready for the next game."

Dr. Robert H. Smith, a Dallas psychologist who specializes in teenage problems, experienced the football phenomenon firsthand while growing up in the tiny West Texas town of Anson. "Football is just so readily available to the kids in this situation," Smith said. "In cities that aren't quite as industrialized, there is a definite interest in the spartan life and football is the best avenue for that."

Bill Spann, coach and athletic director at Dumas High, affirms that theory. "People in this part of the country are still rugged individualists," Spann said. "We believe that hard work and a challenge are good for a man. One thing which disappoints me in our society is our bad-mouthing of athletics and our drift toward uncontrolled discipline. I feel football is the last place where we have discipline."

Shaw said, "Backing football so completely is not a mindless thing that the people do. It is what they believe. They want their sons to be tough, aggressive, competitive."

So into the high school football program goes fanatic enthusiasm and plenty of money. In Dumas, also north of Lubbock, where the average yearly income per family is approximately $7,000, the residents voted a local bond issue in 1964 which built a $316,689 stadium, capacity 6,000. The stadium is constructed of pre-stressed concrete and steel, with fiberglass sheathing on the seats, and is equipped with six light poles and 100 floodlights, plus an electric scoreboard and double-leveled press box.

Beyond the basic cost of its stadium, Dumas paid $2,000 just for grass, $500 for labor and seeding of the field and $600 to provide a watering system for the field. The football coach has a yearly salary almost double the town's average, and five assistant coaches are paid $1,500 above their teaching salaries.

It is difficult to find a Texan who questions the emphasis on high school football. Frank Vollert, Dumas superintendent of schools, does question the emphasis in the lower grades. "Frankly," Vollert said, "I have reservations for starting the kids at organized tackle football in the second grade, because I think it can discourage some of the quick-growing youngsters. A 10-year-old kid with baby fat may get popped a few times by a smaller kid and give up.

"But," he emphasized, "in the high schools, football is a rallying point for the community. There's a genuine spirit and pride in the football team that everyone feels."

So you have magazines like *Texas Football,* with a 77-page section presenting pictures and previews on every school which plays football (more than 700). In the Panhandle area there is a magazine named *Top-o-Texas Football,* 432 pages of pictures, rosters, schedules and praise. Every local town with a local radio station carries the high school game live—except where the station is so small that its license requires sundown sign-off, and then it carries taped coverage of the Friday night game on Saturday morning.

The football team members are treated like dignitaries at all times. On the field, there are new game uniforms at least two out of three years (home uniforms ordered one year; road uniforms the next; skip the third year if there aren't too many grass stains visible). Many teams have special game shoes (usually white) and many have separate, lighted practice fields so that the game field will be in good shape on Friday night.

Off the field, many schools provide blazers to be worn on the day of the game. The player-to-coach ratio at Dumas is 6-1, while the student-to teacher ratio is 18-1. For out-of-town games, the players are excused from classes around noon, bussed to the game and are provided with a snack before the game (usually toast and honey and hot tea) and a full meal after the game (usually chicken-fried steak, potatoes, one vegetable, iced tea). The going rate is $2.50 per player and the school always picks up the tab.

The players are honored at weekly pep rallies, when the entire school and many of the local residents crowd into the gym to sing and cheer and holler while the players sit stone-faced like soldiers. Letter jackets used to be a gift from the schools to all lettermen until five years ago, when a statewide rule banned the practice for fear of violating amateur rules.

"I know just how it is," Dr. Smith said. "You go to church on Sunday morning and the preacher will get up and talk about Friday night's football game for 10 minutes. Or you go to the weekly Kiwanis Club luncheon and the thing turns into a booster club meeting."

Texas state high school rules, governed by the University of Texas Interscholastic League, allow for the maximum in football competition. For the largest class of schools, those with enrollments of 1,120 and up, there is even a three-week period of spring practice, pads and all.

There are seven classifications, including eight-man and six-man football for the tiniest of schools, in which state championships are determined. Each classification breaks down into a five-week playoff system, so that added to a team's regular schedule of 10 games, a state champion would play 15 games.

"When it gets to the playoffs," said Danny Andrews, 25, who played at Plainview, Tex., "People really go nuts. I saw a quarterfinal game last year between two schools with enrollments of about 150 each, and there were four radio stations, two television stations (filming for news reports) and six newspapers there."

In Dumas, they still talk of how former coach Burle Bartlett motivated his team for an important playoff game. He promised that if the Dumas Demons won, he would dye his hair green. They did, and he did.

There is such an urgency to win, in fact, that many small communities have their entire youth program dictated to by the high school coach. "We did a study a while back," said Hollis Biddle, associate editor of *Texas Football* magazine, "and we found that the real fine high schools will have their coach take charge of the whole program down to the second grade. He'll have those second graders running the same plays as the high school varsity. Getting them ready."

It leads to an intense high school program. Dr. Smith said, "Emotions run so [high] for a high school player getting all of this attention. There is pressure from the community as well as glory, so that the youngster can be very happy one week and very depressed the next. Actually there is probably more reality of life in this experience than a 16-year-old can handle, and in some cases it may lead to him going through life looking just for the extremes. In other words, seeing something as an ultimate success or ultimate failure, and nothing in between.

"I see a positive and a negative. Positively, there is a team spirit and community spirit which is truly working. But negatively, there is unrealistic success for these youngsters which can't be duplicated in adulthood."

Shaw feels that small Texas communities will continue to overlook the negative in favor of the positive. "People will move away from football as a basic way of filling community and discipline needs when they find something of value which can replace it. They won't move away from football just because there are some negative things about it," Shaw said.

"I'm not worried about football devouring other important things," said Hereford School Superintendent Roy Hartman. "I have a little proverb for that. Take a dinosaur and an ant, and you know that a dinosaur is so big he could mash ants a thousand at a time. But you look around, and how many dinosaurs survived in this world and how many ants?"

If there has been a sociopolitical "revolution" in high-school sports, it would be nice to let the good folks in Hereford, Texas, in on it. And the good folks in Parma, Ohio, and in Wilmington, Delaware, and in Quincy, Illinois. But no such news is forthcoming. There has been no revolution among high-school athletes. The reason, of course, is that kids who have questioning postures, kids who do not submit without first asking why, are quickly weeded out by the coaches. The kids are too smart, potential revolutionaries or, at least, troublemakers. The coaches say that they are "uncoachable." Only the conformists remain. Apparently, there are still enough high-school kids in America who want to play in varsity games without asking questions. They are "coachable." "Being coachable" is a euphemism for "being a conformist."

Revolution?

Try talking about revolution on a Friday night in October in, say, Hereford, Texas. Some idea. Some revolution.

XIII • Programs: Whom Are They for, Players or the Public?

Programs are the superstructures within which coaches operate. A typical high-school program may start in the seventh grade of the district's junior high schools; players are then funneled, year by year, through the program, which releases them after their senior seasons. Programs are sports bureaucracies.

Sometimes, high-school coaches cannot see their players for their programs. In many schools, the program has a higher priority than the player; many coaches will even tell you that the program itself makes for better players. The program does not adapt itself to the players; the players adapt themselves to it. Critics have said that these programs represent nothing more than job security for the coaches; the coaches convince school administrators that they have devised a basketball or football program that will rival the program of the English department, or the program of the art department. *Program.* The word smacks of computerization, and that is exactly what is happening. Many of these high-school sports programs are 1984-ish in concept; they are regimented, authoritarian, unimaginative, and restrictive, intellectually and creatively. They are the corporate wombs from which young robotized athletes emerge. Kids who buck these programs are eliminated: Their cards are pulled, the buttons click, the machines whirr, red lights blink—they are tossed out of sports. The verdict: Uncoachable. (Unprogramable?)

So, what happens when one of these elaborate programs is threatened? The coaches, naturally, are thrown into states of apoplexy. Early in 1973, in Fort Lauderdale, Florida, such a crisis arose. The spring football programs at high schools were threatened with abolition because they were too expensive. The coaches were irate. Their arguments were:

1. "The entire county program will suffer in not only football, but in every sport."

2. "We need it in order to compete with the other areas of the state."

3. "The more time you can spend with the kids these days, the better. This is twenty days that these kids are busy during a time when there is nothing else going on."

4. "We make money on spring football every year. Players must pay five dollars for insurance themselves. The only other expense is first-aid equipment and tape. Spring games have always paid for the rest."

5. "We pick our team in the spring. In the fall you just about have time to get them in shape."

6. "Broward County is just getting to be representative with other parts of the state in football, and this has taken a long time. Let's not go backward."

7. "Spring practice provides an opportunity to concentrate on teaching, experimenting, and evaluating. There is time to modify or install new systems and work out the fine points of technique that best suit the personnel. Players can be evaluated at different positions in order to fully utilize talent and abilities."

8. "Spring practice is the time for them to set team goals and develop a camaraderie that will carry them through the summer and return them psychologically prepared in the fall."

9. "If omitting spring practice caused a decrease in the caliber of football being played, it's possible that the decrease would be paralleled by a drop in spectator attendance and gate receipts. Such

a decline would financially affect the total athletic program."

10. "Spring practice is necessary if we want our players to have the same opportunity for a college scholarship that others in the state have. Certainly, a player who has participated in spring practice from the ninth grade through the eleventh will be much more experienced and better-prepared than one who has not."

11. "Many college scouts attend spring practice sessions to evaluate athletes and begin preparing their list of prospective college recruits."

12. "Omitting spring practice would probably result in a salary cut for coaches."

George Iannacone, who is the superintendent of schools in Palisades Park, New Jersey, is among a small group of professional educators who feel that all of these programs—indeed, all of interscholastic athletics—are, in Iannacone's own words, "a fraud." Iannacone said that interscholastic sports benefit only a small minority of students—and it is questionable, he said, whether or not that small minority is benefitting or not. He said the myths surrounding interscholastic sports, myths that are composed and perpetuated by coaches, blur the reality surrounding high-school sports. That reality, he said, is that all of these interscholastic sports programs, as they are currently constructed, are not geared for the students. They are geared, instead, for adult sports fans in each community. The programs, he said, belong to the public, not the players.

Iannacone:

To begin at the very basic problem, there is no clear guidelines as to what a coach really is, and there are no clear guidelines as to whether or not a coach is successful. The result is that winning games has filled the void. Coaches in high schools are judged primarily upon how many games their teams win; but does that make a football coach whose team goes eight or zero a better coach than the coach whose team goes zero and eight? The won-loss record becomes the measuring stick for a coach's effectiveness, and this, I feel, is inaccurate. There are also other things that go into determining whether or not a coach is successful, things that have no bearing whatsoever on how he treats his students. One of them is this suspected image of what a coach should be in the community, a man who mixes well with the American Legion and organizations like that. You get a coach who has an eight–zero season, and if he mixes well in the community and shakes a lot of hands and smiles a lot, it becomes unanimous that he is successful. But whether or not he has been successful in giving the kids the opportunity to have a good time through sports does not even enter into the picture. That, I think, is the key question: Did the kids enjoy the experience? And that, I think, is the guideline that has been overlooked the most. Too many school administrators look at the coach's record to determine whether or not he has been effective. That may be valid in the pro leagues, but I don't think it's valid in high schools.

I've always felt the best coaches are the ones who are always around the break-even point as far as their records go. Coaches whose teams have five–three seasons, or four–four seasons, or four–five seasons, seem to have the happiest kids. I have always been wary of coaches who fall at either extreme in the spectrum, coaches whose teams always go undefeated, or coaches whose teams always lose. I think the break-even point is the ideal insofar as high-school sports are concerned. It eliminates the hysteria that undefeated teams create, and it eliminates the despair that winless teams create. It gives the kids a chance to taste both victory and defeat—and tasting defeat is just as important as tasting victory in high school —and it keeps the adult sports fanatics in the community at bay. Nobody gets excited about the teams that are four–four; they get excited, one way or the other, over teams that are eight–zero and zero–eight.

Now, to get into the situation with the kids themselves.

There is this great myth in high-school sports that somehow the kids who play on varsity teams are better off for the experience. I think that myth is one of the most harmful there is. Now, is a kid who plays football really any better off than a kid who is involved in producing the yearbook, or a kid who is involved in producing the school's plays? I don't think so. The problem in sports is that the coach dictates just how much each kid will get out of playing on the team; kids who are first-stringers, say, certainly get a lot more out of it than the kids who sit on the bench. There is, in high-school sports, this tremendous coach-to-player situation; it is the adult in charge, dictating terms and situations to the player. In other school activities, such as the yearbook and school plays, there is a student-to-student situation; interplay and free exchange of ideas are stressed. But in high-school sports you see very little of this player-to-player situation. There is this vertical loyalty, with players looking up to coaches, but there is very little lateral loyalty, with players relating to each other. The high-school players are too busy competing with each other for starting berths, and there is this pecking order of status that goes with being a first-stringer, or a second-stringer, or a bench-warmer. That kills any chance of the kids relating to each other on equal terms. How many stars of high-school teams are friends with bench-warmers?

All of these interscholastic teams, I feel, are geared primarily for the adult community in each city or town. That is a situation that must be reversed; we in education must give the sports teams back to the kids. Now, people in sports will tell you that their games build character in young people, make them morally upright, and all of that. But why is it that in high schools today there is such a tremendous need for riot control at all of these games? That is because the adults who follow the teams become more wrapped up in the teams' winning or losing than most of the high-school students do, and they create an atmosphere of hostility that helps to set the kids off. I would recommend, as a way of defusing this whole issue of adult involvement with high-school teams, playing games in the afternoon, after school, so the school could limit the people in attendance to primarily students. We have to stop processing our high-school teams for the purpose of attracting adult followings. We have to give the teams back to the kids, and let them take it from there. If they want to get excited about the team, fine; if not, fine too.

There also is this argument that adults help pay the way by buying tickets to games. Now, this argument is not valid for two reasons. First, in my school system, we pay between twenty-five thousand and thirty thousand dollars a year on interscholastic sports. Our return, in the form of gate receipts, runs around three thousand dollars a year. That means that the adult followers don't even come close to helping to pay for the programs. But, on the other hand, they already have paid for it—with their tax money. And I raise the question of whether it's valid to charge admission to games in the first place—how can you make people pay to see something that they have already paid for? I think that if some adult, in some city, refused to pay admission to a game, and took the issue to court on the grounds that he already has paid in the form of taxes, he would win the case and establish a precedent for all high schools throughout the country.

Another fraudulent situation in high-school sports is that coaches say that sports make it easier for a kid to get into college. I think this is inaccurate. How many kids really do get college scholarships? One or two, maybe, from each team? Especially if the team is a good one. What happens to the rest of the kids, the kids who are on the bench? Will sports make it easier for them to get into college? No, it will not. This is a myth educators have not challenged. They actually believe coaches when coaches tell them that sports scholarships are available in unlimited numbers; they give the coach all the money he wants, to re-sod fields, buy electric scoreboards, buy new uniforms. The thinking is that college recruiters will be impressed with a school that has all the latest trappings, and that somehow that school's program is superior and, surely, its athletes must be superior. Presto! Scholarships by the dozen. It just doesn't happen that way. In fact, when I hear coaches talk about how sports make it easier for kids to get to college, I become enraged. The truth of the matter is that kids who would be getting athletic scholarships to colleges are going to get them anyway. The kids who won't certainly won't be getting them just because they play on a field with an electric scoreboard while wearing the newest in fashionable uniforms.

All of the money spent on making high-school sports programs more elaborate is wasted. Much of that money, I feel, should be used in a way that would benefit the highest number of students—and what I'm talking about is to use the money to upgrade the gym classes. Now, gym classes in high schools are adominations; they usually become basketball classes and volleyball classes, because they are held in gymnasiums that are geared for those two sports. Gym teachers who double as coaches have always taken the gym classes lightly, while emphasizing the varsity teams. It should be just the opposite. Kids who are not athletes should be introduced to sports; they should have the opportunity to learn about gymnastics, or tumbling, or whatever else it is that they are interested in. As it is now, the gym teacher throws out a ball or two and tells the kids to play. There is no instruction, no concern, no teaching whatsoever. Because of this imbalance, many kids turn off on sports; the feeling is that the only good athletes are playing on the varsity team. There is no such thing as a good gym-class athlete. Yet it is entirely possible that kids may want to do well while in gym classes, but do not want to play on varsity teams. The way things are constructed now, gym classes merely give a lot of varsity coaches something to do with their time before varsity practice starts. They are a waste of time. Yet more kids are in gym classes than in varsity sports. That means we are spending all of this money on a very small minority of students; the majority is being overlooked.

As a solution to all of this, I would recommend that each

school superintendent establish an athletic council; it would include himself, one of his assistants, the athletic director, one or two head coaches, two or three department chairmen. The function would be to continuously study and analyze all of these sports programs, concentrating on two things: first, the amount of time spent on them, and second, the amount of money spent on them. There has to be some kind of independent body set up to act as a check and balance to all of these elaborate programs. In my school district, I've tried some things along this line. For one thing, I've made all pep rallies voluntary; that is, I've made them after school, and the kids have the option of attending them or not. Mandatory pep rallies, during school hours, are merely outgrowths of elaborate sports programs; the school day is a waste of time —the kids don't have their minds on anything else but the rally. Whatever teachers are being paid on that day is wasted money. So now the kids have their choice: They can go, or they can do something else and not feel guilty about it. I think there is something unnatural about forcing this so-called school spirit down the throats of kids. But pep rallies are just small ways in which people in athletics brainwash everybody else. So there are kids who are in school who don't care a single bit about whether or not the football team wins or loses. Should they feel guilty about it? No.

The ultimate danger in all of these elaborate sports programs is that they begin to dictate the very image of a school by their success, or by their lack of it. Unbeaten football teams should no more enhance a school's image than a winless football team should detract from it. When we reach that point, then we can feel safe that we have high-school sports in proper perspective.

XIV • Symbolism and the Patriotism Game: What Do God, Indians, and Anthems Have to Do with Games?

It is no secret that high-school coaches are fond of symbolism. They use symbolism in all of their clichés; they encourage the use of caricatures of fierce animals as their teams' insignia. All of this symbolism is designed to give their domains touches of implied aggressiveness. (Is there a team in the whole of America that has a peace symbol on its helmet?) All this superimposed symbolism is rather thoughtless; coaches say that teams are supposed to be mean and hungry, forceful and aggressive, and what is wrong with having a roaring Siberian tiger on the athletic department's letterhead stationery? Sometimes symbolism takes the form of local history; as an example consider Sleepy Hollow High School in the Rip Van Winkle country of upstate New York. The sports teams at Sleepy Hollow High School are nicknamed "the Headless Horsemen." All of which points out that the symbolism is rather mindless; coaches are usually too preoccupied with game plans and strategy to seriously study the effects of the symbolism they promote. Which brings up one rather distasteful note: In the midst of all of this symbolism, some serious distortions are taking place. Many coaches are actually encouraging forms of symbolism that are dishonest and racist. Since very little of what is traditional in high-school sports is ever questioned, this offensive symbolism has not stopped. There are, for example, two shamefully distasteful symbolic themes that any intelligent, sensitive, compassionate coach would move to abolish immediately. These two themes use symbols involving American Indians and patriotism.

In the United States of America, in the year 1974, there is a professional football team that is actually called the Washington Redskins. The President of the United States has said that it happens to be his favorite team. There are colleges in the United States that have teams that are nicknamed "Tomahawks" and "Scalpers." There are hundreds of high-school teams nicknamed "Red Raiders" and "Screamin' Sioux" and "Warrior Chiefs." Thousands upon thousands of football helmets have emblazoned upon them faces of screaming Indian braves or warriors; at games, mascots are dressed to resemble Indian chiefs, and they do dances that are supposed to resemble war dances, for the entertainment of the crowd. Game programs, scoreboard paintings, and mid-court decals also feature the faces of male Indians, distorted and out-raged, presumably preparing for a violent battle. To anyone who has read about, or studied, the acts of genocide committed against the Indian tribes in America, the distorted symbolism toward Indians in sports becomes repulsive. Apparently, most high-school coaches do not view it that way; the stock answer is: "The nick-names and mascots are meant to honor the Indians, not defame them."

But none of the coaches, of course, bothers to seek out any real American Indians, who are now living in poverty and despair on reservations in (among other places) Montana and Wyoming, to ask them if the symbolism is, indeed, flattering or demeaning. Only in the last few years has the situation been questioned; the people who have been doing the questioning are not coaches or administrators at high schools. The people who are doing the questioning are the great-grandsons of the Indians who were murdered in such places as Wounded Knee, South Dakota. They are young American Indian students. Despite what the coaches contend about Indian caricatures being an honor, the young

American Indian students do not agree. They have considered it to be a damnable insult.

Consider, for example, the following words from Sonny Sixkiller, who was an outstanding quarterback at the University of Washington:

"I'm starting to get an idea of how bad the Indian has been treated in this country, in the past and also today. I've also been going through some changes myself about what it means to be a Cherokee. Like, people are always making a big thing about me being an Indian, like maybe I'm some kind of freak or something. I mean, they keep asking me about my family background and what my father does for a living, like they expect me to say he sits cross-legged all day in front of a tepee, weaving baskets."

In 1968, a group of students at Dartmouth College, assembled by Howard Bad Hand, Dwayne Birdbear, Travis Kingsley, and Rick Buckanaga, demanded that school officials stop entertaining fans at home football games by employing undergraduates dressed as Indians to do war dances along the sidelines and at mid-field during half time. The students said that the practice was demeaning to the American Indian, and that they were insulted when the tribal customs of their ancestors were used to feed the fantasies of the insensitive. Before leaving, they also suggested that Dartmouth consider changing its nickname to something less racist than "The Indians." After several meetings on the subject, school officials decided to retain the nickname, but to abolish the Indian mascots.

In 1970, at Marquette University, a similar incident occurred. Indian students petitioned the governing student organization, the Associated Students of Marquette, asking that the school's Indian mascot, nicknamed "Willie Wampum," be abolished because it portrayed the American Indian in a demeaning manner. The student senate subsequently passed a resolution calling for the mascot's abolition, and in April 1972, the school announced that the mascot would be permanently retired.

"The mascots had been jeered and laughed at for years and we just decided to put an end to that kind of nonsense," said Bill Yellowtail, a student in the American Indian–studies program at

Dartmouth and a member of the group. "The old grads, especially, used to get a big kick out of them every time they'd come back to see a game; they'd point them out to their kids or to their grand-children, just like they'd point out a monkey at the zoo: 'Look, look, there it is, the Indian.' To this day, a lot of the old grads jump on us for what we did; they say we destroyed one of the school's oldest and most enjoyable sports traditions.

"But we feel we did our part in eliminating another false illu-sion. Too many people in this country still think of Indians as savages doing war dances and wearing feathered headdresses and having two-word vocabularies, 'How' and 'Ugh.' People in sports are as responsible as anybody for perpetuating these illusions, with their Indian nicknames and their Indian mascots and their Indian half-time shows. I've often wondered to myself if the people who owned these teams ever stopped to think what goes through the mind of a ten-year-old Indian kid on a reservation in North Dakota when he picks up a sports page and reads a headline, 'Redskins Scalp Chiefs.' "

The Association for American Indian Affairs, in Manhattan, is hardly ecstatic over the number of sports teams in the country bearing nicknames alluding to the American Indian. Six profes-sional teams and ninety-seven colleges, according to the *Blue Book of College Athletics,* have Indian nicknames, ranging from Red-skins (Washington, National Football League) to Choctaws (Mississippi College) to Scalpers (Huron, S.D., College). Jeffrey Newman, assistant director of the Association, said:

"If we had the money, we would file suit against every college and professional team in the country with an Indian nickname we found offensive. I think the first team we would go after would be the Atlanta Braves; if any team in the country is exploiting the American Indian for its own purposes, it is this one. It is outra-geous, I feel, to have a man dressed as an Indian,* sitting in an

*The man portraying the Indian in Atlanta, Levi Walker, said that he is an American Indian, by birth, and a showman, by profession. He said he has never been criticized for his act, but that he was aware of a faction among Indians "that is trying to do away with the feather-leather-skin-and-beads image." Walker also said that he does not feel he is exploit-

alleged tepee outside the outfield fence, doing a silly dance every time some player hits a home run. Even the name they gave him, Chief . . . something or other [Nok-a-homa], is discriminatory. Would they hire a black man to sit in a tar-paper shack out there and come out picking cotton every time a player hit a home run? No, they wouldn't dare."

Newman continued:

The danger in these shows and mascots is this: They keep alive false myths about the American Indian . . . you know, being a savage and a warmonger, and always the aggressor. Young people, like the white, middle-class, suburban kid who may never meet an Indian in his entire life, are particularly vulnerable to them. Subconsciously he's developing an inaccurate image of what Indian people are, and were. The same kid wouldn't think of calling a team the "Blackskins" or the "Yellowskins," but he had Redskins' pennants on his bedroom walls.

I have also found that, while the sports establishment exploits Indian nicknames and mascots, it gives nothing back to the Indian. I lived in a small reservation, Menominee County in northern Wisconsin, for several years, and the Indian kids there would have loved to play baseball and football and basketball. But their parents had enough trouble buying food and clothes for them; there were no baseballs or gloves or spiked shoes around at all. I tried to form a Little League for them, and I contacted the Little League people in Williamsport for some help. Well, I was astonished, because the people there just didn't give a damn; they weren't interested in helping us at all. So we formed our own league and we scrounged up old bats and hand-me-down baseballs, and the

ing the American Indian; that most of his war dances are authentic "in a sense"; and that his most fervent followers are young people—"I get more fan mail from kids than most of the players on the team."

kids had a hell of a time. They even beat the local Little League team at the end of the season.

Somebody once asked me if Indian children look up to and identify with athletes in America. I said I didn't think so, for two reasons: First, there are very few of their own kind in sports—a Sonny Sixkiller, a Jim Plunkett, a Johnny Bench, maybe, and that's about it—and, second, how can you expect a kid to identify with sports people when he can't even identify with his own?"

In 1971, in Cleveland, Ohio, the director of the American Indian Center in that city said that the symbol used by the Cleveland Indians professional baseball team was racist, degrading and demeaning to the American Indians. The director, Russell Means (who is a leader of the American Indian Movement), then filed a lawsuit against the team to collect damages and to halt the further use of the symbol.

"How long do you think the stadium would stand if the team were called the 'Cleveland Negroes,' with a caricature of Aunt Jemima or Little Black Sambo, and every time a ball was hit some guy would come out and do the soft shoe?" Means asked. Through a Legal Aid Society attorney, Means filed a $9-million suit against the baseball team and its owner at the time, Vernon Stouffer, in the Cuyahoga County Common Pleas Court, and he also sought an injunction to halt the future use of the symbol.

The "Chief Wahoo" symbol showed an "Indian" wearing a wide, toothy grin that dominated his features. It had a prominent nose and triangular eyes under arching eyebrows that rose above a headband with a feather in it. The grin bulged the Wahoo's cheeks, and the top of his head, where his hair was parted down the middle, was just short of coming to a point.

"The whole viewpoint America takes of the Indian is that we don't count," Means said. "Can you envision the Washington football team called the Washington 'Rednecks' instead of the Redskins?"

The attorneys, Joseph Meissner, of the Legal Aid Society, and Robert Kates, said in an affidavit that was filed with the suit that the Indian Center claims the caricature "represented the basic attitudes which the majority of the larger society has of the American Indian." It further stated that "Wahoo" is not an Indian word, and "when sounded is a slander upon all Indian languages, and subjects them to public ridicule." The center also claimed that the symbol ridiculed the political and social system of the Indian nations, as well as promoted detribalization, denied the Indians their right to self-determination, and mocked their courage, wisdom, and statesmanship.

"No other nationality, group or race would be expected to tolerate such a caricature of themselves," the affidavit said. "Only the American Indian, whom this country has raped, robbed, ruined and murdered, can be so depicted as a big-toothed, pointed-head, grinning half-wit while we Indians are expected to endure such a racial slur."

The suit sought $6 million dollars for libel, slander, and defamation and $3 million dollars for compensation based on the money the team had earned while using "Chief Wahoo" as a symbol.

A few weeks later, in North Dakota, the Fargo *Forum* sports staff took a hard look at its policy relating to the usage of Indian nicknames as applied to athletic teams. Ed Kolpack, the sports editor, said the *Forum* was not refusing to use any and all nicknames which refer to the American Indians. He said his staff believed some terms were acceptable while others were indeed offensive.

Kolpack said tribal names such as Sioux, Cherokee, Chippewa, and Mandan should not be considered derogatory. However, he said, nicknames in the vein of "Savages," "Redskins," and "Scalpers" were terms his staff felt were not in proper taste, since they were mindful of an often-accepted historical background which does not fit the image of today's American Indian. The paper changed its policy accordingly.

As for Dartmouth College, its sports teams are no longer called

"The Indians," and there are no more Indian mascots parading along the sidelines. Stanford University's sports teams are not called "The Indians" any more either. But the high schools have been slow to follow the acts of the colleges. Given the choice between having his team called "The Ragin' Redskins" or "The Blue Velvet Mist," the high-school coach will still opt for the former. Particularly if there are no Indians, nor Indian groups, residing within earshot or eyeshot.

Now, for the patriotism game:

There is, to be sure, absolutely no connection whatsoever between sports events and patriotism. Being a good athlete does not necessarily make one a good American. But coaches, particularly high-school coaches, have gone to great extremes to imply that high-school sports are very patriotic endeavors. They will say, "What is more American than a high-school football game on a Friday night?" Nothing, of course, except maybe apple pie à la mode; but people in America do not postpone that first sumptuous bite and put down their forks in order for some marching band to play "The Star-Spangled Banner." The separation of sport and state is something high-school coaches find abhorrent; they want their games to be wrapped and bow-tied in Old Glory. The kids, apparently, have had some second thoughts about it all. In recent years at least, some high-school athletes have actually challenged the premise that punts, passes, and pitches are interwined with patriotism.

On September 17, 1970, Forrest Byram, a seventeen-year-old player on the Niles North High School football team in Skokie, Illinois, refused to remove his helmet during the playing of the traditional pre-game national anthem. He said it was his way of protesting American foreign policy while on the football field. David McCarrell, the coach, removed Byram immediately from the team and said that he was a "disruptive influence."

Dr. Gilbert Weldy, the principal, did not agree with McCarrell's actions. He met with the coach privately to discuss the matter. Weldy told the coach that to remove a boy from the team because he voiced a personal feeling was an infringement of his constitutional right of free speech. He asked the coach to reinstate Byram.

McCarrell refused. Weldy told him he had no other choice but to remove him as head coach. Shortly thereafter, the remainder of the coaching staff issued an ultimatum to Weldy that stated, in effect, "If McCarrell goes, we go too." Then the football team banded together and issued a statement with similar feelings, and, as Weldy said, "The entire athletic program at our school was left to hang on the outcome."

But he stood by his decision and insisted that Byram be reinstated. The situation was finally resolved when Byram himself called a news conference and told members of the press that he did "not want to play football at Niles North any longer."

"Personally, I don't feel the national anthem has any place at sports events," said Weldy. "Athletic crowds don't react to it at all. It's not serving any useful purpose. . . . The only thing the national anthem accomplishes before a sports event is that it helps numb the crowd for a minute or two. With this in mind, I did not feel that this boy should be punished for what he did. He was not disrupting the sports program at this school, and he was not disrupting the team. . . .

"Personally, I've never taken a more unpopular stand in my entire life. The reaction around here was incredible. The teachers' union was after me for not backing the coach, parents were after me for being too permissive, the community patriots were after me for allowing such a thing to happen. But I'll tell you one thing—I'm proud of my decision, proud that I stood where I did."

The turning point came when the reaction to Byram's deed started affecting his personal life.

"The boy was receiving obscene phone calls at home; he was receiving letters that were ripping him apart, and even his family was taking abuse," said Weldy. "So he came to me and said, 'I've made a decision. I'm not going to return to the team.' But I think the most crushing blow of all for him was when he discovered that the rest of the team didn't want him back."

Byram subsequently began playing the tuba in the school marching band, and participated willingly in the playing of the anthem.

"The boy told me that now it was just another piece of music, and that he'd like to play it well," said Weldy.

The playing of "The Star-Spangled Banner" and the recitals of the pledge of allegiance to the flag before sports events began during World War II, apparently to remind ribald spectators that there was a real war still going on halfway across the globe. The practice was embraced as ritual after the war ended. One of the first people to question all of the patriotic hocus-pocus at games was the late sportswriter Leonard Shecter; he said that national anthems are nothing more than vehicles by which the establishment attempts to cloak itself in civic righteousness. No matter, Shecter concluded, that some of the most unscrupulous and authoritarian practices in our society actually flourish in the realm of sports.

The people who inhabit the suite of offices on the twelfth floor of 410 Park Avenue in Manhattan, and who run the National Football League from there, took the patriotism game a step further during the 1960s. They instituted the practice of having Air Force Phantom fighter jets fly over stadiums in "missing-man" formations—in sympathy for prisoners of war in Indochina. What prisoners of war in Indochina had to do with the football game about to begin was never clearly defined. But politicians, particularly, have been quick to label sports events as microcosms of reality.

In 1960, the late Robert Kennedy, speaking at a football coaches' dinner, said, "Except for war, there is nothing in American life which trains a boy better for life than football." In 1968, Richard Nixon said in an interview, "Anybody in politics must have great competitive instincts . . . That's the world of sports. That's the world of politics. I guess you can say that's life itself."

The potential danger here, wrote Dr. Bruce Mazlish, author of the book *In Search of Nixon: A Psychohistorical Inquiry,* is getting reality and politics confused with the game of football.

Nixon, for example, took for himself the code name "The Quarterback" when advising Henry Kissinger in secret negotiations with the North Vietnamese. The mining of Haiphong Harbor in North Vietnam was dubbed "Operation Linebacker." The President of the United States described his new economic policy as "my game plan." Nixon's sincere interest in football as a fan, as well as his intensity as a Whittier College substitute football player "with two left feet," are indications that he may have been mixing football with life and politics.

The fixation with being "No. 1" was of concern to the President, as shown in the controversy he stirred in 1969 when he conferred that mythical college title upon the University of Texas football team. One critic of the Vietnam war, and of Nixon, former Senator William Fulbright, a Democrat from Arkansas, has made a point of that.

Fulbright has written:

Perhaps our national tendency to extol competition rather than cooperation as a social virtue and our preoccupation with primacy—with being the "biggest," and "greatest" nation—suggest an underlying lack of confidence in ourselves, a supposition that unless we are "No. 1" we will be nothing. . . .

One detects this cast of mind in President Johnson's determination that he would not be "the first American president to lose a war," and President Nixon's spectre of America as "a pitiful, helpless giant." The perpetuation of the Vietnam war is the most terrible and fateful manifestation of the determination to prove we are "No. 1."

Most high-school coaches still revere the tradition of pre-game anthems and color guards. But many others in the sphere of sports have begun to question the necessity of it all—on the grounds that the anthem itself is being exploited. (Ask not what games can do for the anthem, but what the anthem can do for games.)

· Lee Trevino, professional golfer: "There's no need for the national anthem at sports events. The public doesn't come to hear it. Eighty percent don't know the words; I don't. A short prayer might be better. Everyone respects the flag. You don't have to play the national anthem to prove it."

· Doug Rader, Houston Astros' third baseman: "Too many people have become blasé about it; they don't seem to realize what the song really means. I personally like to hear it played before every game, and I like to sing the words. You don't have to sing it pretty; I sure don't. Maybe there should be a little variety. Play the 'Star-spangled Banner' every third or fourth day and play 'America the Beautiful' and other patriotic songs on the other days. Maybe then people wouldn't be so blasé."

· John Carlos, former Olympic runner: "I don't really have any comment, but I think the question should be put only to amateurs. It's hard to ask a professional athlete how he feels. Pros get paid for what they do, and if the owner says 'I want you to stand up for the national anthem,' they stand. Leave it to the amateurs. They're not getting anything out of it."

· Peter Daland, coach of United States men's Olympic swimming team: "I think it should be played, but perhaps we've overdone it. For example, at swimming meets, we have the national anthem or the pledge of allegiance normally at every session of every meet. That's too much. Playing it at the start of a meet would be fine."

· Jason Miller, Pulitzer Prize–winning author of the Broadway drama *That Championship Season:* "It's not necessary for the performance of a game. If it's a way of large masses of people paying homage to the country, fine. You have to determine if it's essential to the pageant, but it always seems to be played at games of physical competition. What most people don't realize is that the 'Star-Spangled Banner' is a war song. It was written during war, inspired by war and a man's reaction to war. The song has military connotations, and so does sports."

· John Wooden, basketball coach at the University of California, Los Angeles: "I like the custom of playing the national anthem at public gatherings, including major sports events. However, perhaps it is not necessary at every game. Frequently I take my team to the dressing room for last-minute instruction rather than having them stand around cooling off during the anthem. I have received letters from superpatriots taking me to task for that. I wonder if those superpatriots are always standing. Times are changing. I tell my players, 'If you are on the floor when the anthem is played, I don't expect you to stand at attention—but don't do anything disrespectful.' "

In recent years, another new twist of symbolism has been added: religion. Some college and pro teams now have "team chaplains" who lead the players in pre- and post-game prayers. (Oral Roberts University of Tulsa, Oklahoma, has its own evangelist.) After the Washington team defeated Dallas in the 1972 playoff game for the Super Bowl berth, the national television audience was taken into the dressing room of the winning team. Champagne was not flowing; piety was. The team was huddled in a post-game prayer of Thanksgiving, led by its spiritual adviser. Richard Bell wrote about it:

> I believe in the separation of church and football—at least temporally, church for Sunday mornings and football for Sunday afternoons. But Super Sunday is just days ahead, and there appears to be more of a religious imbroglio shaping up than a good old football game. Whose side is God on, anyway?
>
> I knew I was in trouble after the Redskins-Dallas play-off, when the cameras took us into the winners' dressing room. Instead of a bunch of sweating, exhilarated, champagne-

chugging football players crashing around the locker room, I saw a team file in quietly as if following some carefully rehearsed script, get down on their knees, and listen to a self-righteous prayer of thanks for the victory. Even the tv announcers, to their liberal-biased credit, seemed nervous and uneasy with this self-serving display.

Where was Billy Graham, for God's sake? Even if God had been helping the pious Redskins, He didn't have to do much to help subdue the amazingly inept Cowboys. Dallas wasn't going anywhere with the ball, even with St. Peter for a split end.

When Rice University played Notre Dame in football in the fall of 1973, it employed a bit of reverse symbolism on the nation's No. 1 Roman Catholic university: It lined its player bench with priests. Ara Parseghian, the Notre Dame coach, was not amused; he said he lost respect for the Rice authorities because of their act. His players were not distracted, however, by all the white collars; they won the game easily. But the point of it all is that many coaches employ symbolism to promote their own gains. Enter distortion and dishonesty. In the end, high-school coaches, particularly, would be doing their kids—and others—a great service if they took the following steps:

1. Stop sanctioning the use of Indian nicknames and mascots, and really do the Indians a favor.

2. Stop promoting patriotism as by-product of sports, and do the free-thinking players a favor.

3. And stop using religion as a motivating or intimidating force, and let God make His own point spreads.

XV · The Media: Why Coaches Get More Publicity than the Local Mayor

Newspapers, it would seem, are in a position to be the perfect watchdogs of high-school coaches. They have the capacity, through their reporters, to ferret out facts about coaches who are abusive and extremist in their methods and then print these facts for the benefit of the unsuspecting public. In fact, newspaper reporters, who are assigned to cover high-school sports events, are in extremely important positions insofar as high-school coaches are concerned—these reporters are capable of getting close enough to the scene to discover what is really taking place, yet they are not a part of the scene themselves. They have no vested interest in either the coach's success or in the high school; their interest lies in the reporting of the truth.

Now, all of this is nice, idealist reading; in theory, newspaper reporters who cover high-school sports events are the last barriers between the people and the coaches. But the truth of the matter is that a vast majority of these newspaper reporters who cover high-school sports have failed miserably in doing their jobs; the reason is not because the reporters are totally incompetent. The reason lies within the structure in which they operate. Newspapers make money from high-school sports news; in many thousands of cities and towns across America, high-school sports news is the only legitimate sports news there is. Result: Keep the news favorable, and keep the cash registers clicking.

The scenario usually works like this:

From the newspaper's standpoint, high-school sports coverage commands a huge audience; not only are the kids reading the stories, but their parents are reading the stories, and their neighbors, grandparents, etc. Many of these fathers and neighbors and uncles are local businessmen who advertise in the newspaper. The newspaper publisher does not wish to jeopardize all of this advertising revenue because a high-school sportswriter desires to write an exposé on the tactics of a particular coach. The exposé would infuriate the local adults, and the only way they could get back at the newspaper would be to cancel their advertising, if only for a spell. So, no matter what a high-school sportswriter sees, no matter how distasteful, how immoral, how outrageous it may be, it is a pretty solid bet that he will never write it for his newspaper. The result: The most neurotic and the most insecure of all newspaper sportswriters are the people who cover high-school sports; they are programed to overlook what is really going on, and to write about what is supposed to be going on. Invariably, they either ignore the pangs of conscience and embrace the ground rules, or else they move on to another newspaper, another job.

Many newspaper publishers have long since realized the potential profits in pandering to the high-school sports audience, particularly in the last decade. They have gone to great extremes to pander to the high-school sports followers in suburban areas, where sports fanaticism is rabid, and where the most white, affluent people live. Many newspapers publish special sections that are designed specifically for these voracious suburban readers: They publish high-school football previews, and basketball previews, load them up with favorable stories about the glowing prospects each school has for the coming season (and, incidentally, these preview sections also happen to be bulging with prime-rate advertising). It behooves the high-school sportswriter to write that every team has a chance of winning the championship; under no circumstances will he ever write the real, raw truth about a team, such as: "Mount Airy High School's football team, which lost its entire starting lineup to graduation last fall, will be lucky to win a single game this season." No sir; the story will usually read something like this: "Mount Airy High School's football team, depleted by graduation, will be rebuilding this season. Arnold Bombast, the head coach, has not written off the season, however. He said his young team of scrappers 'will be in the thick of things right to the end.' " When the season does end, such schools usually have records of 1–6–1 or 0–8.

The writing about high-school sports in newspapers, then, is really shilling. The writer is forced to be the school's non-paid publicity man. The newspaper for which he works is not interested in in-depth, investigative articles about what the coach's authoritarian tactics are doing to his players; no, the newspaper is interested only in the kind of pablum that will not turn off advertisers or subscribers, who may have sons on the coach's team, and who may happen to support the coach fully, philosophically and otherwise. Since many newspapers have special sections every weekend devoted strictly to high-school sports coverage, the imbalance is particularly noticeable: Almost all the writing is devoted to games, in the form of pre-game advances and post-game reports. Rarely does any of the writing or reporting dip below the surface to find out what is really going on. The result: Coaches have been able to keep the lids on even the most outrageous of situations, and very few people ever find out what is really happening insofar as the Mercury High School Cougars are concerned.

At newspapers, the high-school sports beat is particularly unattractive. It is usually assigned to a young, ambitious writer who has just joined the staff; or else it is assigned to a cantankerous old writer who has been around for a while but who lacks the talent necessary for advancement. So, in most cases, the rookies and the mediocres are doing all the writing about high schools; they are either too unsophisticated or else too stupid to seriously question, in print, anything that is going on around them. Many of them, in fact, are happy just to have the niche, and they write reams and reams of nebulous nonsense to please the sports editor: the sports editor, in turn, tells the managing editor what a great job the new kid (or the old cuss) is doing—even though the new kid (or the old cuss) hasn't written a credible story in months. The managing editor, knowing the publisher's wishes in that area (keep it in-offensive), gives the new kid (or the old cuss) a five-dollar-a-week raise.

The best writers on sports staffs of newspapers stay away from high-school sports as if they were electrified tar babies. First the "star" sportswriters are too busy writing reams and reams of cotton candy about the local college or semi-pro or professional team; they feel that whatever is going on in high schools is beneath them.

Inside newspaper sports departments, there is a caste system. The newest or the poorest writers are usually stuck with the high schools, and only after they have showed a certain expertise in turning out drivel are they considered for promotion. Once they get that promotion and move a step up the ladder, they make fun of their former beats; incredibly, the college writer, who may be writing about one or two local schools that play in the Little Five Conference or the Scioto Valley Conference, has more prestige inside his sports department than has the high-school writer, who may be responsible for thirty-five or forty-five schools in the whole southern sector of his state. Naturally, the high-school writer, desiring that status, will deliver all the drivel he can to get there himself. Once there he can thumb his nose at the poor sap who is sitting in his old chair.

But the truth of the matter is that the most fertile areas for news and feature writing and investigative reporting in all of the thousands and thousands of towns and cities in America is right in the domain of high-school sports. The best writers should be assigned to the high schools, the worst to Marlboro Community College.

That it is the other way around works to the perfect advantage of high-school coaches. They can do just about anything and not have to worry about it appearing in the local newspaper. Sometimes these coaches even make friends with the sportswriter who is covering their teams; that means they will be free from serious scrutiny for sure. When high-school coaches and high-school sportswriters are pals, the people and the players lose.

And this is not going on just at newspapers in backwoods towns and unaware cities. It is going on as well at newspapers that are as prestigious as, say *The New York Times*. During the two years in which I was an editor in the sports department of that newspaper, I twice was assigned to copy-read high-school sports stories during what was called, at *The Times,* "football Saturdays." During these Saturday afternoons, results of football games were pouring into the office from all over the nation, and they were, unquestionably, the busiest and most hectic days of the year.

At *The New York Times,* the scholastic sports editor produced three pages of high-school football results every Saturday during the months of September, October, and November; the stories were written by high-school stringers, or else they were called into the office by correspondents who covered sections of a state. The emphasis was on suburban schools; whatever happened out on Long Island, in Nassau and in Suffolk Counties, invariably demanded large headlines, pictures, and chunks of space. Whatever happened in Bergen County in New Jersey or in Fairfield County in Connecticut or in Westchester County in New York State demanded the same treatments. After all, the paper apparently conceded, the people who live in these areas are the people who buy, and read, *The New York Times;* it did not consider itself to be pandering to a white, affluent, suburban audience while, at the same time, virtually ignoring whatever it was that was going on at high schools in Brooklyn and Queens and Staten Island and Harlem. People who lived in those places apparently did not buy, or read, or advertise in, *The New York Times*.

As soon as the football season ended in the suburbs *The*

Times would cease producing its three-page specials every Saturday afternoon. But the obvious contradiction in *The Times'* handling of high-school sports was this: Suburban high-school football in the New York area is mediocre in quality and majestic in pomp; the kids were only average players, but the local enthusiasm was high, so long as the fires were being fanned by newspapers. Surely, no team from Westchester County in New York State or Bergen County in New Jersey could hope to compete on an equal basis with teams from Texas or Pennsylvania or Ohio.

But when the high-school basketball season started in New York City, *The Times* pretended it did not exist. Now, it is no secret that the best high-school basketball in America is being played inside the gymnasiums of schools in New York City; it is no secret that schools such as Texas Western have won national championships by recruiting kids off the playgrounds of New York City. It is no secret either that most of the best players, and most of the best schools, are black. At *The Times,* mediocre suburban high-school football teams were commanding more space than rocket launchings, while the best high-school basketball teams in the country, who were playing in *The Times'* own backyard, were being ignored. Boats, dogs, horses and new buildings always seemed to get more publicity in *The Times* than did the best high school basketball players in the country.

All of which brings up the relationship between newspapers and high-school coaches. First, make no mistake about it: Coaches want publicity. They want it because publicity makes their success official; no matter how successful a team is, it is not really considered successful by others until that success has been spread out across the tops of pages inside newspapers. Naturally, when the coach is in the midst of a losing season he avoids newspaper sportswriters as if they were walking carriers of the bubonic plague. Successful high-school coaches, who are in the midst of winning seasons, expect newspapers to come to them; then, they play it aloof, smug, dignified. But the same men, when they start losing, become manipulators; they have excuses ready, they twist obvious facts and fit them into their defensive arguments, and sometimes they even butter up the writer, in the hope that he is vulnerable to such tactics and will become soft and purposely omit an unflattering fact from his story. The interplay is subtle and sophisticated because the writer needs the coach, the coach needs the writer, and they both know it. The obligation for accuracy and honesty to the reader is either ignored completely or at least compromised.

The problems in covering high-school sports are legion, among them:

1. *Managing Editors.* One of the biggest obstacles to tough, investigative reporting on high-school sports is the breed of man known in newspaper circles as the managing editor. He is the man who controls what the reporters write and, in many cases, what they actually think. Most managing editors I have worked under have been incredibly naive about what is happening in sports. Ever conscious about repercussions that arise from controversial stories about coaches or high-school athletes, they rarely encourage digging by their high-school reporters. One managing editor I knew, a dour man in his seventies who had spent most of his career at a small newspaper in the Texas prairie land, epitomized how deeply most managing editors think about sports: All he was concerned about was getting the results of Allegheny College's football games into the newspaper. The reason: He had a son who attended the school. So, every Sunday night, people in the sports department would be on the phone to the Associated Press in Pennsylvania, attempting to get the Allegheny scores; the school was so small, and apparently so insignificant, that its scores did not even appear on the regular AP college run-down. Once, an Allegheny score appeared in the paper but "Allegheny" was misspelled; the managing editor, naturally, tracked down the copy to determine exactly whose fault it was. The reporter was chastised unmercifully. Another managing editor I worked under had a teen-aged

son who managed the local high-school football team. Naturally, the son read every line that was printed about his school's football team and critiqued every story with his father. Naturally too, the reporter was subject to incredible second-guessing by the managing editor. Finally, the reporter threw up his arms and told the managing editor point-blank, "How the hell would you like to be in the position of being at the mercy of a fourteen-year-old high-school sophomore?" That ended the armchair quarterbacking from the managing editor. But the examples are hardly atypical.

2. *Coaches' Reputations.* The result of all of this favorable publicity enhances the coaches' reputations within their respective communities. They become more visible than the local mayors and councilmen; dozens of newspaper stories about them during the course of a season give their reputations huge doses of elephantiasis. "So what?" you may ask. As soon as the season ends, the big head atrophies back to normal size. But that is not really the case; the residue from all the publicity lingers. Coaches who are successful, and who have earned reputations in the media for being hard-nosed disciplinarians, seem to skyrocket through the high school's job stratosphere. One of the most noticeable trends in the last decade is the huge number of high-school coaches who retire after years and years of success and step right into the principal's office—as principals. The number of high schools run by former high-school coaches is on the rise. The coach's reputation has been enhanced along the line by all of the favorable newspaper publicity; the anonymous science teacher, who may be ultimately more qualified for the job, cannot compete with the coach's reputation. How many biology teachers command eight-column headlines when they perform successful dissections of reptiles?

3. *Community Pressure.* Most newspaper reporters who cover high-school sports are introduced to the pressure from community high-school sports fanatics very early in their careers. Writing favorably about one school, which happens to be winning, while ignoring another school, which happens to be losing, usually results in an ugly phone call from some adult who accuses the

reporter of being partial to one school and prejudiced against another. The same thing happens when writers select all-star teams: Parents of kids who do not make the first team are on the telephone, screaming obscenities. No high-school writer can write a story without the specter of community reacton to it lingering in the back of his mind. Invariably, he overcompensates in an effort to please all readers. Invariably, he fails in doing this, and his efforts in that direction only limit his effectiveness. Coaches who do not wish to make admonishing telephone calls to sportswriters themselves usually solicit the aid of a local adult booster and encourage him to call instead. Many times, coaches used stories I had written about opposing schools to fire up their own teams: "This son of a bitch writes that Poly Prep is going to beat us by two touchdowns: What does he know? Saturday, we'll show him!" The kids roared with vengeance. All of which means that when they played the game, they were not playing to win—or at least, were not playing to beat the other team: They were playing to prove the newspaper wrong. Chalk up another gimmick for the coaches.

4. *Oversights.* Whenever coaches do something wrong, it rarely makes the newspapers. I can think of two incidents, during the mid-1960s, in upstate New York, to substantiate that point. The first occurred at a high-school baseball game. The opposing coaches began needling each other from their benches. The game was close, and it was an important game, inasmuch as the winner of it took over the league lead. After several innings of needling, there was a close play at home plate; the runner was called out. His coach began arguing with the umpire; the other coach rushed to the umpire's side. Soon they began arguing with each other. Then they began beating each other with their fists. The players joined in. The game was called. The two coaches, welts on their faces and bruises on their knuckles, took their teams home. Not a single newspaper reported the incident—only the score of the game. The second occurred inside a high school. The man who was the school's track coach usually described basketball players as sissies; they were not, in his mind, as tough as track performers were. He

went out of his way to taunt basketball players in his classroom and in the halls of the school. One day, in the hall, one of the basketball players—in fact, the star of the school's team—answered the challenge. He talked back to the track coach. The track coach, enraged, grabbed the kid and heaved him in the direction of a large plate-glass window. The kid went through the window. Then he went to the hospital for stitches. Nothing happened to the track coach; he runs the city's recreation department now. The player, although still bandaged, started the following Friday night in a game. Nothing about the incident made the newspaper. If it had, I felt at the time, the overwhelming support of the community would have been in support of the coach: How dare a seventeen-year-old high-school kid talk back to him?

A similar incident occurred at another high school a year or two later; it involved a football coach who hated soccer players, considering them lesser animals than his superstuds. A soccer player made the mistake of calling the coach's bluff one afternoon in the school's locker room; he said that the soccer team's record was something like 11 and 1 and the football team's record was something like 2 and 5. The football coach hit him with his fist on the jaw, and knocked the kid unconscious. Of course, nothing appeared in the papers. Today, the coach is a school principal.

Solutions. The chances of seeing horror stories about coaches' actions in the newspapers are still slim. Such stories amount to a betrayal of the public trust in the man; outraged parents, upon reading about such incidents, would no longer allow their sons to be under his influence, and the school would probably have to remove the coach from the job. Now, no community or school wants that kind of problem on its hands, particularly if the coach has been successful at winning games. So newspapers play along with the whole charade, playing the role of moral eunuchs. The solution, of course, would be to begin to scrutinize the local high-school coaches with the same skepticism and the same vigor that newspapers use to scrutinize the local sewer inspector. Managing editors love to unearth stories about local building inspectors on the take, or local politicians involved in influence peddling. But they never view high-school coaches with comparable skepticism.

What goes on inside certain newspaper sports departments seems to be just as deplorable as what goes on inside certain locker rooms. In a nutshell, policing high-school coaches has a lower priority than merely publicizing them.

XVI · What Looms Beyond: Are You Ready for Purple Pride and Gator Getters?

Resembling actor Robert Preston playing the lead role in the movie of *The Music Man,* many college coaches travel to the far corners of America selling themselves, their programs, and their dreams of success, to seventeen-year-old high-school seniors. They traffick in gimmickry. To be a college coach today, one simply has to be part charlatan; manufactured euphoria gets people interested in the fate of a college's sports teams as well as anything else, short of unbeaten seasons. ("We're No.1" bumper stickers are big in Indiana; "Hook 'em Horns" buttons are popular in Texas). Bob Cousy resigned as the head basketball coach at Boston College in 1970 because he no longer wanted to participate in that foolishness; he said he no longer could rest his professional fate on whether or not he could sweet-talk some seventeen-year-old kid from Kansas into attending his school. The most successful college coaches remain slick pitchmen, always ready to unleash on the public a new attention-grabbing device.

Even the most distinguished of colleges coaches, most notably John Wooden of the University of California at Los Angeles, are not above employing salesmanship while pretending to be the chairmen of the board; Wooden is of the genre that delegates the sales pitching to subordinates. While appearing to be above the recruiting battle, concentrating strictly on producing winning basketball teams, Wooden sends out his assistant coaches and former players as surrogates; they do the wooing and the selling for him, but nevertheless it is done in his name. When a young man named Ferdinand Lewis Alcindor, Jr., was a senior at Power Memorial Academy in New York City, he received the full surrogate treatment: The late Dr. Ralph Bunche, a UCLA basketball player during the 1920s, sent him a letter that said, in effect, "UCLA is the school for you." Willie Naulls, another UCLA alumnus, who was playing for the Boston Celtics at the time, spent hours with Alcindor talking about UCLA. The late Jackie Robinson, still another UCLA graduate, did the same. Even Sammy Davis, Jr., took Alcindor out to dinner and gave him a UCLA pitch. By the time Alcindor finally met John Wooden—on a visit to the campus in April of his senior year in high school—he had virtually made up his mind to attend UCLA.

The selling of a school is designed to create a sense of hysteria over the school's sports teams. That hysteria serves two purposes: It helps to recruit outstanding high school players, by giving them the impression that the school is an athletic hotbed, and it rallies the community and the alumni behind the team. The newer, younger breed of college coach is an expert salesman: Sharply dressed, glib-talking, superficially liberal, he puts himself and his school across in such a suave manner that his tactics would leave professional recruiters in the Pentagon salivating.

Once people take notice, the rest is relatively easy: Just deliver the goods. Win games. The whole state will be swept up in the excitement. Following are some examples of the marketing techniques of college coaches, which somehow manage to be classified by educators, and by the public, as harmless:

1. *The Hostess Hustle and Purple Pride.* Vince Gibson of Kansas State University was an expert in using the opposite sex to help attract high-school athletes to his school. He assembled a staff of alluring college coeds and named them "The Gibson Girls." Whenever a high-school athlete visited the college on a recruiting

trip, he was taken on a guided tour of the campus by one of the Gibson Girls. Gibson personally screened applicants for the Gibson Girls, and each year selected fifty of them as members. "One year," he said, "we had three hundred girls apply." Florida State University had a similar group of hostesses; they were called "Gator Getters." At North Carolina State, they're called "Sweet Carolines."

Vince Gibson also employed many other tricks of imagery to promote his football program. He took the school's colors, purple and white, and transformed them into the most fashionable colors in his state. He personally set the style: He wore purple shirts and purple blazers regularly; he had a purple telephone installed in his office. Purple carpeting was installed in the team's locker room. He changed the team's insignia from a smiling purple wildcat to a snarling purple wildcat. Purple-and-white-striped ties and purple shoes for women went on sale in the shops of Manhattan, Kansas. Waitresses in restaurants switched from white to purple uniforms. A local men's store stocked three purple blazers in every size. Another store added a line of purple pipes. Gibson said: "I told people that we got to have purple pride. I even wear purple boots, and I wear purple underwear." The purple gimmick went beyond even Gibson's wildest dreams: Fans from all over the state began sending him purple presents. His office was cluttered with purple pillows, purple blankets, purple ashtrays. A nun who worked in a hospital even sent Gibson a purple bedpan. Gibson did not think that gimmickry was a questionable selling device. He said: "There's always a group against athletics. But you talk to the masses. They enjoy it." Gibson parlayed the hysteria and the gimmickry into a bonanza: In the midst of all the purple hysteria, he got an $800,000 athletic dormitory built on campus; he got a new 50,000-seat stadium built; he got a full-time, 10-man coaching staff; and he got a huge budget for recruiting. The dormitory itself was equipped with a swimming pool, a sauna bath, color television sets, recreation rooms, and lounges; students at Kansas State called it the "Sheraton Gibson." Said Gibson: "Nobody has an athletic dorm like this. It's got everything you need for a winning edge."

Gibson earned $26,000 a year as a coach and $10,000 for a weekly television program. In 1970, 6 of his players were drafted by the pro leagues. None of them left Kansas State with a degree. So much for Gibson Girls and purple pride.

2. *The Musselman Mystique.* In 1969, Bill Musselman was an obscure basketball coach at obscure little Ashland College in Ashland, Ohio. But he was clearly a young man on the make; he was itching for the opportunity to coach basketball at a major university. Ashland, Ohio, is a pleasant, agricultural community of approximately seventeen thousand people, located in central Ohio, midway between Cleveland and Columbus. Prior to the arrival of Bill Musselman, the school had only two distinctions in the sphere of sports: It is the home town of Johnny Roseboro, a catcher for the Los Angeles Dodgers during the 1960s, and its major industry produces the golf balls that Lee Trevino pops around on the professional golf tour. In 1968, a third distinction was added by Bill Musselman: Ashland became the home of one of America's most unusual college basketball teams. Musselman's trick made the state of Ohio, at least, stand up and take notice. His team was unusual because the players practiced their pre-game warmup drills more than anything else; the players would rather play defense than anything else; and the players liked defense so much that they actually aspired to hold the other team scoreless some night—a shutout. Musselman's Ashland College Eagles were the nation's No. 1 small-college basketball team in defense that year. Ashland's opponents had been limited to an average of 32 points a game; half of them were held below 30 points, and one unfortunate victim failed to score a single point against Ashland until just before half time. Defense at Ashland College was more than just something to do when the opposition had the ball; it was an obsession. It was planned that way by Musselman, who said: "I've studied every offensive play there is, and I've come up with defenses to stop them." Example: "The big rebounder is usually the poorest passer on any team. We'll give him the rebound, then harass heck out of him, and wind up getting the ball right back when he throws it away."

Pop psychology was another of Musselman's variations. His team dribbled out before a game to the tune of "Sweet Georgia Brown," à la the Harlem Globetrotters. The players formed a large circle, and each got a basketball to twirl on his fingertips. One player was stationed in the middle, where he juggled three basketballs simultaneously. The routine was perfected during regular practice sessions, which opened and closed with twirling and juggling drills. "We figured our pre-game show had to have an effect on the other team," said Musselman. "I know if I were on the other team and just got through watching one of our performances, I'd feel as if I'd just been through double-overtime." After the pre-game show, Ashland settled down to the serious business at hand—holding the opposition scoreless. "We don't think a shutout in basketball is impossible," said Musselman. "One year, we held teams to seventeen points on two occasions. We feel that if we can hold them that low, we can go all the way and hold them to nothing at all."

Musselman theorized that it was easier to have an "off" game offensively than it was defensively. "Good shooting teams always run into 'off' nights," he said, "but good defensive teams never do. Defense is something that's bred into a player. Never will the outcome of our games depend on our ability to put the ball through the hoop."

Offensively, Ashland averaged 53 points a game, but Musselman said that figure would have been higher if so much emphasis hadn't been placed on defense. "We'd score a lot more," he said, "if our players thought about points. But they don't. Our game is defense."

Bill Musselman did not succeed in guiding his Ashland College Eagles to college basketball's first shutout victory. But he did succeed in attracting attention to himself. Ashland was ranked in the small-college top ten, and made it to the small-college playoffs; at one time, during the 1969–70 season, Ashland was ranked as the No. 1 team in America among small colleges. So, when Bill Fitch resigned as the head basketball coach at the University of Minnesota, to become the coach of the Cleveland Cavaliers of the National Basketball Association, the university sought out Mussel-man. This aggressive, innovative young coach was destined, it was assumed, to make the Minnesota basketball team one of the best in the nation. He brought his gimmicks with him to Minnesota, the pre-game warmup drills and all, and his team began to win games with frequency in his first season. But on Tuesday night, January 26, 1972, Bill Musselman's technique lost its innocence.

That night, with thirty-six seconds remaining in a basketball game being played at the Williams Arena on the University of Minnesota campus, Luke Witte, the center for the Ohio State University team, scored an easy basket. The basket gave his team a 50–44 lead, which, considering the amount of time remaining, was virtually insurmountable. After scoring the basket, Witte was knocked to the floor by Ron Taylor, a forward for the Minnesota team. As Witte began to rise, Taylor put out his hand in an apparent gesture of aid; Witte clasped it and began to get up. With Witte halfway up, Taylor rocked slightly and then drove his knee into Witte's groin, and the Ohio State player fell down again, hitting the floor virtually unconscious. Ron Behagen, another Minnesota player, then came over and began jumping up and down on Witte's neck and shoulders, and other Minnesota players ran about the court, seeking out Ohio State players with whom to fight. Some spectators came out of the stands to join the melee, and when some semblance of order was finally restored, the game was ended by officials and Ohio State was declared the winner.

Witte, meanwhile, and one of his teammates, Mark Wagar, were taken by ambulance to a hospital. Two days later, the commissioner of the Big Ten, Wayne Duke, suspended Ron Taylor and Ron Behagen for the remainder of the Minnesota season, and as televised instant replays of the incident were brought into living rooms in slow motion and in color, the public outcries of revulsion began. The Governor of Ohio, John Gilligan, said that it was "the worst incident that I have ever seen in sports." Some people, sportswriters particularly, put the blame squarely upon the shoulders of Bill Musselman; they said that his pre-game warmup routine, the Harlem Globetrotters' "Sweet Georgia Brown" act, had inflamed the emotions of the crowd and of the players. On the Minnesota side, Luke Witte himself was blamed for planting the seeds of the eruption; he was accused of punching a Minnesota player, Bob Mix, in the jaw at half time and later spitting at Ron Taylor as the Minnesota player was helping him off the floor.

Luke Witte was never the same basketball player again. He returned to Ohio State for another season, but never played with quite the same vigor and élan as before. He now is a reserve center on the Cleveland Cavaliers pro team. His father, Dr. Wayne Witte, who at the time was a professor of philosophy at Ashland College, blamed the entire episode on Musselman. Musselman was no stranger to him—while Musselman was the basketball coach at Ashland College, he once tried to recruit Luke Witte himself. In an interview two weeks after the incident at Minnesota occurred, Dr. Witte said:

The players who assaulted my son were comparable, in my mind, to the American soldiers who assaulted My Lai. In fact, their actions were worse; the soldiers, at least, were in some kind of war. These players were only in a game. But I do not blame the players totally; the conditions that led them to commit this act were to blame. To begin with, there is the coach. After this particular incident, I received a letter from a faculty member at the University of Minnesota, who was obviously quite upset about it, and he wrote that the Minnesota players were talking in his classes, a week before the game, that the only way to beat Ohio State was to "get Witte." The letter said that it was the battle cry, so to speak, for the week: "Get Witte . . . . any way you can. Stop Witte and you win the game." The letter said that the seeds for a violent eruption were planted a week before it actually happened and, as far as I am concerned, the entire situation traces back to the coach, Bill Musselman. He was, according to the letter I received, the one who was telling players to "get Witte," and this kind of thing brings up a question I have long had in my mind about the immunity coaches and athletes have from the criminal laws of America.

Now the FBI put H. Rap Brown on the most-wanted list, and it hunted him down for months and years because he was charged with inciting a riot. But if a basketball coach can plant the seeds for an assault and a riot inside a gymnasium, the question of his being charged with a criminal act does not even arise. The fact of the matter is this: If we really wanted to put a stop to this business of coaches inciting crowds and players to frenzies that lead to riots, then we should start subjecting them to the same criminal laws that govern the inciting of riots in the rest of our society.

The same is true for athletes. If Taylor and Behagen had assaulted my son in an alley, the way they assaulted him inside that fieldhouse, both of them could have been arrested and charged with aggravated assault and battery, and possibly attempted murder. But there is that immunity thing again; they are not criminally liable for their actions because the actions occurred in a sports event. They are liable only to the laws governing their sport, and the people who administer these laws decided to suspend them for the season.

Bill Musselman said at the time that he had done absolutely nothing to inflame his players' emotions, and that he never had told them to attack Witte. He is still coaching basketball at the University of Minnesota, but the memory of that January night in 1972 still hovers over him like a rain cloud. It would seem that the coach who made his reputation with defensive wizardry would spend the rest of his coaching career being on the defensive. Not so. Musselman still has difficulty controlling himself. At the 1973 Lobo Invitational Tournament in New Mexico, Musselman set a tourney record for being the coach who was banished earliest from a game. In the championship game of that tournament, on the night of Dec. 29, 1973, Musselman was ejected from the game and sent to the locker room by the referees after he had accumulated his third technical foul of the game. Musselman was banished with the game only 7 minutes old; he averaged a technical foul every 2½ minutes. With Musselman sitting in the locker room, his Minnesota team absorbed a 102–62 defeat from New Mexico University.

3. *The Traditionalist.* Of all the coaches who are employed by colleges in America today, the prototype of the old traditionalist is one Wayne Woodrow (Woody) Hayes of Ohio State University. While many of the other coaches employ purple pride and Globetrotter routines, Woody Hayes uses the reverse twist—his game is tradition. Let all the others change, let all the others acquiesce to the times, but ole Woody is going to stay the same —and any kid who wants to play his football in a hard-line, good old American atmosphere, should come to Ohio State. Woody Hayes makes authoritarianism seem fashionable—his domain is the last bastion of Spartanism. No modernistic trappings, no sweet talk, no Aqua Velva sales pitches for him—and damned if it doesn't work. Woody Hayes, the same old hard-line Woody Hayes who was chewing telephones on the sidelines in 1956, has been taking Ohio State teams to Rose Bowls with the regularity of full moons. He is the protector of the pure ideals of football; no one will infiltrate his domain and contaminate it. Nobody, in fact, will ever infiltrate his domain, period. The man who guards the gate to his practice field is armed with a revolver. Once inside the sacred stadium, visitors are required to wear red caps or red shirts, for easy identification. Hayes commands his players with the voracity of an Army field general; he has admitted his only personal hobby is the study of professional military tactics during wartime. Occasionally, all of this overlaps inside Woody Hayes's head. In a suburb of Pittsburgh one night in 1969, he attended a banquet to show movies of a trip he had made the previous year to South Vietnam (he was there four times). He wound up, in the course of the evening, defending the Army's actions in the massacre at My Lai. He said, among other things: ". . . and I wouldn't be too sure those women were innocent. The children are obviously innocent, but only if they are less than five."

Woody Hayes has 9 full-time assistants and an academic counselor for his players—with a payroll of $357,000 a year. Also, Ohio State spends $64,000 a year for policemen and gatemen; $39,200 for clothing and equipment; $20,000 for game films and practice equipment; $46,416 for meals for the players; and $18,000 for transportation. The entire athletic budget at the university runs to $3.3 million. Said Woody Hayes, protector of the holy grail: "Football is the most wholesome activity on our campus."

Woody Hayes merchandises tradition, and has been very successful at it. Rarely does he have to go outside the state of Ohio for his players; how can a kid in Ashtabula, Ohio, say, pass up the chance of playing for Woody Hayes and becoming a legitimate hero in his own state? To kids in small towns in the Midwest, the purple pride is fraudulent and unappealing, anyway; Woody gives them what they want—real, hard-nosed football, without the frills. So long as the other universities in the Big Ten insist upon liberalizing their regimes and making changes, ole Woody Hayes is going to keep beating them. By resisting change, he has put the past to work for him.

Prior to the 1974 Rose Bowl in Pasadena, California, ole Wayne Woodrow Hayes was at his traditional best (or worst, depending on one's view of him). He worked his Ohio State football team for sixteen days straight, including several two-a-day practices. The players were allowed Christmas Day off, but only Christmas Day. Then, as the game approached, he said: "Yeah, I'm going to get a little softer, but not much." He said his team's morale was as good as the morale of any team he had ever coached, and that he was sick and tired of people who were "questioning the role of football in a changing society—and all of that junk." Hayes' traditional tactics were contrasted prior to the 1974 Rose Bowl by the tactics of his opposing coach, John McKay, of the University of Southern California. While Hayes was bearing down, McKay was saying, "We consider the Rose Bowl a reward, not a punishment. It isn't fair to players who started training in August to beat them to death in December. I gave my team three days off, because I like Christmas, too. After eating a lot of turkey, we came out looking like turkeys in practice." If McKay's words were transmitted to Woody Hayes, there was no report of Hayes' savoring them while wringing his hands with glee. But the inevitable happened in the 1974 Rose Bowl. The traditionalist worked over the modernist.

Ohio State won, 42–21.

Floyd (Ben) Schwartzwalder, a former Army paratrooper, had been successful in using tradition for years at Syracuse University. But he apparently failed to notice the rise in sociopolitical awareness among the black football players he was recruiting. In the late 1960s, Schwartzwalder's entire football program at Syracuse was in jeopardy of crumbling when black players on his team revolted against what they called Schwartzwalder's "racist policies." They quit the team and got substantial student support. The resultant furor and publicity cast a pall over Schwartzwalder's past accomplishments (No. 1 team in the country in 1960; Jim Brown, Ernie Davis, Floyd Little, Larry Csonka were among the players he had coached), and sent him out of coaching in 1973 as an anachronism. His last team at Syracuse was his worst, and one of his last public utterances was: "It's not that victory is everything; it's that losing hurts so bad." Ben Schwartzwalder, it was concluded, milked tradition a little too long, and it all caught up with him.

Sometimes the gimmicks fail. Athletes see through the superficiality and either rebel against it or leave. Charles (Lefty) Driesell took over as the head basketball coach at the University of Maryland in 1969 and immediately proclaimed that he would turn the school into the UCLA of the East. He hasn't as yet (although he did take UCLA itself down to the wire in one game, losing by one point). He used high-pressure coaching tactics and high-pressure recruiting. When he was coaching at Davidson College, the president of the university at the time, Dr. David Grier Martin, actually called Driesell into his office and informed him that if Driesell's antics didn't cease, the school would be forced to fire him. Driesell's antics included screaming at officials, leaping off benches, and delivering a foot stomp which, Dr. Martin said, threatened to bring the walls of the gymnasium crashing down. Once, Driesell called Vic Bubas, the coach at Duke University, "yellow." The reason: Bubas wouldn't play Davidson on Davidson's home court. Two outstanding players, Jap Trimble and Wilson Washington, quit his Maryland teams. Said Washington, who left while still a freshman: "There are several reasons why I left, but mainly I was disgusted with Driesell."

Then there was the case of Jim Harding, the rigid disciplinarian. Harding had produced winning teams at Gannon College in Erie, Pennsylvania, and LaSalle College in Philadelphia, and then he was hired as the head coach of the Minnesota Pipers of the American Basketball Association. While serving as the coach of that pro team, he got into an argument with the team's owner. Harding punched him. He was fired. The University of Detroit hired him. Harding began whiplashing his players verbally; he drilled them intensely, and drove them to the brink of physical exhaustion in practice sessions. He hadn't been there more than a few weeks when he told a player, one Erick Rucker, that if he didn't get a trifle more aggressive out there on the court, Rucker could get his carcass back home to Chicago, because he would no longer have a scholarship. When another athlete, Dwight Dunlap, asked to take a few days off because his grandfather, who had raised him, had died, Harding told Dunlap he "couldn't wait that long," and that Dunlap also had "obligations to the team."

Said Dunlap: "He would scream at you in practice and give you that stare of his. He'd almost want you to defy him, so he could give you laps to run. I know a guy who owed him two hundred laps. He knows basketball. He's a genius when it comes to the game. But he acts like he hates the athletes."

Another player had been feeling bad, mourning the death of a guy he'd known since kindergarten. Harding chewed him out: "What was I supposed to do for the kid? Was I supposed to say mass for the departed? Did he want me to have services? We've got a basketball program to build here. We don't need weaklings."

The players finally banded together and took action: They all quit. The University of Detroit had a basketball coach, but no team. Harding said the players were liars, "all twenty-five of them." Harding was ultimately succeeded at the school by a young coach named Dick Vitale.

Dick Vitale's first job was to make basketball at the school palatable again. He had to sell himself, and his team, to Detroit basketball fans, and convince them that the hard days of Harding had ended. Vitale visited every sports show on Detroit television stations; he spoke at numerous banquets and luncheons. He made his team do a pre-game warmup drill that was reminiscent of the Harlem Globetrotters' "Sweet Georgia Brown" routine à la Bill Musselman at Minnesota. It was, according to Vitale's pitch, a new era for Detroit basketball, flamboyance instead of floggings. Result: The Detroit gym, which had been accustomed to accommodating approximately fifteen hundred people whenever the team played under Harding, began accommodating full houses of nine thousand people. Inspired, one alumnus donated five thousand dollars to the school for a locker room that would be equipped with carpeting and a stereo sound system. Jim Harding, presumably, never would have tolerated that.

Florida State University had the football equivalent of Jim Harding during 1973; his name was Larry Jones. The trouble started during spring football practice, when twenty-eight Florida State players protested against Jones; they said he was conducting barbaric practice sessions. Then, all twenty-eight of the players quit the team. In the fall of 1973, the Florida State University football compiled a won-lost record of 0-11.

Larry Jones was fired.

Some coaches subscribe to the Donald Segretti School of Trickery. They believe that the playing of dirty tricks is justified as long as their teams win. Some examples:

• Paul Bryant, the head coach at the University of Alabama, used one of the oldest tricks of all to help his Alabama football team score its first touchdown of the 1973 season. Playing against the University of California, Bryant's team reached the California 11-yard line early in the game. Bryant sent in his kicking specialist, a player named Bill Davis, for what appeared to be a field-goal attempt. But no player left the field when Davis came onto it; Alabama had 12 men in the huddle. When the huddle broke, Davis picked up the kicking tee and ran off the field; the Alabama quarterback, Gary Rutledge, then took the ball from center—on a quick snap—and pitched out to the right to a running back named Wilbur Jackson, who scored the touchdown. The NCAA Rules Committee decreed that the play was illegal; it said that a team "cannot simulate a substitution designed to confuse an opponent." Alabama went on to win that game 66–0.

· Long Beach State University wanted desperately to recruit two outstanding basketball players named Roscoe Pondexter and Glenn McDonald. Long Beach State wanted the players so badly that it took no chances when it came time for the players to take their entrance exams: According to the NCAA, Long Beach State used two stand-ins to take the exams for Pondexter and McDonald. Although the president of Long Beach State University, Dr. Stephen Horn, denied the charges, the NCAA suspended Pondexter and McDonald anyway.

· Prior to the 1973 season, thirty-six students at Southern Methodist University were ejected from their dormitory rooms. The dormitory was one of the best on campus. The rooms were then taken over by the school's football players. The coach at Southern Methodist, Dave Smith, had requested separate dormitory and eating facilities for football players the previous January, for "control, morale and prideful atmosphere." But the vice-president for student affairs at SMU, Dr. James Wroten, Jr., stalled. It wasn't until early September that the situation reached a head, when the administrator backed down and ordered the thirty-six students out of the dormitory and replaced them with football players. The administrator said that he and the coach were on a collision course. The ousted students were less diplomatic. One of them, Cy Rosenblatt, said: "We really got the shaft."

All of the funny business, however, has apparently paid off. According to the National Collegiate Sports Services Bureau, college football attendance increased for the twentieth consecutive year in 1973, and has nearly doubled over the period of

1953–1973. The final figures showed that 31,282,540 people attended college football games in 1973, an increase of 453,738 over 1972, and nearly double the 16.7 million who attended college football games in 1953.

The South, according to the bureau, showed the greatest increase. Southern schools had 906,776 more fans in 1973 than in 1972. Also, the South led in total attendance for the seventeenth straight year, with a figure of 9,680,820. The South's average of 14,825 people per game also was the highest in that category in the nation.

The Big Ten Conference was the leader in league attendance, with 3,344,742 fans. The Southeastern Conference was second, with 3,279,697. The largest crowd? It is symbolic, perhaps, that the best crowd of 1973 turned out to see Woody Hayes' Ohio State team play. Over 105,000 people were in the stands in Ann Arbor, Michigan, to watch Ohio State play the University of Michigan. But the people left feeling betrayed.

The game ended in a 10–10 tie.

XVII · The Recruiting Game: Who Is Hustling Whom?

In the realm of intercollegiate athletics, one of the most distasteful practices known to coach and athlete alike is recruiting. To the coach, recruiting is the art of convincing the best high-school athletes to attend your school; to the athlete, it is a confusing period during which grown men representing fashionable institutions of higher learning attempt to influence his thinking by very proper methods, or by very improper ones. In recent years, the recruiting battle has been waged with increased intensity, particularly since the National Collegiate Athletic Association decreed in 1971 that freshman athletes were eligible to play on varsity teams. (That means coaches don't have to wait two years to get the player who will turn their losing teams into winning ones; they get him right away.) But as the coaches have pulled out all the stops in the recruiting trenches, the athletes have added some twists of their own. They are hustling the hustlers. Through the years there has been considerable indignation about recruiting practices. Educators, writers, and even clergymen have expressed outrage over coaches allowing athletes to receive under-the-table payments from alumni; new cars as gifts; clothing; even the company of women—not to mention the scholarships themselves. The critics have long been on the record as saying such practices corrupt the young man's values, make him think in terms of how much he can get out of a school materially and socially instead of academically. But such criticism, it seems, is already obsolete; the athletes have passed that point. They are now playing the schools off against each other, taking all the free trips, eating all the free meals, enjoying the social trimmings each of the schools offer them, milking all the favors they can. Then, once they have partaken of all that has been offered them, they go to the school they had decided upon even before all the recruiting business began. The athletes have turned the recruiters' zeal into their own personal bonanzas.

If the colleges are using immoral tactics to recruit athletes, as has been accurately charged, then the athletes have gone the colleges one better. They enjoy all the luxuries that colleges dangle in front of them and then they take that big, luxurious banana-cream pie and stuff it right back into the colleges' faces. They are, in popular lexicon, ripping off the system; that the system itself is immoral only makes the practice more palatable.

One of the few coaches who has ever stepped forward to denounce all of this is Bob Cousy, who in 1968 resigned as the head basketball coach at Boston College after five and a half years, during which he compiled a 117–34 record. He said that he is out of basketball after twenty-three years as one of its celebrated individuals because he no longer could comfortably live with the evils of recruiting and the breed of player the practice produces.

Bob Cousy:

It's appalling what you have to do to get a key player in colleges. I'm fed up with the whole thing. My retirement had been building for a long time. There's more to life than winning and losing basketball games. My feelings about basketball haven't changed per se. But the system as it stands today has created monsters . . . athletes who are spoiled from the time they get out of grammar school. I just reached a point where I could make a choice of coaching or not coaching for more esthetic reasons than money.

Look, I don't want to make a blanket statement, but it may not be possible to finish in the top ten in the college polls without cheating. That's what the whole recruiting mess has come to. There also is this grotesque overemphasis on winning . . . a value system gone astray. As for pro basketball, it's degenerated into a big business.

The same situation exists to a degree in other sports, but it's more flagrant in basketball. It starts with the recruiting system spoiling the kids so badly. They're pampered and catered to from the time they're playground players. They have an exaggerated opinion of their role in society. They expect instant recognition, exposure, and financial rewards, while men are going to the moon, doctors are working on cancer cures, and others are spending their lives trying to effect meaningful changes.

Everybody knows that there is a great deal of money at stake in college basketball. Recruiting starts the whole vicious circle. Naturally the athletes take advantage. Hell, any of us would do the same thing. There are parallels throughout society. If Nixon was involved in Watergate, is he a crook or is he simply playing by the rules as they've been established? What we're talking about is a problem with roots deep in American society.

Another strange situation took place in one of Cousy's favorite cities—Boston. It involved Boston University and a man named Leon Abbott, who had been that college's hockey coach. He was fired in December 1973 after a bizarre series of events that involved two countries and two collegiate athletic associations. Begin with the 1971–1972 college hockey season:

Leon Abbott produced a fine team, but on February 2, 1972, the Eastern College Athletic Association declared one of his best freshman players, a Canadian named Dick Decloe, ineligible. The ECAA said that Decloe had failed to report that he had played for a team in Canada (the London Knights), and that that team had paid an education tax for him. As a penalty, Boston University was forced to forfeit eleven victories in which Decloe had played. Then came the 1972–73 season.

Two more freshmen players from Canada, Peter Marzo and Bill Buckton, were ruled ineligible prior to the start of the season by Boston University, the ECAA and the NCAA, because they had accepted money while playing in their homeland. The controversy went to a federal court, which ruled in favor of the players and advised the three complainants to take no action against the pair and to allow them to play without restriction. Boston University appeared to take the judicial black eye in stride. The school's hockey team thrived, in fact, winning four of its first six games, including three straight against Harvard, Princeton, and Providence.

Then Abbott was fired.

In announcing the dismissal, Boston University's athletic director, Warren Schmakel, said the action was taken because Abbott had deliberately evaded NCAA and ECAA eligibility rules in his recruiting of foreign players. Schmakel added that Abbott's conduct was personally deplorable and that his "unilateral actions" had been detrimental to the university, the team, and amateur athletics.

Said Abbott:

I think the ECAA and NCAA want to protect their rule concerning the eligibility of players, and BU wants to avoid censure and still keep the boys eligible. To do that, they needed somebody to blame, and I guess I'm the scapegoat. Since the Dick Decloe affair of last season, I have known that I had to choose between the support of my players in their right to attend BU as student athletes and a set of rules I have known were unjust and which, within the past month, have been found unconstitutional by U.S. district judges in Massachusetts and the District of Columbia. The university has been willing to sacrifice three of its students, and now its coach, for this set of sham rules. These violations have occurred in ECAA Division I schools, and I know the ECAA

Western and Central associations are all guilty of these alleged violations.

Leon Abbott's mistake, of course, was that he got himself involved with foreign players and ECAA and NCAA power chau-
vinism. But hundreds of coaches are doing much worse things with
athletes right under the ECAA's and NCAA's noses—with
American athletes. Following are some accounts from the front
line of the recruiting war; they show what coaches offer and how
the young athletes twist things their ways.

The Al Hornyak Case

There was a time when the college recruiting of high-school
athletes was a simple process: offer the hotshot a free education,
give him a train ticket, and tell him where to report.

Not any more.

College recruiting has become an elaborate—and expensive
—ordeal. Untold thousands are being spent behind the scenes to
impress prospects. Assistant coaches and recruiters have been
known to park themselves for weeks on the doorsteps of players
they covet. Head coaches annually place hundreds of long-distance
calls to chat informally with kids from towns they never before
knew existed.

Campus visits are arranged, summer jobs lines up, and the social
advantages of each college (coeds, of course) discreetly pointed
out. It is not uncommon for universities to spend over a thousand
dollars trying to land a basketball prospect (two round-trip plane
tickets, meals, phone calls, coaches' visits to his home) and then
lose him to a rival school. A few years ago, one high-school
All-American basketball player made dozens of trips to campuses
all over the country. Then, to the dismay of all concerned, he
announced he would attend a college fifty miles from his home.
"The trips were great," he later said. "I got to see places I never
thought I would see. All free, too."

In 1969, one of the prime targets of college recruiters was seventeen-year-old Al Hornyak, a 6-foot-2, 175-pound guard who was an ambidexterous—and extremely accurate—jump shooter. He averaged 44 points a game for St. John's Central High School in the southeastern Ohio community of Bellaire (population: 12,000), and was offered basketball scholarships by 157 colleges.

He made the weekend trips to four major colleges early in his senior year: Michigan State, West Virginia, Alabama, and Ohio State. Then he visited North Carolina and UCLA, then the University of Miami, Kentucky, Davidson, Tennessee, and Houston. To him, the recruiting race was fun, but there were times when the whole business left him perplexed.

"Everybody was so nice to me," he said, "I didn't know what to do. When I visited Michigan State, I left impressed and thought I might go there. Then I went to Alabama, saw its new fieldhouse, and changed my mind. Same thing happened after I visited Ohio State. Every time I made a trip, I came home all mixed up. Then another weekend came, and another trip, and I came home again mixed up even more."

Hornyak's weekends started at 5:15 A.M., when he left his Bellaire home and drove sixty-two miles to Pittsburgh to catch a plane to his destination. He was met upon arrival by an assistant coach and promptly taken on an auto tour of the campus, where points of interest were painstakingly brought to his attention.

"When I went to Michigan State and Ohio State," he said, "the first things they showed me were the football stadiums. But when I went to Alabama, the first thing I saw was the new fieldhouse. I met some of the varsity basketball players at each school, and one of them was assigned as my chaperone. The first thing he did was take me on a tour of the dorms, where I met the other athletes, and everybody wound up telling me what a great place their particular school was.

"After I saw the dorms, the assistant coaches took me to an expensive restaurant and urged me to help myself to anything on the menu. I usually did. After we got through eating, it was about four in the afternoon, and I was so tired, I just wanted to sleep. But I was usually taken on a tour of the business-administration buildings, because I wanted to major in business. Sometimes I got to meet some professors, if they were around.

"Then I met my chaperone again, and he took me on a tour of the campus social spots. Coffee shops and hangouts, you know. I got to meet some of the non-athletes. If I wanted a date that night, it was arranged for me. Nothing elaborate: I usually doubled with another player and his date."

Hornyak said he didn't meet the head coach personally until just before he went home, on a Sunday night.

"I met the coach in his office, and he talked to me about the future of basketball at his school. Where I would fit in, and all that. A couple of coaches told me I could get summer employment any place in the country if I came to their schools. They said alumni would arrange it. Then the coach gave me a talking-to about his school being the perfect place to play my college basketball.

"I didn't get back to Bellaire until Sunday night midnight or later. And it usually took until Tuesday to get myself back to normal."

Al Hornyak grew up right across the street from the only outdoor basketball court in Bellaire. He said he was six years old when he first popped a jump shot. In the winter, he said, the kids would shovel snow off the court and play for hours, shooting a water-logged ball through a rim that never had a net. "There was nothing else to do," he said. "If you didn't like basketball, you were dead."

The only person who could get Hornyak off that outdoor court was his mother. "Usually she'd yell for me to come home for supper," he said. "But I remember one time when she yelled, 'Allen, get into this house immediately. It's five below zero. You'll freeze to death out there.'"

When Al Hornyak was thirteen, he broke into the starting lineup at St. John's Central High School and averaged 12 points a game. As a sophomore the next season, he averaged 22 a game, and right after the season ended received his first two feelers from colleges.

"They were from Notre Dame and the U.S. Military Academy," he said, "asking me if I would be interested in attending their schools. I was thrilled. I'll never forget it. That whole summer I went around wondering what it would be like playing for Notre Dame or West Point."

As a junior, Hornyak averaged 42 points a game, with a one-game high of 70, and the deluge started. As a senior averaging 44 a game with a one-game high of 86, over 150 colleges were after him. He said he averaged at least one telephone call a night from a college coach or recruiter once the basketball season started.

"After a while, it stopped being fun," said Hornyak. "When I came home from school I knew there would be a message waiting, and if there wasn't, some coach would wait until later in the evening, when he knew I'd be home, and then call. They asked the same questions, and I gave the same answers, and when I hung up I sometimes wondered if there was any purpose to all of it."

Despite Allen's notoriety at the time, the Hornyak family went about its daily business unaffected. His father, John Hornyak, worked in the Bellaire post office. His two sisters were in junior high school; his mother was a housewife. The family is of Hungarian descent, strict Roman Catholics, and had lived in no other place but Bellaire.

"We didn't let the turmoil bother us," said John Hornyak. "Allen had a big decision to make, and we let him alone. We had confidence that he would make the right choice. The only unusual things I noticed is that the telephone rang a lot more, and there were a lot of strangers with smiling faces dropping in."

Hornyak's high school coach, Sy Kolesza, who went to college nights while working in a steel mill, said most of the college recruiters came to him first before talking to Hornyak personally. "They felt me out," he said. "They wanted to know if I tried to push Allen toward a certain school. I assured them I hadn't. Then they usually said, 'We'd appreciate it if you'd tell your boy he wouldn't go wrong if he came with us.'

"It really got bad after Al's biggest weekend. He scored eighty-six points on a Friday night, sixty-one the following night.

The next weekend, scouts were all over the place. Assistant coaches from UCLA, North Carolina, and Davidson were seated side by side. After the game, they wanted to talk to Al. The rest of the team was showered and dressed, but Al was still sitting there, sweating and listening to them. I finally broke it up by threatening to turn out the lights."

Kolesza said he sometimes wondered how Hornyak withstood all the pressure. "If I thought for one minute the pressure was going to affect him," he said, "I'd have stepped in. But he looked as if he was doing all right for himself. I wanted him to get out and talk to as many people as he could. It was the only way he was going to remove all doubts."

Hornyak himself said pressure was not his biggest concern. The fear of a wrong decision was.

"I thought about what happens if I pick a school and don't like it when I get there? Or if somebody tells me something to influence my choice and things don't work out? Then I wondered if I'd look back and say, 'Gee, if I had gone here or maybe there this wouldn't have happened. Why did I pick this school in the first place?'

"More than anything else," said Al Hornyak, "the thought of a wrong decision scared me."

So, after a year of traveling around the country free, after a year of eating free meals in expensive restaurants, Allen Hornyak made his decision: to go fifty miles up the road to Columbus, Ohio. He chose Ohio State. He played well at Ohio State for four years, and was drafted by the Cleveland Cavaliers of the National Basketball Association. His basketball career ended in the fall of 1973, when the Cavaliers cut him.

The Mike Young Case

In the spring of 1973, Mike Young was a student at Westchester Community College in upstate New York. A fine basketball player, Mike Young got to see the other end of the country free. One of the colleges attempting to recruit him was Washington

State University. George Raveling, the coach there, had made a tremendous reputation as a recruiter while serving as an assistant coach at such schools as the University of Maryland. George Raveling specialized in recruiting black players. Mike Young is black.

"I was at Westchester Community College, and I was getting letters from all kinds of colleges about playing for them," Young said. "I saw these letters from Washington State and just tossed them aside. I'd never heard much about them. Then one day I decided to open one up, and they were inviting me out for a weekend, and I thought, 'Hey, that's not a bad trip.' Anyway, me and four other dudes they were recruiting were flown out there, and when we got off the plane there was coach Raveling and three of his assistants. The first one would say 'How-do-you do' and pass you right on to the next one. It was a receiving line right there in the airport. Then they handed us this schedule telling us what we would do and when we would be doing it for the whole weekend. One of the events was a meeting with coach Raveling.

"He said, 'We have alumni who can take care of you. They don't give you any money but if you want to go home for a weekend or anything like that. . .' You knew just what he was talking about, even if it was in an indirect way. But I really liked the cat; his personality overshadowed everything. Then I got home, and a few days later he's on the phone. I said I wasn't sure what I was going to do, and he said, "There aren't many scholarships left, but if you really want to come, I'll see if I can work something out.' I'm not the kind of person that goes running to anyone, so I decided to wait and see what happened."

What happened was that Mike Young decided to take a half-hour ride south on the New York State Thruway instead of four-hour flights west to Washington. He now plays for Manhattan College. The cost of his free weekend in Washington presumably was written off by Raveling under "Prospects Lost."

*

The Jim Chones Case

When Jim Chones decided to drop out of Marquette University in 1972 to sign with the New York Nets of the American Basketball Association, his coach, Al McGuire, did not discourage him. Said McGuire: "I've looked in my refrigerator and I've looked in his."

Mrs. Mamie Chones of Racine, Wisconsin, used to shop on a day-to-day basis because her family was too poor and the refrigerator too small to stock up. (J.W. Chones died in 1969, leaving Mamie with their six children, ranging from Jim, then nineteen, to Sylvia, then eight.) There would usually be a dozen eggs in the refrigerator, and possibly a small piece of salt pork, and maybe some sausage. Rarely milk. The family drank Kool-Ade or tea. No bread, except for the biscuits Mamie Chones baked when she wasn't too tired after work. (She was the sole support of her family, and earned ten dollars a day making salads in a restaurant.) No vegetables. No fruit. No ice cream. "Not much of anything," she recalled.

In February 1972, Jim became a professional basketball player and the Chones family became millionaires. Sportswriter Ira Berkow called Mamie Chones to ask what she had in her refrigerator now. "You'd be surprised," she exclaimed. "It is a new two-door, seventeen-cubic-foot Whirlpool. What's in it? A ten-pound ham, a three-pound roast chicken, a three-pound fried chicken, two three-pound packages of round steak, six slices of Wisconsin cheese, a whole gallon of milk, a whole bag of apples, a whole bag of oranges, twelve cans of frozen orange juice, two loaves of sandwich bread, two family-size bottles of catsup, two large jars of Miracle Whip salad dressing, a jar of dill pickles, a package of frozen mixed vegetables, a package of frozen butter beans, a package of fresh blackeyed peas, a couple packages of frozen turnip greens, and a gallon of French vanilla ice cream."

The setting for the new refrigerator was also new. The Chones family moved into a finer neighborhood and a grander house. "We had lived in an old wood house with no siding, no anything—the plumbing was bad, and the water would run down all over the kitchen all the time, and we weren't able to pay to get it fixed," Mrs. Chones said. "But the house wasn't quite as bad as some slum places. It had two floors and three medium-size bedrooms."

A few months after Jim Chones began receiving his pro basketball money, the family moved from Edgewood Avenue to a two-story brick house on Haven Avenue. "It's got five bedrooms, with two and three closets in each bedroom. A big living room, a big dining room, a den, and a big recreation room in the basement. And a *big* kitchen, twice the size of the one in the old house," said Mamie Chones.

The old house was still fresh in her memory. It was in that house that Jim, one wintry night, came home and woke up the family: "Mama, come downstairs; I've got something to show everybody." When they had gathered around the dining-room table, Jim put down the signed contract from the New York Nets. "Read this, Mama," he said.

"My prayers have been answered," she recalled saying. "Little Sylvia ran around the next day shouting, 'Bunny'—that's Jim's nickname—'Bunny signed a contract! We rich! We rich!' "

Mamie Chones said she did not fly right out and start buying food and clothes and houses and cars. "I kind of wanted to settle down first, didn't want to get too excited," she said. She eventually traded in her "junk" of a 1967 car for a 1970 Oldsmobile. And she bought much-needed shoes for the family. "Before," she said, "I had two pair of shoes with holes in them. One for work and one for home. Now I've got six pairs of shoes. More than I've ever had in my life. The same for all the children."

Maimie Chones also quit her job. But she said she is looking around now to do some part-time work. "I get sort of bored just doing house-cleaning," she said. And she still has worries. "A mother always does," she said. "Jim had a tonsillitis, and then he had a cold, and he hasn't been playing as well as he'd want to. And there's always something with one of the kids, school, or a fall, or something. But I don't worry any more about having food to feed them. And I haven't forgotten those old days. I'm not really too religious, but I think that this was all something that happened from God. I often think about that, of why me that this dream should happen to? Well, I really think that I deserve it. That after a lot of hardship we have a lot of happiness now. I thank the Lord for Jim and for all my kids. I think way back and remember scolding Jim for going out to play ball instead of doing his homework," she said, laughingly. "I'm happy now, I didn't discourage him from his ball-playing."

Archie Roberts Hustles the Browns

It was 6:56 in the evening during the spring of 1969, when the ambulance pulled into the admittance gate at the Veterans Administration Hospital in New Haven, Connecticut, and the young intern, about to go home for the day, heard his name called on the public address system again.

"Dr. Roberts, please," the voice said softly, as it does in all hospitals. "Doctor R. . ."

Hurrying down a corridor, Dr. Arthur James Roberts stopped and made a brief call home, to say he'd be late again, then reported to Admissions. Two hours later, in pinstriped business suit of dark gray, he would finally emerge through a side door and drive home to the two-bedroom apartment on Treat Street, for another late supper and, as usual, another late look at the sports pages.

"I still follow football religiously," he said at the time. "But, let's face it, I'm just a plain old fan now. Football is out of my life . . . forever. I always said I'd rather be a doctor than a football player, and things have worked out pretty well for me, so far."

Dr. Roberts is the former Archie Roberts, All–Ivy League quarterback at Columbia University, who in 1965, in the midst of pro football's contract-signing war, commandeered an agreement with the Cleveland Browns that, to this day, ranks as one of the game's most unusual and one-sided contracts. He simply told the Browns, who drafted him along with the New York Jets that year, that he was going to become a doctor, and that pro football was not going to interfere with his plans for medical school, and that if they wanted him they would have to make some unusual, if not unheard of, concessions.

At the time, the Browns needed a backup quarterback for Frank Ryan. So they signed Roberts to a four-year contract and agreed to pay a salary of fifteen thousand a year to him and all tuition and expenses for him and his wife, Barbara (she's also a doctor now), to Case Western Reserve Medical School for four years. In return, Roberts was not even obligated to play for the Browns—all he had to do for the first two years was report to practice every day, study the offensive system, and take a spot on the taxi squad.

As it turned out, Roberts never did get to play in a single game for the Browns, but in June 1968 he received his degree from medical school, and his contract with the team—which was worth forty thousand dollars—was finally terminated. For the free education and generous salary, he said he was grateful to the Browns, of course, but he also credits the war between the leagues for making it all possible.

"I know I couldn't have received a contract like that today," he said. "I guess I'm just a product of the pre-merger period. The last couple of years I felt kind of bad, because I couldn't contribute anything to the Browns, but now I rarely think about it. I'll always be grateful to the Browns and especially to Art Modell, who stuck by me the entire four years and lived up to his part of the bargain all the way. I know the situation wasn't easy for him.

"When the Browns finally traded me to Miami of the AFL, in my last year of med school, I wanted to give football one more try. But I got there the same time Bob Griese did, and it was evident right away that I was going to be the number-two or number-three quarterback. So I decided right there to forget about football for once and for all and return to school. Had I stayed with the Dolphins, it would have cost me a year of schooling, and I didn't think playing pro football was worth that."

Roberts' ultimate goal was to become a cardiotherapic surgeon, and, in 1969 he said he faced at least eight more years of formal training.

"After I finish my internship here, I'll put in a year of residency, then go to the National Institute of Health in Washington, D.C., for two years to study cardiac surgery. After that, I'll finish my residency, study general surgery for three years and cardiotherapic surgery for two more.

"Then I'll be ready for private practice, sometime in 1977."

Courtesy of the Cleveland Browns, for whom he did not play a single down.

As for policing the recruiting battles, the college athletic associations try. The University of Oklahoma was caught doctoring up high-school transcripts of top players and was put on probation for two years. (That means the university's football team will not be able to play on national television or in bowl games.) Southwest Louisiana College was caught in 1972 in the biggest single recruiting scandal of all times: The NCAA said the school had been guilty of committing seventy-nine different violations (no national television ever?). But so long as colleges want sports teams, the schools will use tricky tactics to get players, and the players will use the schools to eat, sight-see, and socialize free of charge. There apparently is no solution to the problem.

As Bob Cousy said, "It's the system. . ."

XVIII · How Colleges Keep
Their Players' Lips Zippered:
The PR Industry

Inside the administration buildings at virtually every college and university in the United States of America is a public-information office. Inside these public-information offices, there is a two- or three-room office called the sports-information office. Inside these little suites are men who are paid to function as advertising men for their college's sports teams and coaches. They are called sports-information directors or sports-publicity men. Their jobs are not designed to guarantee a free flow of information concerning the teams and the coaches to the public. Their jobs are to manage the news concerning the team and the coach so that the news reaches the public with a favorable flavor. These men will not tell you why a coach suspended a black player from his team; they will merely tell you that so-and-so has been suspended from the team by the coach for an indefinite period for reasons that will have to remain confidential. *Wordwash.* But, at the same time, these men will have prepared elaborate, three thousand-word press releases to inform the public that a Wittenburg or a Muhlenburg will be on the basketball schedule for the 1977–78 season.

Rarely does a reporter from a newspaper or wire service, or a feature writer from a magazine, or an author of a book, get to interview a coach without first getting clearance from the sports-information director. The sports-information director interviews the interviewer, feels him out, attempts to discover whether or not the interviewer is preparing to do a hatchet job on the coach. If he is interested only in writing about Wishbone-T formations and zone defenses, the interview with the coach is arranged. If the sports-information director detects any sign of irreverence in the writer, he immediately informs the coach, and one of two things usually happens: (1) the coach avoids the interview, claiming higher priorities, such as an urgent recruiting trip, or (2) he consents to the interview, but is on his toes throughout the encounter. Either way, this collaboration works against the writer, and the public which may read his material. The coach has been tipped off in advance and, suitably forewarned, usually discusses only the weather or the next arrival of Halley's Comet. One of the sports-information director's duties is to keep the coach protected from writers who may actually write the truth about him. For this most valuable of services, the sports-information director earns an annual salary that ranges from fifteen to twenty-five thousand dollars a year, depending on the size of the college.

Another important duty of the sports-information director is to prepare the team's annual press brochure. Now, press brochures do offer some valuable information: They give to media people the height and the weight of each player, his home town, his position, and the correct spelling of his name. They also furnish the team's schedule and a listing of members of the coaching staff. But the rest of these brochures usually consist of nothing more than the usual public-relations puffery. Some schools, like the University of North Carolina, go to great extremes to publish lavish press brochures; they come into newspaper offices in magazine size, with full-color covers, action profiles of each player, and scouting reports of the opposition. Some schools, in order to attract newspapers' attention to their brochures, pose coeds wearing bikini bathing suits on the cover of their brochures. One Southern school has been posing a blond coed on a black bearskin rug for years now (she is wearing a flesh-colored bikini). Another school in the South poses coeds wearing red, white, and blue togas.

And the schools compete with each other to produce the most lavish and elaborate brochures; every year the College Sports Information Directors Association has a contest to select the No. 1 sports brochure. The University of North Carolina has become the UCLA of its field; it has won it three of the last five years. The reward: a trophy for the school's trophy case.

The brochures are supplemented by weekly press releases which inform newspapermen of the team's latest statistics, the coach's comments on the previous game and on the upcoming game, and perhaps even a nebulous feature story on some second-string guard who is an immigrant from Transylvania. Some 75 percent of these releases wind up, unopened, in newspaper trash cans; but some newspapers, lacking ingenuity, paste them up and print them as legitimate news ("Coach Wilson Sees Bates as Rugged Foe"). Sports-information directors apparently are content with flooding newspaper offices with their canned drivel; most of the envelopes are addressed to a sports editor who has been dead for five years, or to a college sportswriter who has left the paper and has become a sports-information director himself.

The trick in all this is to beat the newspapers at their own game. Flood the office with releases and, sooner or later, a lazy editor, or a lazy writer, is going to use one. Then two. Then regularly. And when some bloodhound of a reporter comes sniffing around the campus, all they have to say is: "Didn't you get our latest release? It's all in there."

The sports-information office also is reponsible for keeping the players quiet. Frequently, the sports-information office informs reporters that athletes are not available for interviews, as a matter of university policy (UCLA has been great at this ploy). That way, dissident athletes do not get the opportunity to vent their spleens on the local sports pages or, horror of horrors, on the national wires. But occasionally an astute reporter seeks out a disenchanted athlete and the young man's thoughts reach print anyway. When that happens, sports-information directors usually look upon the reporter as a traitor, not as a professional who is merely doing his job. Following are some incidents in the continuing battle between sports-information directors and media people over what version of the truth the public will get.

The Ken Wyrick Case

Several days before the Army-Navy football game in November 1970, I visited the United States Military Academy at West Point, New York, to collect material for a pre-game story on service-academy football. While there, I interviewed the captain of the Army team, a cadet named Ken Wyrick, who was a defensive tackle on the Army team playing in his final season. How I happened to be in a position to interview Wyrick is in itself worth reporting. The West Point sports-information director, a young, affable fellow named Bob Kinney, was sitting with us in a room near the gymnasium when his takeout lunch arrived. Apparently embarrassed because he had not bothered to ask if Wyrick or I wanted lunch, he excused himself and went into another room to eat alone. Once he was gone, all hell broke loose. Wyrick turned out to be one of those festering boils of players waiting to be lanced; the interview was astonishing. During it, he made some of the most irreverent statements ever made by a cadet at West Point. When the interview was published, it outraged the academy, the Pentagon, and presumably, military commanders from Germany to Indochina. Wyrick was made to apologize to the team; he did, saying that he was trying to make things better at the academy, not worse. But much of what he said about academy football proved ultimately correct—four years later, Tom Cahill, the Army coach, was fired after a winless season (0- 10), including a 51–0 trouncing by Navy. Had Cahill, among others, listened to Wyrick's pleas for reform, and made some corrections—instead of blaming their misfortunes on the war in .Indochina and tough schedules—the 1973 Army football season might not have been the shambles it was. Excerpts from the interview with Wyrick, as it was published, follow:

Ken, there is this image of the Army football player being the epitome of discipline and rigidity. Is it accurate?

I'm well aware of the image, and I don't think it's accurate at all. In fact, it disturbs me very much. People who don't know us personally think we go around thinking, "Kill, kill," all the time. That's not so. I'd say the football players are the most liberal-thinking cadets in the whole academy.

Liberal in what way?

For one thing, you ask any of the kids on the team about Vietnam and they'll tell you it weighs very heavily on their minds and that they're asking the same questions about Vietnam as any other college kid is asking. Personally, I don't particularly want to go to Vietnam, and I'm not going to volunteer to go, but I know it's inevitable that I'll be over there someday. I know other cadets who can't wait to go to Ranger School and Airborne School and get over to Vietnam. I don't think that kind of attitude is typical among football players here. If you polled the team and asked everybody about Vietnam, I think the feeling would be over-whelmingly in favor of our getting out of there.

Do football players express their opinion around the academy?

No, not vigorously. But I think you can detect that football players are less gung-ho than a lot of other cadets. For one thing, I'd say, the football players are not caught up in all the military spit and polish. I think our appearances are a lot sloppier than most cadets'. I think our uniforms are sloppier, our shoes aren't shined as much, and our hair is a little longer. In general, I'd say that football players are a lot less military-conscious than other cadets.

You said the academy isn't being fair to its football players. Can you elaborate on that?

I think the big thing is that the academy expects us to be outstanding football players and outstanding cadets at the same time. I don't think it's possible. I feel there should be some adjust-ment made in our military life-style during the football season. It seems as if we are getting punished, from a military standpoint, for being football players. Yet we are doing everything everyone else is doing—and more.

I'll give you a couple of examples. On Friday nights before games, there are inspections of living quarters, and we have to stand them just as every other cadet does. If we get demerits, they won't keep you out of the game the next day; they wait until the following week and give us extra duty. I don't think we should be liable for this kind of punishment, because on Friday nights before games our minds are on football, not inspections. This really upset me when I talked to some football players from the Air Force Academy, which I feel is the most liberal of the service academies. They told me that on Friday nights before games the whole team is quartered in a motel, relaxing. I feel the academy should be thinking along the same lines, and that's what I mean about "bending."

Are non-football-playing cadets in sympathy with your problems?

No, and I'll tell you why. The cadets around here think they are supporting the team by showing up on Saturdays and sitting up in the stands, screaming and yelling. But these same guys are battalion commanders and such, and they're the ones who put the screws to us during inspections and things. They have no mercy on us in day-to-day military life, yet just because they scream and yell in the stands every Saturday, they think they're supporting the team. I don't think they're supporting the team. In fact, some of them are actually hurting the team. You can get guys off the street to scream and yell every Saturday. That's not support as far as I'm concerned.

Do you think, then, that the football program at West Point is due for a few revisions?

Yes. It's back to the bending again. I don't think the players here are wrapped up in the memories of Glenn Davis and Doc Blanchard and Pete Dawkins. I think the military people and the grads are the ones caught up in all the tradition, not us. I think we have some excellent players this season, and I think we should have a lot better record than one, eight, and one. It's not the coach's fault, and I don't think it's entirely the players' fault. But I do think West Point is going to have to ask itself something about its football program—does it want outstanding football players or outstanding prospective officers?

What about your own future? Do you have plans for a military career?

No, I have a five-year commitment to the Army after I graduate from the academy in June. I don't know what will happen after that. But I do know I would like to be part of the change that is taking place in the military right now. I would like to be a company commander and be able to tell my troops, "All right, you have to do such-and-such job today and when it's finished go home." I'd like to help eliminate a lot of the bullcrap that is going on. I would like to be part of an Army that teaches. I would like to be in an Army that everybody is proud of, that I'm proud of.

Are you proud to be a cadet?

Right now, I like to think of myself more as a football player and less as a military person. I know I'm looked up to because I'm a cadet and because I'm captain of the football team, especially back home in Knoxville. But socially, I play it down. When I go out with a girl, especially on the first date, I try not to mention that I'm a cadet at West Point. When I go out with girls who know I'm a cadet, they don't mention it to me. I've found that it's not exactly the perfect topic for social conversation.

After that interview appeared, I received telephone calls from Army public-information officers at the Pentagon in Washington and the academy at West Point. Both said they wanted my notes from the interview. I offered to give them Xeroxed copies of my notes, and I said that I would put them in the mail immediately. They said that they would call me back. They never did. A week or so later, a gray-blue, unmarked car pulled in front of my home in New Jersey; two men in gray suits got out and began taking pictures of it. Then, for several days, strange noises were coming out of the receiver of my home telephone: beeps, buzzes, clanks.

Was I under surveillance because of my piece on Ken Wyrick? To this day, I assume that I was.

The Wooden Philosophy

It was during a timeout in the second half of UCLA's semi-final victory over New Mexico State in the 1970 NCAA Basketball Tournament in College Park, Maryland: John Wooden, obviously incensed, said something to Sidney Wicks, his star forward. Sidney Wicks looked him straight in the eye and said something back.

Wooden raised his voice even more, and then Sidney Wicks started waving his hands in John Wooden's face and said something else. The rest of the players, sensing perhaps a budding emotional scene, huddled around them and shielded the episode from further public exposure. The next time anyone saw Sidney Wicks, he was sitting down, toweling his face, and John Wooden was standing over him, presumably adding the final word.

What transpired during that incident was never discovered, because John Wooden does not allow his players to talk to the working press, and he himself is an old master at answering direct questions with indirect X's and O's. Which brings up the question that emerged rather vividly during the playing of the final rounds of that NCAA Tournament: Just how much freedom, if any, does a college basketball player have to speak his mind?

The NCAA is apparently doing its best to maintain the silence quo. It ruled that locker-room doors would be closed to the working press at all times during the semi-final and final rounds of its basketball tournaments, then relented somewhat and left the decision to the participating schools. Of the four at College Park in 1970, only Jacksonville removed the police guard and opened its doors.

And, as if to add the ultimate insult to the imagination of newsmen, who by this time felt as if they were drawing empty buckets from an over-flowing well, the committee distributed mimeographed copies of coaches' quotes at the end of each game. (It was delightful, indeed, to learn that Larry Weise was still proud of his St. Bonaventure team even though it lost.) As one NCAA official said, while passing out the canned goodies, "They're better than no quotes at all."

A reporter stopped John Wooden in the lobby of the Shoreham Hotel in Washington on the tournament's off day and asked him just why he forbids newsmen to talk to his players after a game.

"Are they big boys now, John," the reporter asked, "or what?"

Wooden removed his dark-rimmed glasses, wiped his blue eyes for thinking time, replaced his glasses slowly, and blinked the reporter back into focus.

"Newsmen are too smart for college kids. They are in the business of selling papers. They will trick players into saying things, then twist it for purposes of controversy. I do not want controversy," he said.

"Are you saying, in effect, that college athletes are not smart enough to deal with newsmen?" the reporter pressed.

"No," said Wooden. "That is not the point. I just will not allow controversy to disrupt my team. My main concern is for my team as a whole. I will not allow anything to interfere with the team and the direction in which it is heading. I want my players thinking about basketball. I don't want them going around talking about politics and racial issues and social change. Such things have a negative effect on the team as a whole."

Later that day, the same reporter sought out Joe Williams, the young Jacksonville coach. He found him wearing a dark brown double-breasted sports coat with sky-blue pinstripes, a Navy-blue tie four inches wide, and buckled alligator shoes. Williams said he opened his locker-room doors because it was standard procedure for him.

"Dealing with newsmen is part of the total experience of being an athlete. I want my players talking to the press, but I also give them the option of saying 'No comment,' if they wish. My kids are smart enough to know that what they say after a game is going to be printed, and they act accordingly. I don't see any sense at all in locking them in hotel rooms and sneaking them in and out of back doors. They're human, too, aren't they?"

Many feel that Williams' method of coaching, permissive yet effective, may indeed become a trend for the next decade.

"I will not try to eliminate the human element," he said. "Who needs all this rigid discipline, rules and regulations, game plans and scouting reports? Just give me some kids who want to play basketball. That's what it's all about."

The Columbia Riot and Dave Newmark

The smoke had pretty well cleared from the campus battleground at Columbia, the Ivy League school where athletes aren't synonymous with animals and the locker room is secondary to the library. Dave Newmark, the seven-foot center who had helped the Lions to their first conference basketball championship in seventeen years, reflected on the riot at his school.

"I tried to stay away at the outset," he said. "I knew the issues and what the students were trying to accomplish. In principle, I was in favor of them, but their tactics [barricading themselves inside the campus buildings] were illegal, so I had mixed emotions. Since I do have somewhat of a name in sports, I was asked to be interviewed, but refused. Frankly, I was afraid of being misquoted, and also I didn't want to hurt my future career by making statements that many people would probably disagree with."

What happened when the New York City policemen, reporters, photographers, and cameramen moved in was enough to convince Newmark that some changes were needed, however. For the first time since the trouble had started, he happened to be on campus the night violence erupted. "I had always assumed that 'police brutality' was just a catch phrase and that people who shouted it were just looking for a crutch to justify illegal actions," Newmark said. "But I was amazed to see the cops using violence for its own sake. Innocent people who were doing nothing but sitting were clubbed on the head. After the buildings had been cleared, the cops all lined up along the walks in the center of the campus like troopers, which infuriated the crowd.

"The cops started charging the crowd, and people were tripping over each other, trying to get away. I was completely appalled by what was happening. Then I came across Bill Ames, one of my teammates. He was sitting on the ground sobbing."

"I asked him what happened.

"He said a lady who had been trying to get out of the way of the fleeing students and charging police had caught a spike of her shoe in the grass and tripped. A cop ran and clubbed her in the back of the head. Bill ran over and was leaning over the bleeding woman, trying to help her, when another cop clubbed him from behind. He said, 'I'm just trying to help this lady,' and the cop told him to move along.

"The real atrocity was that the administration showed no moral regard for life or limb. They took no steps to alleviate the problems. All they accomplished was to have campus activities suspended altogether."

Newmark also claimed the media distorted the true picture. "The networks and the papers didn't report the incidents the same as I saw them," he said.

"I've talked to students from the two factions in one of the buildings. In the event the cops came, the 'moderate' group decided to go and not cause trouble. The 'resistance' group chose to sit, lock arms, and sing. That was the extent of their actions.

"The 'majority coalition' was made up largely of athletes and was against the strikers. They also wanted reforms, but did not go along with the strikers' actions. But after the cops moved in they changed their minds. Morality transcends legality in this instance. I'll tell you this. I was never prouder to be a student at Columbia than I was then."

His remarks were not cleared through the Columbia sports-information office.

*

The Carlos Alvarez Case

Carlos Alvarez, an outstanding receiver at the University of Florida in the early 1970s, was another example of a college athlete speaking out on the issues of the day despite all attempts to silence him. Carlos Alvarez arrived in the United States after the Cuban revolution. He received the usual indoctrination about freedom of speech which America offers, and apparently he believed in it. A decade later, football made him doubt it. He first upset football fans in Florida when he told a reporter that he had misgivings about American involvement in the war in Indochina. After four students were killed by National Guardsmen at Kent State University, Carlos Alvarez addressed a campus rally and pleaded for more understanding. Result: more hate mail from angry Floridians. But what finally outraged followers of Florida football was Carlos Alvarez' attack on the university and the athletic department during a change in head coaches at the school. Alvarez said that he and his teammates had been misled, and that he was "shocked, embarrassed, disappointed, and bewildered." Alvarez said that the team had been led to believe that if a coaching change occurred, Gene Ellenson, an assistant coach, would be considered the head coach.

Instead, the job went to Doug Dickey, who had coached at the University of Tennessee. Said Alvarez:

"What disturbs me most is that people I had placed a great deal of confidence and trust in went out of their way to deceive and mislead us. I've learned some things about the ugly aspects of football, and it'll never be the same again."

Alvarez' remarks brought a flood of mail, much of it saying, "Spic, go home." Alvarez shrugged it off. He said: "If the sport doesn't change and bend a little, it might not last. I think the coaches will be made to change by kids coming up and not wanting to play under a lot of restrictions, where everything has to be done by the rules and you can't ever question the rules. Football is like a rose. A rose is nice, but it's not essential."

At the same time Alvarez was taking his stand, Jim Calkins, who had been captain of the football team at the University of California, had a few things to say as well. Calkins said: "When I first came to California, I'd do anything for the coach. I'd take what he said as the word, without question. Now I've come to the conclusion that I had better say something. That's been part of the problem. You see so many black athletes speaking out now. But the white players are gutless. They don't want to take a stand. They are so entrenched in the system and so full of all of this super-patriotic stuff. So the coach is all-dominant, all-powerful. I've never seen one player call a coach a bleephead, like coaches call us all the time. Sometimes I look inside myself and I think I won't be leaving school with my dignity because of what I had to go through. The most degrading thing is being treated like a child. I was programed to act and function in a certain way. And they talk about learning things from football! I don't think I learned a single thing. The attitude is that you're getting paid to play football so you can't gripe. If that's the way they want it, fine. But I say to them, *You don't pay enough.*"

XIX · Colleges Are the Athletic Melting Pots—the Dreams End There (Sometimes Tragically)

The dreams of athletic success, the dreams that begin in Little Leagues and are nursed through high schools, invariably end in colleges. College sports are the athletic melting pots. All of the thousands and thousands of high-school hotshots are mixed together as college freshmen; after four years, one or two of them from each college can legitimately aspire to a professional sports career. The others will return to their home towns, become insurance salesmen or accountants, their sports careers over. It is a rude and shocking experience, one which college coaches never mention in the living rooms of the high-school hotshots they covet. But the truth of the matter is that college sports serve as the minor leagues for the professional leagues, especially for the National Football League and the National and American Basketball Associations. Only the very best college athletes make it to the professional leagues; the very good, the average, and the mediocre don't have a chance. The National Football League has 26 teams of 40 players each; that means there are merely 1,040 men who make their livings by playing football. Fewer than a hundred rookies stick with the league during a given year. The pro basketball leagues—there are 24 teams in both leagues, 14 men to a team—

have 336 jobs. A rookie's chances of sticking in pro basketball are even smaller than in pro football. But in their recruiting talks, coaches always seem to dangle the prospects of a pro career in front of outstanding high-school players, as if making a pro team is easily within their grasps. Example: "Don't go to Ohio State. You're a great quarterback, son. You know how many Ohio State quarterbacks made it with the pros? None. Ohio State quarterbacks don't throw the ball, son. They hand it off." The implication is that the recruiter's school will offer the boy a better chance to play in the pro leagues merely because it will give him the chance to throw the football, as if a good passing arm, alone, will guarantee him a job with the Baltimore Colts.

The reality of the situation is that the overwhelming majority of high-school hotshots will never make it to the pro leagues. Coaches are rarely honest about this when they make their recruiting pitches; during these talks, they always seem to emphasize the list of players who went on to play pro ball from their schools. They never mention the staggering number who have failed.

It is March, 1968: The voice from the shower was half blubber and half cry. A soapy gurgle. It asked a question: "Hey, Butch, whatcha gonna do now?"

Angular Butch Beard, honorable-mention All-American basketball player at the University of Louisville, leaned his head back against the locker-room wall and rolled his eyes in a comic, Eddie Cantor manner.

"I'm going to play ball in Vietnam," he replied, loudly. An appreciative snicker followed. "I'm going to run the fast break against the Viet Cong."

The scene: Locker room No. 6 in Madison Square Garden. Louisville had just lost to Boston College in the National Invitational Tournament quarter finals. The seniors took their time dressing. For most of them, there wouldn't be another time.

"I'd like to go somewhere and sleep for four weeks," said Beard, lolling naked on a bench. "All of a sudden I'm so tired."

Ultimately, Beard would live to play another day—with the pros. For others the time had come to hang it up.

"I've been playing basketball all my life, since I could lift one," senior guard Dennis Deeken said. "I'm better right now than I've ever been. Now, all of a sudden, I've got to stop and go to work or join the Army or something. It's going to be quite a change."

Quite a change, indeed. As a University of Tulsa senior put it earlier in the tournament, "I'll probably have the best jump shot in the marines . . . for all that's worth."

Deeken, for instance, was a good college guard. Fine shooter. Adequate passer. But too slow. Nobody in the Louisville dressing room asked him what he was going to do.

Each year, colleges and universities release hundreds of former athletes on the nation—fellows like Deeken, honed to a competitive edge in the prime of their lives.

Then it's over. For a few years, the ex-athletes may haunt local YMCA's, astonishing unknowing patrons with their talents. During a pickup game, the ex–college star may sink three or four straight from the corner.

On the sidelines, men whisper their admiration the way cheerleaders used to scream it. "Didn't that guy used to play for State U.?" they'll ask. Sure, sure he did.

After four years of free gym shoes, clean uniforms, and cheering crowds, the day finally comes when the former college basketball player must buy his own equipment.

"It's about this time that you really realize the show's over," St. John's alumnus John Ringle pointed out. "Basketball gives you four years of college, sometimes five, and an opportunity to play the game. A man can't ask for much more than that."

The elite, the lucky ones like Butch Beard, go on—never knowing the pride their former teammates will swallow to buy, for the first time, a pair of white wool socks.

Bruce Clark Gardner, of the University of Southern California, was the collegiate pitcher of the year in 1960. Eleven years later, after an aborted pro career in the Los Angeles Dodgers' farm system, Bruce Gardner was a suicide. Death came as a result of a self-inflicted gunshot wound at the scene of his proudest moments: a few feet away from the pitcher's mound at the University of Southern California's Bovard Field. His death, at thirty-two years old, was bizarre: His college diploma was clasped in his right hand, and an All-American plaque, emblematic of collegiate baseball's pitcher of the year, was lying nearby, alongside an unaddressed, unsigned note.

Only the few people who read the note found near the body know why he actually committed suicide, but the motive became apparent in the reminiscences of those who knew Bruce Gardner closely, and in the pages of a personal scrap book in which he chronicled his life's triumphs and setbacks. Most of the scrapbook's pages revealed a life of accomplishment: awards, pictures, complimentary letters, and so on.

But there was a bitter refrain, as well—it was a resentment toward those who talked him out of signing a lucrative major-league bonus contract when he was a seventeen-year-old left-handed pitcher fresh out of Fairfax High School in Los Angeles. Foremost among those who insisted that he go to college instead of turning pro were his mother, Mrs. Betty Gardner, who now lives in San Diego, California, and the man who recruited him to USC, the head baseball coach, Rod Dedeaux.

"He was always looking back, wondering how things would have been if he'd gone into baseball right away," said Mrs. Gardner, a plump, white-haired woman, of her only child. She spoke of him with little emotion, calmly, quietly.

"His first love—and only love—was baseball," she went on. "But I didn't approve of his signing a contract when he finished high school. He needed security for the future, after he would be through playing. The trouble, I supposed, was that he felt I was interfering with his goal."

Dedeaux, on the other hand, said Gardner "gave every impression, more than most kids do," that his college days were the "happiest of his life."

"There was never a finer, more cooperative guy in any way," said the Trojan coach. "He was so totally happy with college, yet he could have signed at any time while he was at USC, as Ron Fairly and Len Gabrielson did. There was no restriction whatsoever on keeping kids from signing in those days.

"When he signed out of college," said Dedeaux, "he actually got a better chance to make it to the majors than he would have if he'd signed out of high school. He started at Montreal, a much higher level than Class D, where they often started high school kids in those days."

At USC, Gardner not only became an outstanding pitcher—his varsity record was 40 victories, 5 losses, a Trojan record—he was engaged in numerous campus activities as a member of Delta Chi Fraternity, of Hillel, of such honorary groups as Blue Key and Skull and Dagger. He also performed in the school's stage presentation of *Damn·Yankees*, as Joe Hardy, who made a deal with the devil to become a great ballplayer.

Then, in a summer of 1960, he stood on the threshold of fulfilling his lifelong dream. The Dodgers signed him to a contract, but for a bonus of twenty thousand dollars, less than what he reportedly had been offered (about fifty thousand dollars by the Chicago White Sox) as a teen-ager four years earlier. From that point, his life apparently became one of unfulfilled promise, of injuries, and of frustration.

He was inducted into the Army (shortly after signing) for six months of training at Ft. Ord, California, where he suffered an injury to his pitching arm. And when he reportedly tried to hasten his conditioning a few years later, his arm was stricken with bursitis. His career read like a road map: 0–1 at Montreal (then a Dodger farm club); 20–4 at Reno; 1–5 at Spokane; 10–4 at Great Falls; 1–2 at Salem. It was a downhill road to baseball oblivion: an arm shot, a dream shattered, a life tormented.

"He often talked about how he should have been in the majors," said a close friend, a singer and bandleader named Barry Biales, "about what a waste it was that he went to college."

Still, even in the face of frustration, Gardner lived a life of fulfillment in many areas. He was handsome and articulate, a bachelor who was described as being "particular" about the girls he dated. He also was described as meticulous and introspective, "not really outgoing," inquisitive and sensitive.

Still another reflection of the man was conveyed in his modest, immaculate apartment in West Los Angeles. The bookshelves suggested a variety of interests: *The Fountainhead,* by Ayn Rand, *The Grapes of Wrath,* by John Steinbeck, and *Psycho-Cybernetics,* among many others.

So did the small piano near the door (he learned to play at age ten), the stacks of albums flanking his stereo (George Shearing, Ray Charles, Erroll Garner, Ramsey Lewis, Los Indios Trabajaros), and the large oil seascape on a wall over the stereo.

Music, his friends said, was the sunshine in Gardner's life, particularly after his baseball career fell on hard times. There were nightclub stints as a ballad singer and a classical, jazz, and pop pianist. There were also jam sessions at parties with high-school buddies—notably, a fellow named Herb Alpert on trumpet, Phil Spector (renowned rock producer) on guitar, Sandy Nelson on drums, his pal Barry Biales on vocal, and Bruce Gardner on piano.

He worked as a stock and mutual-funds broker, during which he struck up a friendship with a business associate, Eddie Allen, who also was an assistant coach on Dedeaux's staff at USC.

"Even when we talked only business, the talk would always relate to baseball," said Allen. "He also was very concerned about America; he seemed to want to talk with kids, to help keep them from making mistakes in life, to keep them from drugs."

Gardner ultimately turned his thoughts into action. He quit what friends described as a lucrative career in the brokerage business and became a teacher—first as a substitute, then as a junior-varsity baseball coach at a Los Angeles high school, where he guided the team to its best season in history (13–2), as well as to a league title.

Several players said he was "strict, but fair and understanding," while one player said, "He seemed to need someone to talk to. And the more he kept things inside him, the more it drove him crazy."

Ken Bailey, a tennis coach who shared a locker with Gardner, said he discovered, after hearing the news of Gardner's death, that Gardner had already completed recording final grades for everyone in his four gym classes, even though the school was not to close for several weeks more.

"I found all his grade books—all up to date—with a note that was signed 'Farewell,' " said Bailey.

The student who was then the sports editor of the school paper, Mike Terry, wrote a tribute to the coach, entitled: "Coach Gardner, Why, Oh Why?"

"Coach Gardner seemed to be very bitter about not being able to play major league ball," Terry wrote. "When I interviewed him for the school paper, he was somewhat emotional in his talk. Yet I felt he would not do what he did whenever I saw him during the semester.

"Coach Gardner had a brilliant baseball mind. . . There will be mourning for Coach Gardner, for he was well liked, They say the good die young. But Coach Gardner, Why, O, Why?"

XX • Seminole College: The Black Team in a White Town . . . and Why

One of the most socially significant college basketball games ever played took place in the Cole Field House on the University of Maryland Campus in College Park, Maryland, on Friday night, March 25, 1965. It was a game between the University of Kentucky and Texas Western College. At stake was the championship of the National College Athletic Association tournament. What made that game significant, from a sociological standpoint, was that it brought together, on the same floor, two schools that represented opposite extremes insofar as black players were concerned. Texas Western (which is now called the University of Texas at El Paso) had recruited most of the players on its team from the playgrounds of New York City; people such as Bobby Joe Hill, Nevil Shed, and Dave Lattin were the stars of that team. The entire starting five were black. Kentucky's team was entirely white; its outstanding players were Pat Riley, Louie Dampier, Tom Kron, Larry Conley. At the time, Adolph Rupp, the Kentucky coach, still had not recruited a single black player for one of his Kentucky teams, and the whispering along the press table on that night in 1965 was that the old Baron of the Bluegrass would never win another NCAA title without having a black star on his team. What happened that night was this: The all-black team from Texas Western defeated the all-white team from Kentucky, 72–65. The exploiter defeated the excluder; very little was left to the imagination when the teams were on the playing floor. Street-wise kids from New York City won a national championship for a school they had never heard of until they got there; and they defeated a school that had been keeping other young men of their race from representing it on basketball courts.

A few years later, Frank McGuire, the coach at the University of South Carolina, gave the New York City "shuttle system" a new twist: He went out and recruited from the city's playgrounds outstanding white players. Tom Riker, Kevin Joyce, and John Roche kept South Carolina's basketball teams nationally ranked for several years. But it was the black players whom most of the colleges coveted most; there were men in New York City who actually spent their time watching playground basketball games in New York City and then tipping off colleges on the top prospects—for a fee, of course. (They were, derisively, called "flesh peddlers.") A man who was called "Freddy the Spook" actually had dozens of colleges paying him for his information. So the best young black players, from impoverished homes and blighted environments, were being snapped up by colleges with exotic-sounding names in faraway, distant places; they were taken by these colleges for one reason: to give the school a winning basketball team. Coaches of course denied that they were exploiting these young black men who happened to be outstanding basketball players; the coaches said they were giving these poor kids an opportunity to get an education and to escape from their detrimental surroundings. Somewhere in between was the truth.

In 1972, one of the most blatant examples of exploitation of black basketball players involved a new junior college in Seminole, Oklahoma. For want of a reputation, the two-year school opted to put itself on the academic map by having an outstanding basketball team. Seminole, Oklahoma, is a town right out of the movie *The Last Picture Show*. It is located on the dead-brown plains of central Oklahoma. The inhabitants of Seminole do not exactly covet social or economic change. They will tell you, point-blank, that they like things the way they are.

So when the Seminole Junior College Trojans basketball team began winning games in 1971 and early 1972, the people of the town were not exactly affected by its success. They stayed away from the team's game in droves. Tornadoes, it seemed, were more popular in Seminole than junior-college basketball teams composed of black players.

One night during the 1972–73 season, when the Seminole team played its archrival, Northeast A & M Junior College of Miami, Oklahoma, the gate totaled $67. The head coach, a man named Bailey Vanzant, said: "The referees cost us sixty dollars, and Cokes for the players came to four fifty. We made a profit of two dollars, fifty cents." Earlier that week, the Seminole team had had a won-lost record of 13–1 and was ranked fourteenth-best in the nation among junior colleges in the wire-service polls. After routing Northeast A & M, the team moved up to No. 11 in the polls, and was scheduled to play in the featured half of a unique doubleheader—the opening game was between two outstanding local girls' teams. The take that night was $94. The top ticket price: $1.50. The average paid attendance per game: 160 people.

Clearly, something was wrong. What was wrong became evident when the Seminole team dribbled onto the floor. The players differed in height, from a high of 6-foot-7 to a low of 5-foot-2, but they were all black. The city of Seminole has very few black people living in its environs. At the school, there were 705 full-time students; merely 35 were black—including the basketball players.

The townspeople apparently resented having an outstanding team of black players in their midst.

W. G. Lynn, a realtor in Seminole, said: "Today, this is nothing but a basketball training ground for four-year colleges. I won't go out and root for a bunch of dumb buck nigras from somewhere else. If these were local colored boys, I'd root for them." The leading optometrist in Seminole, Dr. Hubert Callaway, said: "Junior-college basketball here is a new idea. We've only had a team two years, and it takes longer than that for a rural community to cotton to anything new. They also have a lot of competition. High-school sports are big in this county. But the main thing is that the junior-college players are outsiders, black strangers. Nobody knows them."

The president of the college, Elmer Tanner, said that an outstanding basketball team was essential to the success—and survival—of the school itself.

Said Tanner: "When I first came here [to Seminole], I wondered what I was getting myself into. So I stopped into several places on the outskirts of town—even downtown—asking for directions, just to hear what the people would say. Many of them didn't even know they had a junior college. They directed me to the high school. Now we have a beautiful little campus—all they had when I first got here was a couple of little rooms in a building. But even with the campus and all, we need the basketball team. Before we had the team, there were people ten miles away who didn't know that there was a Seminole Junior College. I don't care how good you are academically—and we think we've made a fine start in that area—it takes 'activities,' as they call them, to attract attention to your school. And I know of no finer 'activity' than intercollegiate sports."

Vanzant, the basketball coach, said: "I have five thousand dollars for scholarships. After tuition and rooms, that means three fifty a day for meals. Who the hell wants to come to Seminole?"

He answers the question himself, smiling:

"A hell of a team. I have a lot of friends around the country, particularly in New York and the Southeast, and this year I sent out three hundred letters, for one thing. I also ran up a twelve-dollar phone bill one day, and I made a trip or two. We got fifteen players in from Louisiana, Texas, and New York, and nine of them stayed."

The miracle is that any of them stayed. Their "dormitory" downtown is on the second floor of a sagging, peeling tenement building that has been condemned by the Seminole fire department. Said Vanzant: "You should see where they stayed last year. It was a motel, an abandoned motel, and they chased us out. The rats chased us out."

Greg McDougald, one of the team's best players, did not remember that. He was the star of the "new" team, and the basketball experts of Oklahoma believed McDougald, 6-foot-7, could write his own ticket someday to UCLA or Louisville or anywhere in between—if he got out of Seminole with the grades he had never been able to get anywhere else.

"I'm just an average student," Greg McDougald said. "My goal is pro ball, but before that I've got to play college ball. And my only chance is better grades. That's why I'm here. This is such a small school, they can give you a lot of individual attention. And they don't mind doing it. This is all that keeps me in Seminole."

He said he was not surprised that the spectators are few for games. "It's a little, narrow-minded town. We and Oklahoma weren't made for each other. But I'd put up with worse than this to reach my goal. The hardest thing, at first, was eating on three fifty a day. Once I didn't think I had ordered a big breakfast, but it came to two dollars. Now I've learned to pace myself. Food isn't important. At the junior college they treat me as an individual. That's important."

On the basketball floor, Greg McDougald and the other members of the team (who share McDougald's ambitions and some of his talent) put on the best shows ever seen around Seminole. But nobody came to see them.

"These are hard times," said W. D. Graft, a retired oil driller. "I think a dollar fifty for a basketball game is too much."

"It doesn't matter how good their team is," said a Seminole barber, George Hays. "It's a new team, a new program. People don't move that fast around here."

"It's an all-colored team, you know," said Mrs. Ward Lynn. "We're not educated to that yet."

Mack Gillham, who ran a Gulf Station, said, "Honestly, I don't think it's a racial thing. The big problem is it's basketball they're playing. That's a lousy sport. Who wants to pay to see basketball? I don't even watch it free on television. Now, if they played football, I'd never miss a game."

Bob Jones, manager of the Seminole chamber of commerce, said: "The junior college is so popular here that the people of Seminole voted a sales tax on themselves to support it. The one-cent tax raises a monthly seventeen thousand dollars, which, with some state aid, keeps the school going." But just keeping it going isn't enough for president Tanner, who said: "The health of any school depends on two things that have little to do with education as such: morale on campus and public relations beyond the campus limits. A winning basketball team is the finest thing we have going for us at Seminole Junior College in the areas of morale and advertising."

Apparently, black men are in Seminole, Oklahoma, to stay.

On December 9, 1973, New York City metropolitan-area college coaches, the Eastern College Athletic Conference, and black community leaders held a meeting. The topic: exploitative recruiting. The coaches spoke of money offers, cars, department-store credit cards, and off-campus apartments offered to blue-chip players, the majority of them black. The coaches, ECAC members and representatives from community groups in attendance wanted to find methods to halt what they termed "flesh peddling." The coaches warned that if the recruiting methods were not changed, another basketball scandal was in the offing.

"This won't be a point-shaving scandal like the one in the 1950s," said one coach. "It will make that scandal look like nothing compared to the bases this one will touch."

One of the major targets of the meeting was the recruiting-information sheets that are being sold to colleges and may contain a prospect's grades, class ranking, college-board scores, and playing potential. Though the New York City college coaches had a motive in trying to keep local talent playing in New York, some, like Jack Powers of Manhattan College, expressed concern about what actually happens to some of the players: "These recruiters do more harm than good to these kids. The kids are not ready for the pressures they are subjected to and they come home. I spoke to six blue-chippers in the playgrounds last year, and the first thing they told me was, 'I don't want to stay in the city. You can't offer me enough.' "

Other coaches expressed the view that many of the colleges are becoming basketball factories. When a player's eligibility ends, he returns home with nothing. He is without a diploma and an education; he had illusions of becoming a pro player, but doesn't make it.

"These recruiting sheets are immoral," Jack Prenderville, the St. Francis College coach, said. "I coached in high school last season, and the questionnaires sent to the coaches ask for everything but the size of a prospect's underwear. They are actually a violation of a youngster's privacy. They shouldn't be flaunted around the country."

Ron Smalls, the Long Island University coach, said: "A seventeen- or eighteen-year-old kid is very impressionable. They have delusions of grandeur. They envision themselves as great players and these out-of-town colleges as ivory towers. What they are doing to some of these kids is wrong. We know college football is big business, and basketball is moving in that direction. The rich are getting richer, and the poor poorer."

None of the coaches present had ever heard of Seminole College. So much for good intentions.

XXI · A Modest Proposal: From Tots to Teens, Why Not Soccer?

By no means does the hysteria over boys and organized sports end with the games of baseball, football, and basketball. In New Hampshire, and in Maine and Massachusetts and the extreme northern states, little-boys' hockey is popular—and as organized —as any Little League baseball program, or any junior football league. Every year, in Minneapolis and in Duluth, Minnesota, there are national pee-wee hockey championship tournaments. In Saint Clairs Shores, Michigan, for example, a city of 88,093 inhabitants, the recreation department sponsors hockey leagues at three different age levels, each accommodating approximately 500 boys—at a cost of $100,000 annually. In 1969, teams from each division of that league simultaneously won national championships; the city of Saint Clairs shores then began calling itself "Titletown of Boys' Hockey, U.S.A." All of which underscores one rather lamentable fact: Little boys' games are so organized, and so institutionalized, that the old informal sandlot games, with their rag-tag lack of pretension and their improvisational character, are now virtually obsolete. Kids don't stuff an old sock with newspapers and go out to a vacant corner lot for a game of touch football any more; now they study playbooks and game plans in their bedrooms to prepare themselves for Sunday's two-o'clock kickoff (or tipoff or faceoff).

Following are some thoughts on the situation:

1. The institutions, and not necessarily the men who coach, are the real problems. Well-intentioned men who volunteer their services to coach in a boys' league are inevitably corrupted by the league's by-laws and guidelines—most of the time without even recognizing it themselves. For example: A man may decide to become a Little League baseball coach, but he is personally against cutting any boy from his team. He gets to the tryouts and is told that he can have only fourteen players on his team. Twenty-five boys, say, are trying out for his team. The man is faced with his first—and most important—decision: If he goes along with the institution's rules that state that only fourteen players can be on his team, he must cut eleven players and betray his own convictions on the subject. If he refuses to cut the eleven players, then he is ousted from the program himself. Cutting the eleven kids in order to comply with the rules of the institution is a form of institution-induced corruption. What the man considers to be beneficial for the boys involved does not really matter; what matters is what the institution decrees is beneficial. Most men who are enthusiastic about becoming a coach of a little-boys' team ultimately buckle under to the rules of the institution; once they do, they become further corrupted by all the other rules the institution has already set down—rules that force them to compromise their own better instincts. Men who become involved in leagues with the best interests of the boys at heart usually wind up coaching with the best interests of the institution at heart.

2. In that context, the men who become coaches in these boys' leagues do not really coach at all—they merely act as enforcers of the laws and the guidelines set down by the headquarters of the organization. On-the-spot improvisation is virtually nonexistent. After a while, not only are these men ruthlessly cutting kids from teams, but they are whipping them into professional form because the institution is dangling a state tournament, or a regional tour-

nament, or a national or a world tournament, in front of their noses. The institution also decrees exactly how much emphasis there is going to be on the winning of games; so long as there are such things in existence as Little League World Series, the emphasis on winning is going to be great. And who promotes all of these world series and national tournaments? Not the local folks, but the institution's hierarchy.

3. Men who coach little-boys' teams do not necessarily pattern themselves after the late Vince Lombardi; that is an overblown and innaccurate analogy. The vast majority of them pattern themselves after other men who have been successful in the same program. A Little League coach I once knew, who had one of his all-star teams win a Little League World Series in the early 1950s, said that his own tactics—many of which were rather harsh—were dictated by the tactics other men had used to beat his teams in previous years. Once, he said, his team was beaten by a team from Montreal. That Canadian team was quite physical—its pitcher was throwing at batters' heads, its base-runners were taking out shortstops with chest-high slides to second base, its infielders were applying tags not to the body, gently, but to the head, fiercely. One of his players, after being tagged out at third base, came into the dugout crying, and was reluctant to play in the game again. The next year, the coach said, he instructed his players to do the very same things—to be, in a nutshell, ruthlessly rough. With the experience of that Canadian team in mind, he also began selecting a different type of player for his all-star teams. No longer did he choose players who merely possessed outstanding baseball ability. He began choosing players who were more street-wise, kids who would not come back into dugouts crying.

This is a succinct example of how well-intentioned men become trapped in the institutional vice: On one hand, they are forced to do things they do not wish to do, things that are not exactly beneficial to their young players; and, on the other hand, they must do these things if they wish to win games—which is what the institution says the program, or the tournament, is all about. What is happening, then, is this: Little League baseball and football coaches are picking up, and implementing, the tactics used by coaches whose teams beat them—and there is no intermediate position. If one is going to win in these institutionalized leagues and tournaments, one must keep up with the most successful tacticians. Unfortunately, the tactics of successful coaches on this level are not scrutinized by the leaders of the institution; sadly, roughhouse play, subtle intimidation, coaches calling pitches from dugouts, gang-tackling and piling on, and bean-balling have already been institutionalized into these boys' leagues. Parents have two choices: to accept it all as being, in the lexicon of the institution, "a part of the game," or to remove their boys from the program. The boys are the losers, either way.

4. In little-boys' football leagues particularly, there is an inordinate amount of emphasis on physical violence. It is the essence of the game of football. So long as the game is called "tackle" football, physical violence is going to be encouraged—does the passive team ever win? Power sweeps, bombs, and blitzes certainly do not connote expertise, finesse, or style. In little-boys' ice-hockey leagues, there also is an undercurrent of encouraged violence. All of which means that there are millions of prepubescent boys in this country who are being conditioned on the advantages of physically overpowering their less awesome peers. The mental damage in all of this is indescribable because it is not visible, and probably won't manifest itself until the boys' later years. When eleven-year-old boys look forward, with relish, to physically obliterating other eleven-year-old boys, the mental damage has apparently already been accomplished. A certain amount of aggressiveness, psychologists will tell you, is healthy; but to acquire a blood-lust, a "killer instinct," is certainly a disconcerting, if not jaded, goal. But, again, the institutions which promote this philosophy—yes, the little-boys' football and hockey leagues—have failed us all, in that they have never followed up on their own products. None of these institutions has studied what effect this acceptance of violence has had on the minds of boys who have passed through their programs; they have never tracked down their alumni, as adults, and studied their adult attitudes toward violence. It could be that these leagues

have produced the current generation of armchair quarterbacks lodged in front of the television sets in living rooms every Sunday afternoon from September to March, watching professional football and hockey games, taking their violence vicariously. It could also be that they have produced a generation of pacificists who, having tasted violence in football leagues, have denounced it forever. But the practice of conditioning young boys to an acceptance—indeed, a relish—of violence has totally escaped serious study. Coaches, managers, and parents become distraught whenever a Little League player suffers a physical injury; that very few of them are concerned about the very same players incurring mental injuries is a tragic oversight.

5. One of the most corrupt practices concerning all of these little-boys' leagues—a practice that also helps to corrupt the coaches and managers in them—is that of keeping under wraps statistics involving the thousands upon thousands of physical injuries that occur to young boys within their own spheres every year. Just how many boys die every year in the United States of America while playing in these leagues? The institutions—the people in the national headquarters' offices—will never come forward with public accountings of how many deaths and how many serious injuries occur within their domains every year on a national basis. The reason: If the headquarters of the national Pop Warner League, say, announces to the world that seven young boys died as a result of injuries suffered in football games, and that four hundred boys suffered broken limbs, or that two hundred boys suffered concussions and fifty-eight boys suffered fractured skulls, the shock wave might destroy the very institutions they command. If the facts come out, fifty-year-old men wouldn't be making twenty-five thousand dollars a year much longer as the presidents of national junior-football organizations. Parents, of course, would be terrified in the wake of such statistics; most of them would not allow their young boys to play in these leagues, once they had digested the statistical carnage. If the Little League headquarters in South Williamsport, Pennsylvania, say, announced that four boys died, that two hundred boys suffered broken limbs, that eighty

boys suffered concussions, and that thirty boys had their skulls fractured, the same result would occur: Parents would be hesitant—indeed reluctant—to allow their boys to play in these leagues.

Now, for a modest proposal:

The reason little boys become so enamored with the game of baseball is very simple: Their little hands can grip and control baseballs. These same little hands cannot grip or control footballs and basketballs. Taking that theory a step further may also be taking a step in the right direction toward correcting and eliminating the exploitation, the abuse, and the corruption that is now omnipresent in many little-boys' leagues. Forget about the little boys' hands for a minute. The answer may lie deep to the south, with his feet: Soccer is a perfect alternative.

If little boys in America were introduced to soccer balls instead of footballs, things could change for the better for them; they might even be able to play a game again just for the fun of it all. Why? Some reasons:

1. Soccer is a fast-paced game that demands full participation. Boys do more running in soccer games than in any other; substituting is an essential part of the game. With eleven players to a side, forty-boy teams would be standard. Everybody would play. That would eliminate all the eleven-year-old bench-warmers that Little League baseball and junior football leagues have produced.

2. Boys would learn how to use their feet in soccer; also their heads and their torsos. The game demands that they use parts of their bodies that lie dormant in other sports. The only boys who kick in football are the placekickers, and there aren't too many of them. Every player kicks in soccer.

3. There is no grandiose strategy in soccer as it is played on the lower levels in America. The boys simply go out onto the field and run and kick to their hearts' delight. Game plans and playbooks are nonexistent, yet teamwork is necessary, in the form of passing and positioning. The emphasis in soccer is on spontaneous action; this

diffuses—and makes unnecessary—all elaborate, intricate strategy sessions football and baseball coaches employ. No X's and O's; just I's.

4. Soccer is cheap. No shoulder pads or hip pads or helmets are necessary; no gloves, no bats, no bases are necessary; no ice skates, no hockey sticks are necessary. Only a ball and a body are necessary. Boys would not have to go out into the streets, soliciting money, to pay for equipment and loudspeaker systems; sponsors of teams are not necessary. The only expense is a soccer ball.

5. Soccer can be played virtually year-round. It is a spring sport, a summer-evening sport, a fall sport. It is even a winter sport, if the field isn't covered with a foot or two of snow.

6. There are no size or weight restrictions in soccer. The smallest and the fastest boys are wings and forwards; the biggest and the strongest boys are defensive players. The most agile of players are goalies. No boys will have to sweat down in sauna baths to meet weight restrictions; no boys will have to be pulled from a game because they have already played in the allotted number of innings which the institution has decreed for them.

7. Soccer is the only game that has already proved to totally satisfy young boys' energy and excitement capacities. The constant movement, the improvisation, the atmosphere of involvement, is not conducive to bored players. It is the most invigorating game for little boys; it sends them home thoroughly satisfied that they have played in an athletic contest, and it sends them home pooped.

8. There is no structural hierarchy in soccer in America. There are no glamourized professional leagues from which coaches can glean new formations and new twists and new subterfugal strategies—all of which take the game away from the players. There are no legendary soccer figures in America: no Vince Lombardis, no Ted Williamses, no Bobby Hulls with whom to identify. A man who would coach a little-boys' soccer team could not possibly consider himself to be following in the footsteps of Don Shula. (Quick now: Who is America's foremost soccer coach?) The soccer coach, like the boys, would be liberated from

the overbearing tradition that descends from the higher levels of the game. There is no soccer tradition in America. It's virgin territory, with no stereotypes, no legends, no superstars, no specialists.

9. Soccer does not require fancy trappings. Electric scoreboards, loudspeaker systems, manicured diamonds are not necessary. The game can be played on any kind of surface—on grass, dirt, even plain, old mushy mud.

10. Soccer develops individual skills in its players, unlike baseball or football, which develop interchangeable, communal skills. The game is adapted to the players, not the players to the game. In soccer, every player must be able to run; every player must be able to kick. A certain bodily élan is acquired through the extensive footwork and balance involved in the game. The smallest player on a soccer field may indeed be the best; in Little League baseball and junior-league football, the biggest players are almost automatically the best. The very nature of the game of soccer neutralizes size as a factor; 5-foot-8 Little League fastball pitchers might be reduced to 5-foot-8 second-string defensive fullbacks in soccer.

11. The game of soccer encourages aggressiveness in young boys, which is not altogether a negative trait, but it stops short of overt violence. Soccer is not a contact game. Players may indeed scramble for a loose ball, feet first, but there is no tackling or holding involved.

12. Soccer is a girls' game as well as a boys' game. Soccer leagues for girls can be established just as easily as can soccer leagues for boys.

13. Soccer is not an "American" game. Unlike baseball, football, and basketball, soccer has no roots whatsoever in the American frontier. It is not the city game, or the national pastime; it did not begin with peach baskets in Springfield, Massachusetts, or with two frantic fraternities at Rutgers University. In reality, soccer is the closest game there is to being a truly "world" game. Only in North America (including Canada) has soccer failed to become a popular sport among young boys and girls. The reason is because Americans and Canadians have their own sports, which sprang

from their own distincitive roots, and because Americans and Canadians have emphasized them to their young boys instead. But it may be time to give the rest of the world a chance: Instead of trying to convert the rest of the world over to Little League baseball, it might be beneficial for Americans to try what the rest of the world is doing. (After all, more people on the planet Earth are familiar with Pelé than are familiar with Joe Namath.)

14. And, finally, a word of caution, as well: If the day ever arrives when there exists a national Little League Soccer headquarters, and that headquarters promotes a Little World Cup international soccer tournament, then it is time to begin the dismantling process . . . and time to begin investigating, say, gymnastics.

XXII • A General Guide for Parents: What to Look for in a Coach (or, How to Preserve Your Son's Health and Sanity)

Following is a guide that will help parents to cope, and be copious, when that fateful day arrives when their son bursts through the kitchen door and says, "Hey, guess what? I made the team."

1. *Know Your Son's Abilities.* The kids who suffer most at the hands of coaches are the average athletes. The outstanding ones will always get preferential treatment, and the poor ones will not make the teams. The average athletes actually hold the key to the coach's success; if the coach can make the average athlete better, then the team will be better. So the coach will concentrate on making the average player do things that the athlete never envisioned he could do. That opens the door for abuse in the form of high pressure, constant needling, etc. The best thing a parent can do to prepare for the sports experience is to take a long, hard, uncompromising look at the son's ability. If the boy is outstanding, chances are the coach will bend the rules in his favor. If the boy is lacking in talent, chances are the coach will not waste his precious time attempting to develop him. But if the boy is average, watch out. He is vulnerable to the coach's dreams. If the coach is determined to develop the boy into an outstanding player, the process

itself could lead to disaster. If a parent determines that the boy is, indeed, only average, the first thing to do is to seek out the coach personally and ask him what plans he has for the boy. If the coach says, "I'm going to make him a star," the next question is "How?" His answer will determine how much of a price the boy will pay en route to the galaxy. Coaches have a way of sweet-talking parents into giving their approval; they say such things as "The boy has outstanding character, thanks to you, and with some work he's going to be a tremendous player." Flattering parents, coaches long ago discovered, is a very effective way to neutralize them.

2. *Do Some Research.* The best way to find out what a coach is capable of doing to a boy is to seek out former players whom the coach labeled "troublesome." These are the kids who didn't make it because they didn't conform to the coach's wishes and demands. They were subsequently dropped from the team. Because they have nothing further to lose, they always seem happy to tell you about the coach's tactics. The parents of these so-called troublesome boys are also excellent sources insofar as finding out what the coach is really like. They, like their sons, have seen a side of the coach that the coach does not project to "new" parents and "new" athletes. If you, as a parent, suspect the coach of being an extremist, compile a list of his former players who were dropped from his teams and find out why they were dropped. This will prepare you to deal with the coach from a position of strength if he attempts to use the same tactics on your son. Also talk to the school's athletic director, or to the school's principal, as well (or to the president of the Little League or the Pop Warner League). Try to find out what the institution's goals are so far as sports are concerned. Does the principal want to build an athletic power-house? Be No. 1 in the state? Such goals are a tipoff to how the coach acts (he pulls out all the stops in order to achieve the institution's goals). Pete Newell, who coached the University of California to the national-basketball championship in 1960, once summed up the dilemma of coaches who happen to work for institutions that are hellbent on producing winning sports teams: "It's rationalized by some coaches today that 'If I don't cheat, the

other guy is going to get me,' and 'I have to cheat to keep my job.' Now, a lot of coaches have lost their jobs because they haven't won games, and a lot of coaches have lost their jobs for such things as illegal recruiting, but I've never seen a college president lose his job for doing either one."

3. *Interview the Coach—Subtly.* To determine what kind of man the coach really is, it is wise to talk to him on an adult-to-adult basis. Ask him about his political feelings, about his religious beliefs, about his feelings on the news topics of the day. Ask him what his plans for the future are. Probably, one of two things will happen: He will avoid giving you direct and honest answers, which means he doesn't want you to know what he is really thinking—he's keeping you off guard—or he will tell you what he assumes you want to hear. Most coaches will try to keep parents of their players at arm's length; they do not covet adult-to-adult relationships. But in the event that the coach does come clean and answers your questions honestly, then cherish him. Coaches who can relate to other adults usually have their roles in proper perspective; it is the coaches who avoid dealing with adults who become suspect. Many coaches use invisible stiff-arms to keep parents of their players at bay. Some have been known not to answer their telephones during the season. Keep ringing.

4. *Be Wary of the Periphery.* Coaches like to win parents over to their sides by offering the parents semiofficial spots on the periphery of the team. The coaches recruit parents for the Pep Club or the Booster Club, or they ask parents to hold the sideline markers during football games, or whatever. What they are really doing is giving the parents a nebulous piece of the action in exchange for the parents' silence. Once a parent commits himself to a coach in some peripheral role, he loses his objectivity, unconsciously or not. Many parents who are seduced into these kind of roles actually become subservient to the coach, and in so doing relinquish the right to speak on their son's behalf.

5. *Be Wary of Painkillers.* One of the most frightening trends of the last decade has been the increasingly authorized use of painkillers to keep players in games. There are coaches in Little

Leagues, Pop Warner Leagues, and high schools who use spray-type "freezers" on sprained ankles, knees, and elbows; the pain disappears, the youngster continues in the game. But in many cases the young player damages the "frozen" knee or elbow even further—but he does not know it. He doesn't feel anything until the anesthetic wears off. Novocain injections are still popular among high-pressure high-school coaches, who authorize doctors to "shoot" injured kids with Novocain before games so that the players can perform without pain. Again, the chances of the injury becoming further aggravated are great. The passing out of amphetamines and steroids was a problem for a while, but the practice aroused the ire of enough parents (and enough publicity) to discourage the continuance of it. If a young athlete is injured and he comes home and says that the coach has suggested a painkiller so that he can play, the wisest course of action is to consult the personal family physician at once. He has the professional—and moral—authority to stop this horrendous act. The practice allowing coaches to authorize painkillers for players is not exactly widespread, but it occurs often enough for parents to be on guard against it.

6. *Establish a Grievance Procedure.* It is essential to establish a chain of command for parents' grievances. In Little League baseball, say, the best way to do it is to designate one of the league officers as liaison between the coaches and the parents. All complaints would be directed to him. In the high schools, an assistant principal might be a good choice. Parents must have a responsible person to whom to turn whenever they feel the coach is getting out of hand where their sons are concerned. As it stands now, in most sports organizations there are no independent arbitrators linking coaches and parents. Too often, parents are forced to confront the coach directly; in those cases, the coach almost always wins. Third parties, independent but yet concerned, are essential if coaches are to be monitored responsibly.

7. *No Psychic Profiles.* In some high schools and in many colleges, coaches are beginning to give prospective players batteries of psychic-profile tests. The results of these tests are used by the

coaches to screen out undesirables, to weed out potential malcontents, to regulate attitudes among the players. It is in the best interest of young athletes if parents fight—vehemently fight—these tests. Coaches use the results to effectively manipulate the young athletes; if the tests show that a boy is a slow starter, for example, the coach knows even before the season begins that he must prod and pressure the boy into action. The tests do not benefit the players; they have been conceived by coaches to benefit coaches. If a boy returns home and informs his parents that he has just taken a long test, administered by the coach, the parents should immediately go to the school, demand a copy of the test, read it, and then pass it on to the school's higher authorities. Psychic-profile testing seems to be becoming more popular; it all started in the professional football leagues, and is now filtering its way down to the lower levels.

8. *Demand Answers.* Too many parents allow serious problems to continue by not confronting them. Young boys who return home from practice sessions limping, or who return home silently and lock themselves in their bedrooms, have obviously experienced something traumatic. It is then that parents should ask questions. Many boys, under the pressure of coaches, will attempt to hide injuries or unpleasant incidents from their parents because they are afraid that their parents will confront the coach and their position on the team will be jeopardized. But too many "slight limps" result in more-serious injuries, and too many "blue moods" result in serious emotional problems. At the first sign of such trouble, physical or mental, parents must act. Call the coach. Call the principal. Call a teammate's parents. Call somebody. But find out exactly what happened.

9. *Don't Believe in Myths.* Myths are readily available substitutes for hard thinking. When coaches wheel out their bags of myths, be wary. They tell you that football is not a dangerous game at all, that it is perfectly safe. But they do not tell you that at the turn of this century the president of the United States, Teddy Roosevelt, actually asked the Congress to abolish the game on the grounds that it was too dangerous. It was a coach, Amos Alonzo Stagg, who

met with Roosevelt, recommended some changes, and saved the game. Coaches hold up the late Vince Lombardi as a myth; they say he is a legend, the prototype of what a successful coach should be. But they do not tell you that the last team that Vince Lombardi coached, the Washington Redskins of 1969, failed to make the National Football League playoffs. Or that Vince Lombardi returned to coaching because, he said, he "wanted to destroy the legend of what Vince Lombardi was." Actually, Vince Lombardi was considerably more humane, and considerably more sensitive, than many of the coaches who now attempt to emulate him. As Frank Gifford once said: "I played for Lombardi, and I'm sick and tired of hearing what an ogre, what a madman, he was. Actually, he was a big, warm bear of a man, not a raging animal at all." Vince Lombardi, Jr., who is now a member of House of Representatives in Minnesota, said of his father: "He has been a great influence on a lot of coaches—not just in the pros; but on the lower levels, down to pre–high-school football coaches. And from what I've seen and heard, I'm not convinced that younger kids are prepared for the strain that some well-meaning coaches place on them. Maybe you can't overemphasize the striving for excellence, but I think you can overemphasize the striving for victory. Some of the things my father stood for I have accepted and live by too. But there are pluses and minuses. I had great respect for my father. I was in awe of him. But we were never what you'd call buddies." Myths not only replace thinking, but, when strung together, they always form surrealistic moats around the truth.

10. *The Option of Quitting.* The most important thing a parent can do for a son who is involved in sports is to give him the option of quitting. Too many parents force their sons to continue playing for coaches they do not like; too many parents still feel that quitting a team is bad, that quitting is a sign of weakness, a stigma that reflects upon the entire family. This is nonsense. The best-adjusted young athletes are those who know that if they come home and inform their parents that they have just quit the team, their parents will smile and simply say, "Any particular reason why?" The option to quit with honor will relieve a lot of pressure for the

young athlete; if he knows that his parents are behind him, that they respect his judgment, that they will not force him to continue in something he no longer wishes to do, he can deal more effectively with his coach's demands. The option of walking away is imperative for young athletes: It eliminates the life-and-death aura of sports involvement, and keeps the coach on his toes. Once a young athlete quits a team because he no longer enjoys playing on it, parents should respect his decision; he is on his way to becoming a young man with convictions and a sense of individuality. All of which will eventually make him a star in a different league, the human league.